Gandhi

Across The Boundaries

Gandhi

Across The Boundaries

Edited by

Dr Devendra Kumar

Associate Professor
Department of History and
Convenor, Gandhi Study Circle
Ramlal Anand College
University of Delhi

Shivalik Prakashan

Delhi India

Price : ₹ 995

First Edition : 2021

ISBN : 978-81-945562-1-3

Publisher:
Shivalik Prakashan
4648/21, Ansari Road, Daryaganj
New Delhi-110002
Phone : 011-42351161
Mob. : +91-9811693579
E-mail : shivalikprakashan@yahoo.com

International Branch :
64, Grant Boulevard, Dundas
Ontario, Canada L9H 4MI

Published In India

Published by Virendra Tiwari for Shivalik Prakashan, 27/16, Shakti Nagar, Delhi-110007, Type Setting Friends Graphics and Printed by R.K. Offset Printers, Delhi.

Gandhi : Across The Boundaries Edited by : **Dr Devendra Kumar**

Contents

Preface

Mahatma Gandhi was a very empowering and popular leader, not only in India but in the entire world. The whole of Gandhiji's philosophy based on non-violence was all pervading and it could not be restricted within any definition or a set of words that's why he inspired the Indian people to follow the path of non-violent struggle. A true devotee of Truth, Gandhi maintained that God is Truth and Truth is God and further that God is Love (of humanity) and love is God. He resorted to simple living, just like millions in the country, hence people look at Gandhi as one of their own and he emerged as a leader of the masses. In 1893 at the age of 23, he arrived in South Africa on a one year assignment to assist an Indian merchant in a civil suit. He had shown little interest in politics and had less experience in organizing and leading people. But he had a strong sense of duty, an attachment to truth and an open mind. In South Africa, Gandhi protested against the discriminating treatment meted out to Indians. He also protested the Asiatic (Black) Act and Transvaal Immigration Act and started his civil disobedience movement. The South African government repealed most of the obnoxious acts against the Indians. In 1915, Gandhi returned to India and in administration of his services to his countrymen began to be called Mahatma. The next four years he spent in studying the Indian situation. In 1917, the first major initiative taken by Gandhi was the Champaran Satyagraha. It was not with any political ambition that Gandhi started the movement in Champaran. It was to invite the attention of the authorities to the existing poor living conditions which denied indigo workers in large numbers basic minimum living facilities and freedom to live like human beings. Gandhi was invited to visit the place and make a study of what was happening. On his arrival, Gandhi was prevented and was barred entry there. Undeterred, he continued his mission and made a report which altered the situation, almost overnight. And the awakened people convincingly demonstrated that they could never be subjugated by a tyrannical setup of rules and formulations whosoever be the perpetrators of this crime-be it the biggest empire in those days, over which the sun never set.

Gandhi himself said that South Africa was very essential to his personal achievement. He spent 21 years – 1893 to 1914 in South Africa. The passive resistance: Satyagraha (of truth force in Sanskrit) was born and evolved in South Africa before coming to India. At the age of 46, Gandhi left the country, he also left the way of thinking and acting that found an echo in many of the country's struggles, most notable that of Nelson Mandela. Even as Gandhi's adventure in South Africa started in Durban, Johannesburg witnessed his main struggle. The Satyagraha House is thus a place that left its imprint on the life of Mahatma. His ideal of non-violence inspired, besides India, several other countries who willingly adopted them. The Frontier Gandhi, Abdul Gafar Khan is also an ardent follower of this principle. Similarly, Martin Luther King was a staunch devotee of non-violence and an earnest follower of Gandhiji. He connected the Christianity to Gandhi's teachings that the Christian doctrine of love operating through the Gandhian method of non-violence was one of the most potent weapons available to oppressed people in their struggle for freedom. It shows that Gandhism has influenced in the world and even today his name is revered everywhere and by everybody.

On one occasion Gandhi wrote, "non-violence is a plant of slow growth. It grows imperceptibly but surely." He worked for universal human values and his life is a sure guide to a meaningful existence for all of us in 21st Century. Gandhi had a dream for India but realizing his dream has become a nightmare. Today, we are living a life with constant adjustments to changing conditions, which call for a different kind of discipline. Now it rests on our shoulders to see that the democratic values remain intact. The time-tested communal harmony and composite culture must be maintained while ensuing social justice and gender equality for all. If we are able to achieve this, we shall be helping in fulfilling Gandhi's cherished dream.

Gandhi's unfinished task is the biggest challenge before us. He had faith in his mission because he had infinite faith in the individual's capacity to change. He firmly believed that the human nature is capable of radical reorientation; all one needs is a will to explore his own true self. This explains why Gandhi, all through his life, was striving to take humanity on to the path of spiritual and moral growth. The progress of civilization, as it has evolved through the ages, is proof that human nature is a developing entity, capable of change for the better.

Remember that the contemporary crisis demands not only a careful analysis of the roots of current social disorder and strategies of transition away from the current violent system but also demands a total rejection of some of our present narrow minded beliefs while restructuring our life-style and socio-economic institutions on radical moral lines.

Gandhi's thoughts need to be disseminated. It is these ideas which have an impressive role in taking the human society forward towards the desired goal. It is said that, it is not the empire builders but the thought of human being, individually powerless, who are ultimately the rulers of the world.

Today non-violence has become inevitable. Mankind has put a seal on the validity of non-violence when United Nations declared 2nd October as the International Non-Violence day. It is never too late to retrace the steps and follow the non-violent path of recovery shown by Mahatma Gandhi. Life whether individually or socially or at the level of nations practiced as per the Gandhian principles beings back the peaceful coexistence of nations.

Taking into considerations the role of Gandhian philosophy in present scenario, Gandhi Study Circle of the College organized a Two Day International Conference on "Gandhi Across the Boundaries" on 23rd, 24th October, 2019 in collaboration with Gandhi Smriti and Darshan-Samiti on the 150th Birth Anniversary of Mahatma Gandhi. This conference was organized in seven sessions with various themes such as – Gandhi's Contribution to Humankind, Relevance of Gandhian Thoughts in Today's Society, Gandhi and Global peace, Gandhi and Multiculturalism, Gandhi: Caste, untouchability and apartheid etc. Papers related to the themes were presented by various scholars in which plagiarism of each paper is checked by our plagiarism check committee through URKUND software.

Gandhi Study Circle was established in the College more than 3 decades ago. It provides an active platform to the students to express diverse opinions on different topics going beyond mere promotion of Gandhian values. The main aim and objective of this circle is to promote Gandhian Values and Nation Building. The Circle of the College has been organizing Talks, Seminars, National Seminars & conducting Quiz Competitions, Essay Writing Competitions, Debates, Inter-College Debates & Paper-Presentations since then. On the basis of these events and activities the circle of the college was honoured by Hon'ble Vice Chancellor, Delhi University, Prof.YogeshTyagi on

150th Birth Anniversary of Mahatma Gandhi.

The work of this proceedings has been accomplished under the supervision of our Principal, Dr.Rakesh Kumar Gupta, who has always been interested in encouraging such activities in the College and boosting up the morale of the students. I fail to assemble all my words while expressing reverence to him who guided me with his valuable guidance and generous help at every moment I needed. His benevolent disposition and readiness to take responsibilities pacified the despondent moments during this work.

I am very thankful to the Chairman, Governing Body, Ramlal Anand College, Padmashri Daya Prakash Sinha and former Chairman, Sh. Brij Kishore Sharma who not only encouraged but guided me for organizing this International Conference in the College and preparing a proceedings of papers. It would not have been possible for me for the publication work of this proceedings without their constant moral support and affection.

All members of Gandhi Study Circle, Dr. S.C. Dabas, Dr. Neena Mital, Dr. Sanjay Kumar Sharma, Dr. Krishan Gopal Tyagi, Sh. Vikas Kumar, Ms. Pragya Deshmukh, Sh. Rajinder Singh & Dr. Swagata Karmakar and student coordinators Deepak Kumar Trivedi, Ayush Bhagat, Neelam, Manshi Bisht, Pratibha Yadav, Sachin Chauhan and several others also deserve a lot of thanks who always stand with me for organizing and conducting various events related to M. K. Gandhi.

I am also thankful to Sh. Virendra Tiwari, Shiwalik Publication who has done me a great favour in publishing this proceedings with great speed and efficiency.

Dr. Devendra Kumar

1

Creating Sattva in Ourselves*
Remarks on Gandhi's Interpretation of Gita

Gianluigi Segalerba

Introduction

In my contribution, I would like to analyse some of Gandhi's considerations on Gita[1]. Throughout his meditation on Gita, Gandhi aims to show that the knowledge of the Revelation of Gita can give the correct moral education and the correct moral foundations to people. Only the process of learning obtained through meditating on the whole Gita can give us the knowledge of Truth, of God, of reality, and of ourselves, and only through this process are we able to organise and modify our own mind towards goodness. Learning proves to be, therefore, indispensable for strengthening in ourselves our good component, sattva, and for diminishing in us the influences exercised by our negative components, rajas and tamas[2]. The three factors are in us constitutively, and we ought to decide which factor we want to strengthen. If we wish to strengthen sattva, we ought to follow the learning process which enables us to understand what we ought to know, what we ought to do, and

* I would very much like to thank Prof. Dr. Rakesh Kumar Gupta, Dr. Devendra Kumar, and the Ram Lal Anand College of the University of Delhi for inviting me to take part at the International Conference "Gandhi Across the Boundaries", held at Ram Lal Anand College on 23-24 October 2019. I wish to thank very much all the members of the audience present at the Ram Lal Anand College for the attention they gave to my lecture. The title of my contribution refers to the following statement of Gandhi: "If a person overcomes *rajas* and *tamas*, he can create *sattva*. (All the three exist in us. We should make a special effort to cultivate that which we want to strengthen.)" ("The Collected Works of Mahatma Gandhi. XXXII (November 1926 – January 1927", p. 316).

what we ought to avoid. Through and thanks to the Revelation of Gita, education finds the due foundation. Only the morally correct education is the basis of a correct political and social order, since it represents the indispensable foundation of the dialogue between individuals and of the pacific coexistence between individuals.

The human condition: Human beings are battle fields

Throughout his meditation on Gita, Gandhi is searching the contents for a correct moral education. This education consists in establishing in individuals a correct disposition that will enable individuals to take the morally correct decisions and to have the morally correct dispositions. The Revelation of Gita explains to us, among other things, that our own condition corresponds to that of a battlefield: the human condition is to be compared with a battlefield where reciprocally hostile moral potencies fight against each other. Our moral starting point is, therefore, not positive and not easy at all. The first step we ought to take in order to begin a process of moral self-improvement consists in our becoming aware of our own condition, essence, and constitution because only through this awareness can we understand the necessity of finding a correct formation for our moral constitution. As regards our moral condition, Gandhi expresses the following positions, basing his reflections on his general interpretation of Mahabharata:

> "… the epic describes the battle ever raging between the countless Kauravas and Pandavas dwelling within us. It is a battle between the innumerable forces of good and evil which become personified in us as virtues and vices."[3]

Gandhi interprets the Mahabharata in a metaphorical way. The battle of Mahabharata is, actually, the battle between the good and evil present in ourselves. This means that we are composed of forces of evil and of good. Therefore, we cannot wait and see. We ought to take a decision in the direction we want to give to our moral constitution. The morally correct disposition will not come about on its own. Gandhi adds on the internal division of the individuals:

> "… here the physical battle is only an occasion for describing the battlefield of the human body. In this view the names mentioned are not of persons but of qualities which they represent. What is described is the conflict within the human body between opposing moral tendencies imagined as

> distinct figures. (…) It is the human body that is described as Kurukshetra, as *dharma-kshetra*."[4]

We are constitutively divided in different forces which are able to produce in us virtues or vices, such is our own constitution. There is a conflict in us in that we have in ourselves mutually conflicting forces. Therefore, once again, we cannot wait and see. We ought to act. Once we know that we are internally divided entities, our responsibility is to decide whether we want to let virtue or vice grow in ourselves.

Truth, Knowledge, Atman

The learning process of truth and the assimilation to truth are the remedy against the forces of evil present in us; truth gives us the contents, the foundations in order that we can successfully develop the forces of good which are present in us. Gandhi express the following general consideration on truth:

> "… there can be no exception in the matter of following truth, for truth is God and, if exceptions were admitted in relation to it, God also would be sometimes truth and sometimes non-truth."[5]

Truth is to be followed by everybody. In order to follow truth, a learning process is indispensable. Learning and knowledge are indispensable aspects of the process of the education of individuals. Gandhi clearly affirms that obtaining spiritual knowledge is open to everyone; nobody is excluded:

> "It is stated in the *Gita* itself that everyone, whether a woman, a Vaisya or a Sudra, can acquire spiritual knowledge if they have devotion to God. All the same, learning should not be slighted. To understand any matter, one must have the knowledge which comes from learning."[6]

Learning proves to be fundamental. The spiritual knowledge is the foundation for understanding everything.

The knowledge of Revelation modifies the mind of the individual; the meditation on and the absorption in the Revelation will modify the individual. Gandhi is moreover seeking a foundation in order to receive directions for political action; the possibility of coexistence in a society finds its foundation in Atman being the common essence for everybody:

"And so Krishna says:

> "Though I was never born in time, though I am the Lord of all creatures, I incarnate Myself and am born as a human being."

This is the essential nature of the *atman*. If we realize this truth, we would always act in conformity with that nature; we then act, though born as human beings, as if we were never born. If the *atman* in each of us is identical with the *atman* in everyone else, one *atman* born in a body means all of them born, and all others born means that one born too. This is a difficult idea to grasp. "This is *maya*," says Shri Krishna, "and through it I incarnate Myself in this world time and again."

We can follow reason only up to a point. What, then, does avatar mean? It is not as if God comes down from above. It would be right to say, if we can say it without egotism, that each one of us is an avatar. The *atman* in ever body is as potent as the *atman* in any other, though outwardly we see differences. In our awakened state all are one, though in our ignorant state we may seem separate existences. In real truth, there are not several, there is only one.

If we constantly reflect over this essence named the *atman*, we shall regard no one as an enemy to be killed and shall have nothing to get angry about. We shall then see that anyone who hits us hits himself too."[7]

Human beings have Atman as their common source and principle; the common belonging to Atman is the foundation of the connection between the living beings: if we are mutually connected by our common belonging to Atman, if our authentic self is Atman, to commit injustice against other people means to do something bad to ourselves. Thus, belonging to Atman represents the foundation of our solidarity with the other beings.

Limits of individuals and responsibility of individuals

Gandhi insists on our limits. We are not perfect; we have constitutive defects that can only be limited, diminished, but that cannot be completely eliminated, since they belong to our very nature:

> "The only way of rising to this state beyond the three *gunas* is to cultivate the *sattvik* quality, for in order to rise to that state one is required to cultivate the virtues of fearlessness, humility, sincerity, and so on. So long as we live in the body, there is some evil, some violence. The most, therefore, that we can do is to be *sattvik* in the highest degree possible."[8]

We cannot be free constitutively from any form of violence until we are in the corporeal dimension. We ought to cultivate the virtues connected to sattva in order that the balance that exists in us among sattva, tamas, and rajas could be shifted to the advantage of sattva; thus, sattva will increase, whereas tamas and rajas will diminish. Notwithstanding, even in the best condition of development for sattva, tamas, and rajas present in us will not completely disappear:

> "... the reign of the three *gunas* prevails throughout the universe. A cooking or other utensil is an inert object, but it contains air inside; likewise, everything is pervaded by the spirit. Existing apart from the three *gunas* is God. We have to merge in Him. Even if we cultivate the *sattvik* qualities to their highest perfection in us, something of *rajasik* and *tamasik* will remain. But, without worrying ourselves about this, we should continue to strive and cultivate finer and finer *sattvik* qualities in us, for the impulses which agitate us the least and consume the least amount of our energy are *sattvik* impulses."[9]

In spite of the fact that negative components will always be present in us, we ought to continue our work of self- improvement. The fact that we are constitutively imperfect beings entails that we have to educate ourselves continuously. Nothing is given, morally, and nothing is morally reached once and for all. We must reach an ethical foundation by ourselves. We must steadily pay attention to the stability and endurance of our ethical character, and we must try to reach, maintain, and strengthen it. Gandhi clearly expresses that we cannot manage in the corporeal dimension to fully follow ahimsa:

> "It is impossible in this body to follow Ahimsa fully. That is why *moksha* is laid down as the supreme end of life. Violence is inescapable. (...) Evil is inherent in action, the *Gita* says further on."[10]

There are clear limits put on human capabilities. Everyone ought to become aware of one's own limitations. In the corporeal dimension, it is not possible to concretise in ourselves a perfect doctrine of ahimsa. This point, of course, may not lead to renouncing any attempt to realise ahimsa as best as possible. On the contrary, the awareness of one's own defect ought to lead everyone to multiply the efforts towards the realisation of ahimsa.

Conclusions

I would like to synthesise the results of my analysis in the following way:

i) Individuals are moral battle fields. They are mentally divided in good factors and in bad factors. The responsibility of every individual consists in strengthening the good factor, sattva, of their own self.
ii) Gandhi firmly believes in the power of transformation exercised on

individuals by the knowledge of the truth. Knowledge of the truth expressed in the Revelation of Gita successfully modifies men as regards their moral dimension.

iii) Knowledge of truth and the learning process needed in order to obtain this kind of knowledge is indispensable in order to reach the foundation both of an individual and morally correct disposition and of a politically correct order.

iv) Individuals are morally limited entities. They cannot completely eliminate bad factors within their own corporeal dimensions. The presence of limits does not mean that men have no responsibility. On the contrary, since they have limits, men ought to fight against them. Individuals ought to become aware of their own limits, ought not to despair, but to be confident in what they can actually do.

References

1. For my analysis of Gandhi's interpretation of Gita, I relied on Gandhi's "Discourses on the "Gita", in "The Collected Works of Mahatma Gandhi", XXXII (November 1926 – January 1927), pp. 94-376. I also relied on the work of Mahadev Desai, "The Gospel of selfless action or The Gita according to Gandhi". As regards further commentaries and studies on Gita, I consulted the following works: S.M. Srinivasa Chari, "The Philosophy of Bhagavadgîtâ"; "The Bhagavad Gita. With Text, Translation, and Commentary in the Words of Sri Aurobindo"; "The Bhagavad Gîtâ (Sanskrit Text, Transliteration, English Translation & Philological Notes). Introduction by W. Douglas P. Hill. Translated by John Davies"; Ithamar Theodor, "Exploring the Bhagavad Gîtâ. Philosophy, Structure and Meaning".
2. Sattva, Tamas, and Rajas are defined, in the translation of Gita contained in Desai's work, in the following way: "6. Of these *sattva*, being stainless, is light-giving and healing; it binds with the bond of happiness and the bond of knowledge, O sinless one. 7. *Rajas*, know thou, is of the nature of passion, the source of thirst and attachment; it keeps man bound with the bond of action. 8. *Tamas*, know thou, born of ignorance, is mortal man's delusion; it keeps him bound with heedlessness, sloth and slumber, O Bharata. 9. *Sattva* attaches man to happiness, *rajas* to action, and *tamas*, shrouding knowledge, attaches him to heedlessness." ("The Gospel of selfless action or The Gita according to Gandhi", p. 330). To be noted, among other things, is the connection of sattva with knowledge.
3. "The Collected Works of Mahatma Gandhi. XXXII (November 1926 – January 1927)", p. 95.
4. "The Collected Works of Mahatma Gandhi. XXXII (November 1926 – January 1927)", p. 96.
5. "The Collected Works of Mahatma Gandhi. XXXII (November 1926 – January 1927)", p. 106.
6. "The Collected Works of Mahatma Gandhi. XXXII (November 1926 – January 1927)", p. 96.
7. "The Collected Works of Mahatma Gandhi. XXXII (November 1926 – January 1927)", p. 189.

8. "The Collected Works of Mahatma Gandhi. XXXII (November 1926 – January 1927)", p. 320.
9. "The Collected Works of Mahatma Gandhi. XXXII (November 1926 – January 1927)", p. 336.
10. "The Collected Works of Mahatma Gandhi. XXXII (November 1926 – January 1927)", p. 106.

Bibliography

Srinivasa Chari, S.M., The Philosophy of Bhagavadgîtâ. A Study based on the Evaluation of the Commentaries of Úa•kara, Râmânuja and Madhva, with a foreword of MM.V. Srivatsankacharya. New Delhi, 2005, reprinted 2014.

Desai, M., The Gospel of selfless action or The Gita according to Gandhi (Translation of the original in Gujarati, with an additional introduction and commentary). By Mahadev Desai. Ahmedabad, 1946.

Gandhi, M.K., The Collected Works of Mahatma Gandhi. XXXII (November 1926 – January 1927). The Publication Division. Ministry of Information and Broadcasting Government of India. Ahmedabad, 1969.

The Bhagavad Gita. With Text, Translation, and Commentary in the Words of Sri Aurobindo. Edited by Parmeshwari Prasad Khetan, Jhunjhunu; Rajasthan, 333001, 1992.

The Bhagavad Gîtâ (Sanskrit Text, Transliteration, English Translation & Philological Notes). Introduction by W. Douglas P. Hill. Translated by John Davies. Delhi, 2006.

The Bhagavad Gita in English. The Sacred Song. Translated by Philippe L. De Coster, B.Th., D.D. Translated into English from the original Sanskrit into English along ancient manuscripts, and various other sources and research material. Split up reading – Transliteration Word for Word translation. Gita Satsang Ghent Centre (Belgium). Copyright (Belgium) 2006 – 2007. Revised and Enlarged, November 2010.

The Bhagavad Gita. The Original Sanskrit and An English Translation. Lars Martin Fosse. Woodstock NY, 2007. The Bhagavad-Gita, or Song Celestial translated by Sir Edwin Arnold. The Harvad Classics, New York, 1909-

1914. Downloaded from: https://www.bartleby.com/45/4

The Mahabarata. A Prose English Translation of the Mahabarata (Translated literally from the Original Sanskrit Text.) Adi Parva. Edited and Published by Manmatha Nath Dutt, M.A., M.R.A.S. Calcutta, 1895.

The Mahabarata of Krishna-Dwaipayana Vyasa. Translated into English Prose from the Original Sanskrit Text by Kisari Mohan Ganguli [1883-1896]. Scanned at sacred-texts.com, 2003. Downloaded from: https://www.holybooks.com/the-mahabarata-of-vyasa-english-prose-translation/

Theodor, I., Exploring the Bhagavad Gîtâ. Philosophy, Structure and Meaning. Farnham, England / Burlington, USA, 2010.

2

Rethinking and Transforming Swadeshi, Swaraj and Satyagraha for Our Contemporary Times: Ethics, Aesthetics and Responsibility and the Calling of a New Planetary Advaita and Lokasamgraha

Ananta Kumar Giri

Swadeshi, Swaraj and Satyagraha are important themes, concepts and modes of *sadhana* and struggle in Gandhi and Gandhian engagement with Indian freedom struggle and world emancipation. In our contemporary world, we can learn a lot by engaging ourselves with these themes and modes of *sadhana* and struggles. In our present day moment of resistance to globalization in the name of local and national economic well-being and prosperity, we can engage with the Swadeshi movement of Indian freedom struggle and transform Swadheshi mode of doing economy and politics without jingoism, hatred and xenophobia. During Indian freedom movement this was a challenge and Sri Aurobindo, Gandhi and Tagore in their own ways tried to grapple with ways of making Swadeshi less xenophobic and serve the cause of local and national economic regeneration as well as solve the problems of social and economic inequality especially revolving around poverty of religious minorities such as Muslims.

We can relate contemporary resistance against globalization to the task of building local and national economies and relate it creatively to movements of regionalization with and beyond contemporary national boundaries. For example, Swadheshi movement which started in Bengal at the turn of the last century now has to be done in a creative way by bringing the economies of West Bengal, North East India, Nepal and Bangladesh as part of creative regional economic, social, cultural, political and ecological development going beyond nation-state boundaries. Swadeshi now needs.to be creatively linked to other *deshas*—land and regions and we need to cultivate a related movement of Sahadesh (lands and countries together) as part of emerging movements of localization, regionalization and planetary realizations.

Similar challenge of rethinking, reconstitution and transformation awaits us in the discourse and practice of Swaraj. In *Hind Swaraj*, Gandhi offers us a plural vision of Hind or India. Note here Gandhi's insistence that nation and religion are not synonymous[1] *Hind Swaraj* is a foundational critique of modern civilization which erases the plural in the name of the singular conflations of multiple kinds such as nation and language or nation and religion. But the plural understanding of the self and the other now needs to be cultivated at the very heart of the project of *Swaraj*. In *Hind Swaraj* Gandhi hints at several places that the *Swa* or self is not singular and it does not exist in dualistic opposition to the other. Here Gandhi's critique of egoism and drawing upon sources of *Advaita* (non-duality) in Indic traditions does contribute to a plural realization of self. Nevertheless, in its free-floating formulation in Hind

Swaraj and in its common sense rendering Swaraj as self-rule does not always contain a project of pluralization of the very self striving towards self-rule. In other words, the self in Swaraj is not always realized as a plurivocity of Being (cf. Connolly 1999). But building on Gandhi and post-Gandhian developments in transformative philosophy and creative experimentations, we now need to interrogate a linear rendering of Swaraj as self-rule without at the same time making the self undertake a journey of what I have elsewhere called meditative verbs of pluralizations (Giri 2012). Self in Swaraj takes part in meditative verbs of pluralizations by realizing the plural dimension in self, other, society and the world which helps it overcome imprisonment in a fixed embedding of self and other and realize emergent blossoming of all concerned.

Similar challenge us awaits us in rethinking and transforming the vision

1. In the words of Gandhi: "If the Hindus believe that India should be only by Hindus, they are living in a dreamland. The Hindus, the Mahomedans, the Parsis and the Christians who have India their country are fellow countrymen, and they will have to live in unity, of only for their own interest. In no part of the world are one nationality and one religioni synonymous terms; nor has it ever been so in India" (1938: 43).

and project of Satyagraha. Satyagraha in Gandhi is not only a political instrument, it is a multi-dimensional movement of being with and fighting for Truth. It is not entrapped in a logic of opposition of self and other.

Satyagraha is a movement to create a field of searching and fighting for Truth but this field of struggle is a field which holds both the satyagrahi and against those this fighting is on together. It is a field of contestation, compassion, confrontation and co-realizations. To develop this line of reasoning further, we can build upon the idea of zone of proximal development from Russian educationist Leo Vygotsky and argue how Satyagraha is a zone of proximal development in which all participants are challenged to develop further in the direction of co-realization. We can also bring the vision and practice of three *gunas* (three qualities) from Indic tradition—*Sattva* (Truth), *Rajas* (power) and *Tamas* (darkness) and explore the link between Satyagraha and work and meditation with these three *gunas*. We can realize how Satyagraha is a *sadhana* and struggle to overcome Tamas and Rajas in self, culture and society and realize Sattva (Truth) in a spirit of gunatita (transcendence of gunas).

We can also relate work and meditation with Truth in Satyagraha to translation and travel.

Satyagraha as translation of self and other and inter-cultural translation thus can be linked to creative foot work as part of a cross-cultural memory work. This is also a truth work and meditation where one walks and meditates with Truth. This truth work is an aspect of Satyagraha and it has both an epistemic and ontological dimension. Translation as *satyagraha* is thus part of an alternative epistemology and ontology which is a creative dynamics in the work of ontological epistemology of participation in our lives (see Giri 2006; 2018) . This has implication for transforming a predominantly political conception of *satyagraha*. Satyagraha is also related to travel—both inner and outer—which helps us go beyond fixed conceptions of self, other and the world. We thus cultivate a new hermeneutics and practice of Satyagraha.

With a new hermeneutics and practice of Satyagraha, we can realize how Satyagraha is an integral part of constitutional democracy and without Satyagraha, constitutional democracies become mere legal stones. Scholars such as Jurgen Habermas (1996) help us realize how constitution is a project of mobilization of hope and this calls for continued Satyagraha. We thus need to rethink Ambedkar's one-sided critique of Satyagraha in constitutional democracies and his view that we do not need it in it in our democratic setting, and realize its crucial significance when democracies and constitutions themselves have been turned into tyrannies.

We can also realize Swadeshi, Swaraj and Satyagraha as fields of ethics, aesthetics and responsibility. Swadeshi, Swaraj and Satyagraha raise ethical questions such as their possible and historical closures and abuses. Their fuller realization also calls for a new art of living, an aesthetics of creative practice and ways of being with the world. All the three also embody vision, practice and the calling of responsibility. They also challenge us to go beyond the dualism of self and other and realize Advaita (non-duality) at the levels of self, other, culture and the world—both local and planetary Advaita. With Gandhi, this non-duality draws upon multiple religious, spiritual and philosophical sources such as his deep walking and meditation with Jaina philosophy, practice and *sadhana* of anekantavada (many- sided approached to Truth), Tolstoy' vision and practice of Kingdom of God, and philosophies and practices of John Ruskin and Henry David Thoreau. Thus the sadhana and striving of realizing non-duality in Gandhi had multiple sources of inspiration leading to what can be called planetary Advaita—planetary non-duality. We need to work and meditate with Swadeshi, Swaraj and Satyagraha as fields, circles and movements of overcoming unhelpful and harmful dualism between the self and the other and realize varieties of creative and contingent non-duality at local, regional, national, transnational and planetary levels. This process contributes to bringing self, other and different people together which is the other name of *Lokasangraha*—gathering of people for welfare of all. Srimad Bhagavad Gita talks about *Lokasamgraha*. *Lokasamgraha* also involves *atmasamgraha*-gathering of Atman, soul. Happiness and Welfare of all in *Lokasamgraha* is related to creativity of soul, self, society and people (Giri 2020). We need to rethink and transform Swadeshi, Swaraj and Satyagraha as fields and movements of creativity and co-creation of *Lokasamgraha* at the levels of self, other, society, national and planetary levels.

References Cited and A Related Bibliography

Connolly, William E. 1999. *Why I am not a Secularist.* Minneapolis: University of Minnesota Press. Dalai Lama. 2009. *The Middle Way: Faith Grounded in Reason.* Boston: Wisdom.

Dallmayr, Fred. 2002. *Dialogue Among Civilizations.* NY: Palgrace Macmillan.

2005. *Small Wonder: Global Power and its Discontents.* Lanham, MD: Rowman & Littlefield.

2016. *Against Apocalypse: Recovering Humanity's Wholeness.* Lanham, MD: Lexington Books.

Gandhi, M.K. 1938 [1909]. *Hind Swaraj.* Ahmedabad: Navajivan Publishing House.

1929. *The Story of My Experiments with Truth.* Ahmedabad: Navajivan Publishing House.

Gandhi, Ramachandra. 1993. *Sita's Kitchen.* Delhi: Penguin.

Galtung, Johan & Graeme MacQueen. 2010. *Globbalizing God: Religion, Spirituality and Peace.* Transcend U. Press.

Giri, Ananta. 2006. "Creative Social Research: Rethinking Theories and Methods and the Calling of an Ontological Epistemology of Participation." Dialectical Anthropology.

2012. "Beyond Adaptation and Meditative Verbs of Pluraliztions." Ananta Kumar Giri,

Sociology and Beyond: Windows and Horizons. Jaipur: Rawat Publications.

2018. "With and Beyond Epistemologies from the South: Multi-topial Hermeneutics, Ontological Epistemology of Participation and the Calling of Planetary Realizations." Madras Institute of Development Studies: Working Paper.

Habermas, Jurgen. 1996. *Between Facts and Norms: Contributions towards a Discourse Theory of Law and Politics.* Cambridge, MA: The MIT Press.

2006. *The Divided West.* Cambridge: Polity Press.

Heehs, Peter. 2008. *Lives of Sri Aurobindo.* New York: Columbia U. Press. Holzman, Lois. 2009. *Vygotsky at Work and Play.* London: Routledge.

Parel, Anthony J. 2016. *Pax Gandhiana: Gandhi as a Political Philosopher.* New York: Oxford U. Press. Rathore, Aakash Singh. 2016. *Contemporary Indian Political Theory.* London: Routledge.

Rawls, John. 1971. *A Theory of Justice.* Cambridge, MA: Harvard U. Press. Sen, Amartya. 2009. *The Idea of Justice.* Harvard.

Sri Aurobindo. 1972a *Foundations of Indian Culture.* Pondicherry: Sri Aurobindo Ashram.

1972b. *Bande Mataram.* Pondicherry: Sri Aurobindo Ashram.

Thoreau, David. 1975. "Walking." *The Portable Thoreau.* Edited by Carl Bode. Penguin. Tolstoy. 1908. *Letter to a Hindu.*

Vattimo, G. 1999. *Belief.* Cambridge: Polity Press.

Veeravalli, Anuradha. 2011. "Swaraj and Sovereignty." *Economic and Political Weekly* XLV1 (5): 65-69, Jan 29, 2011.

3

Mahatma Gandhi's Vision for Ideal Man and Society: Spirituality as the Underlying Spirit

Harpreet Kaur

Abstract

An *ideal society* is where people of varied religions, diverse cultures and different backgrounds reside together in an amiable manner. Individual and collection amelioration, welfare of all and spiritual progress is the permeating feature in any good society. The idea of a good society is built around social setup which aims to create *individuals and institutions* that endorse social and human values including justice, equality, liberty, human dignity etc. and endorses good governance without discrimination on the basis of gender, race, religion or caste etc. The political theorists and philosophers across various epochs like, Plato, Aristotle,

J.S. Mill, Mahatma Gandhi etc. have focused and the religious thinkers like, Mahatma Buddha, Guru Nanak Dev Ji etc. have pronounced their teachings to guide the people to lead an ideal life in a good society. Guru Nanak Dev Ji, Founder of Sikhism has given an everlasting legacy to the mankind by envisioning an all-inclusive and all-embracing society based on the eternal values. Truth and Truthful Living was the basis of conduct. Mahatma Gandhi, 400 years after Guru Nanak Dev Ji, laid stress on firm norms for the individual and collective emancipation. Mahatma Gandhi based his entire philosophy on Truth that was the basis of thought, speech and deeds and this was to be combined in the private as well as public domain. With 2019 an auspicious year that marks 550th Birth Anniversary of Guru Nanak Dev Ji and 150th Birth Anniversary of Mahatma Gandhi, a befitting tribute to them would be the focus the efforts on creating an ideal society as envisaged by them and *this paper focuses on individual and collective welfare imbued with values and spirituality as elucidated by Mahatma Gandhi.*

Key Words: Mahatma Gandhi, ideal society, Truth, Ahimsa, non-violence, Moksha, bread- labour, individual and collective emancipation

Introduction

The year *2019 marks 150th birth anniversary* of *Mahatma Gandhi.* The teachings of Mahatma Gandhi are reiterated in varied forums of the countries of the world in many ways, that are celebrating and remembering the legacy of the Mahatma and his all-encompassing vision. ***His all-inclusive vision for an ideal society was based on the personal and societal values like,*** Truth, non-violence, social justice, soul force, love, dignity, bread labour, ahimsa etc. He strived to create harmony amongst the society and between the components of the society i.e., individuals by establishing an organic unity amongst them, creating a fine balance between society and societal concerns (*Sarvodaya*) and reiterating enduring commitment to social justice, swaraj, civil disobedience etc. He says, "The best way to find yourself is to lose yourself in the service of others". Mahatma Gandhi's efforts were naturally directed towards creating a harmony between nature and human beings. The aim of one should be harmony of an individual with himself along with the mutual relationships between individuals of the society and balance in various components of society and harmony with nature and one's surroundings. He says, "Happiness is when what you think, what you say and what you do are in harmony". The concerns of religious pluralism, normative economics and magnanimous civil society, all of which are excruciatingly important in the present day context were addressed by the Mahatma. One finds in it a profound awareness of the concepts of the earlier philosophical heritage of the Indian thought while having relevance for the future being certainly progressive even in the modern pluralistic and multi-cultural societies.

Spirituality is the very basis of thought, belief and conduct of Mahatma Gandhi. The mundane and worldly concerns were inter-woven with the other-worldly concerns and *Moksha,* instead of being just an after-life undertaking was woven into the praxis of an individual in one's very life. Spirituality was the basis of thoughts and deeds for creating ideal man and ideal society. The ideas of Gandhi Ji are a beautiful blend of its roots in our rich historical past while embracing the progressive ideas of modernity.

The essence of ***knowledge and education*** has been elaborated by Mahatma Gandhi. He says, "Man is neither mere intellect, nor the gross animal body, nor the heart or soul alone. A proper and harmonious combination of all three is required for the making of the whole man and constitutes the true economics of education". He aspired to reach the depths within before the darkness outside could be dispelled through balance between mind, body and soul and illuminated the masses with definite guiding principles that could lead them in this world and liberate them in other-worldly affairs. An ideal society would be possible if the enlightened men work towards the upliftment of all.

The idea of ***individual emancipation*** permeated the very thought of Gandhi. An individual is complete in oneself and yet, a part of the broader society. If an individual enjoys right place in the social organization, the society will flourish. An individual is a complete circle and a part of other oceanic circles and so, is an independent entity despite being a part of the larger whole. ***Collective upliftment*** or *Sarvodaya* is welfare of all till the last rung of the ladder and this concept as envisaged by Gandhi Ji should be deliberated and if replicated in present context, can be extremely beneficial for us. Moreover at the spiritual level, the Mahatma gave a prescription for a person to live in this world and yet, be emancipated in the other world seems to be vague but if delved, can be an elixir in the present setup. The means and end are compatible in both the personal as well as public space.

Mahatma Gandhi's vision of ***Ram Rajya*** had essential spiritual and religious dimensions. The teachings of Mahatma Gandhi are imbued by deep religious precepts that influenced the entire gamut of his activities in all the arenas including, political, cultural, religious and economic with no strict compartmentalization of any of these arenas. "Ram Rajya for Gandhi meant the rule of dharma, rule of justice. And above all, it meant self-rule of an individual upon himself. He also identified it with a Biblical saying that 'the Kingdom of God in within you'. Swaraj is a multi-dimensional concept including 'Inner Swaraj' that is to be achieved by individuals within oneself through a rigorous process of transformation and Swaraj is also check the 'immoral and selfish' government constituted by many and not merely freedom from the

British colonial rule. Swaraj takes into consideration localism along with avoiding the extremes of liberalization and globalization. "Such balanced and nuanced view might give a lead for a genuine universal culture without making individuals, groups, regions and nations losing their inner and local cultural moorings' (*Pradhan, Ram Chandra, 2011*).

So, Gandhi's ***deep philosophical insight based on the religious precepts*** and many ***concepts, ideas, programmes and movements*** that were instrumental in leading India towards an ideal

state and society are discussed in the paper along with the lasting contribution of Gandhi's philosophy in the present context.

What is an Ideal Society?

An *ideal society* can be envisaged as a place shared by people with varied religions, cultures and backgrounds residing collectively in an amiable way. The core guiding values of the society include democracy, freedom, equality, human dignity, good governance, fraternity, amiability and rationality. The foundation stone of such a society is its spiritual progress and detachment from excessive material possessions. Honestly performing one's vocation in life is its integral aspect. The aim of such a society is create institutions and build character of individuals. This conceives the idea of a good society embracing the '*idea of welfare for all*'. The need for a good and ideal society arose for we needed to establish such system of relations amongst people that is conducive to the ***individual as well as to the well-being of a society as a whole***. Many theoretical concepts, both political and religious emerged from this idea. The political theorists or religious thinkers have pronounced with this objective to achieve a good society. Their methodologies may differ and when the means are compatible with the end, the impact is more lasting.

A good society has been given different definitions by different authors at different times. ***Plato's*** idea of the conception of an ideal society was primarily that of a just society and a Philosopher King, where justice was the highest virtue of the state. An ideal place is 'a where everyone lived harmoniously and without the fear of violence or material possession'. For ***Aristotle***, the function of the state is to stimulate goodness of man. ***J.S. Mill*** supports individual liberty for creation of a good society. ***Mahatma Gandhi*** believed that politics divorced from religion is valueless. He asserted, "What is morally wrong can never be politically right".

Rabindranath Tagore, in his poetic composition elaborates an ideal society beautifully: "*Where the mind is without fear and the head is held high*

Where knowledge is free
Where the world has not been broken up into fragments By narrow domestic walls
Where words come out from the depth of truth
Where tireless striving stretches its arms towards perfection Where the clear stream of reason has not lost its way
Into the dreary desert sand of dead habit Where the mind is led forward by thee Into ever-widening thought and action
Into that heaven of freedom, my Father, let my country awake."

The conception of ideal society has changed from the times of Plato, Socrates, Jeremy Bentham or Gandhi. Such an ideal society endorsing political and social freedom is the aim yet, elusive in the present globalized scenario. ***Vasudhaiva Kutumbakam*** *or 'the world is one family'* that is engraved at the Entrance Hall of the Parliament House is the crux of the Indian rich religious tradition. Inclusive society was key since times immemorial but diluted over the centuries. Many prophets, seers, great men, emperors or kings etc. have manifested it in words and deeds. The contribution of those great men is the true legacy of our country and the message disseminated by them is to be reiterated so that our present and future generations get direction from it.

A desired society have been an ideal space in any epoch, yet elusive. *Philosophy and Religion* both are expressive way of the human creativity and are instrumental in creating a progressive society. A desired ideal society is based on *philosophical insights* that can be taken as '*head*' i.e., one's mental or rational undertakings and *religion* is all about one's '*heart*' stimulating our faith and emotions either towards fanaticism or towards tolerance and empathy. There is a close connect between the two and it is vital to understand the *philosophical insights provided by religion to create a firm foundation of an ideal society*. Almost all the religions of the world envision a society free from immoralities, divisions and evil. Many great philosophers of the world have endorsed these religious precepts to enlighten the humans and to create a conducive society. These philosophers challenged, lead and created a new epoch and had a lasting impact on the society.

In this vein, I would like to elaborate the teachings of Mahatma Gandhi imbued by deep religious precepts that distinguishes him elevating his stature as Mahatma. ***The Gandhian philosophy aimed at self-realization of individuals along with the collective growth of the society at large making him unique granting him a special place in the history.***

Uniqueness of Mahatma Gandhi

A recent survey in 2019 undertaken by PWC 'raked Gandhi as the third most admired leader of all times, after Winston Churchill and Steve Jobs. Gandhi, born 150 years ago, continued to capture the imagination of leaders attempting to change the world. He influenced Martin Luther King Jr's 1955 Montgomery Boycott, the seminal event in the US civil rights movement. Vietnamese revolutionary leader Ho Chi Minh considered himself Gandhi's disciple. He is hero to Jack Ma and Al Gore. Gandhi also inspired John Lennon's music. "Imagine " (*TOI, 2 October 2019*).

Gandhi's uniqueness can be established in all his actions and accomplishments along with his preaching. He was a man of strong conviction, steadfast action and deep faith. Gandhi lived a very hectic life as a politician but despite this 'the process of the enrichment of his spiritual life and embellishment of his syncretic faith did not come to a dead stop'.

His uniqueness is his journey from Mohandas Karamchand Gandhi to Mahatma Gandhi. Despite his privileged upbringing, he transformed himself so radically that Mahatma was prefixed with his name and he came to be called as 'half naked fakir' through his strong will and resolve to carry on with his sadhana. Babu Jagjivan Ram believed the personal qualities like, austerity, humility and saintliness of Gandhi were exemplary. The journey of Gandhi to his ascend as Mahatma Gandhi is mainly due to his teachings and his own refined and exemplary life. His ascend as a saint while living a normal person's life and also of a nationalist leader leading the national movement with a fervour, also makes one marvel. It is worthy to note that the Father of the Nation, *Mahatma Gandhi not only, moulded the lives of millions but also, moulded the national character.* His contemporary society was torn apart and Mahatma Gandhi unified the nation by propounding unworldly philosophy to lead life based on the spiritual tenets that the masses could connect themselves with. He came to known as icon of the Indian freedom struggle. The downtrodden were given a new identity. Communal harmony and brotherhood were the key principles encouraged by Gandhi Ji radically changing the social outlook and landscape.

Sadhanas, his steadfastness and determination tempered his resolve and charted his journey from Mohan into a Mahatma beginning from his South African sojourn. ***He lead an example from his own life proving even an ordinary person can reach to the Himalayan heights in the personal and spiritual space as well as public and political space.*** His fearlessness and introduction of morality continues to shape many till date.

The concept of the ideals of human life directly pertain to the belief in the Providence. Even the vital values of religion, which are *met by the character of God as wisdom, love and goodness*. In this sense, remarks Dr. Radhakrishnan, "Values acquire a cosmic importance and ethical life becomes meaningful". The uniqueness of the Mahatma is that he made ethical conduct the true foundation of the human life. Truth and the pursuit of truth as a one's goal of life was accorded primal place. Acquisition of spiritual knowledge would serve as a check on individual passion, self-centeredness, egoism, frenzy, hate and rage and elevate the human beings in their lives and create a liveable society. The subtle power of love based on sacrifice was promoted in all his endeavours. This is the need of the present hour for the warmth of relationships have gone missing. Abraham Maslow says, "We must study love; we must be able to teach it, to understand it, to predict it, or the world is lost to hostility and suspicion" (*Maslow, Abraham in Rubin, Z., 1997*). Love and Truth go hand and hand and without love, truth is incomplete. Love allows one to take into account the truth of other persons, which would make the truth complete. The love of the Divine is within us all but needs to be realized and that was the mature love advocated by Gandhi Ji.

As a *Nationalist leader*, his stature was very high for he was a *political ethicist*. His Movements were imbued with the principles of non-violence and civil disobedience. The Movements initiated by him stirred the British to the core. The mass appeal of these movements was tremendous and many thousands blindly answered and followed his call making all the movements initiated by him a grand success. Yet, civil disobedience and non- violence was strictly followed in all movements. Even British could not get a pretext to imprison him. His renunciation of any political post despite being the obvious choice of the topmost position in the Indian government after Independence places him on a very high pedestal. Even as a political activist, ethics remained a basis of all his actions and he never compromised on the same, raising his stature.

So *Mahatma Gandhi's* personality can be described as *multi-faceted as a visionary, social and political reformer and a spiritual leader who shaped New*

India. His personality was forceful for he combined many roles working on many fronts as a freedom fighter, a nationalist leader, an ashram dweller, a social leader, a saint, a journalist, a writer, a satyagrahi, a great organizer of the masses and so on.

Essence of Gandhi's Vision of an Ideal Society in the Ashrams

A Social organization is a network of social relations that is embracing. Any form of social construction is credible if based on truthful and honest relations and virtuous deeds. This formula aiming at individual and collective emancipation was taught to the people. Gandhi's vision for the modern Indian society imbued with the religious and socio-economic philosophy is a significant landmark that was put into practice at the Ashrams.

The reflections on self-realization of an individual is the basis of the philosophy elucidated by Gandhi. An individual is complete whole in oneself and yet, a part of the broader society and so, inter-relationship between the two is vital for a balanced society. If an individual enjoys right place in the social organization, harmony in the society would be possible flourishing it.

The concept of an ideal society envisioned by Gandhi envisages a place for other religions and castes and this place is a space where tolerance is firmly rooted based on the precepts of morality and spirituality. The Mahatma created a bond of God and love for humanity breaking all social alignments underlying an essential unity amongst them all. The caste hierarchy, rituals and customs that had divided the Hindu society pained him urging for corrective measures for the same. Gandhi's vision for man and society was all-embracing and inter-dependent. At one side, he fights to give rights and equality to each human being irrespective of any differences and divisions and lay a correct course to the individuals and at the other, creates an all-embracing society. He strongly based them on morality and spirituality and laid such a path that have relevance even in the changing epochs and charted a course for the future.

Ashrams were the experimenting grounds where the members of the diminishing civil society were promoted to live together amicably endorsing his all-inclusive vision of the society based on spirituality. "Gandhi had a vision of transforming the socially and morally degenerated and separated individuals in a manner where individuals can enjoy their freedom in a spirit altruism (*Biswal, S.K., 2012*). Individual emancipation and collective upliftment was envisaged by Gandhi Ji and replicated in the *Ashramic* life outlined by him. The individual life was directed under self-imposed vows creating foundation of a society where the growth of all was the permeating feature and upliftment of all till the lowest rung of the ladder would became possible. Ashrams were used to build bridges and propagate universalism. Gandhi Ji himself would retreat to such a community of fellowship when he desired to do some soul searching. He was also one of the *Ashramite* like others in the fellowship created by him although he was aware of the instability of his stay being an itinerant due to other commitments. Yet, see his resoluteness that wherever he would go, he would instinctively adhere strictly to the ashram observances even if the inmates of ashram did not accompany him during his sojourns. "His need for the physical space called ashram and community decreased as his reliance upon the *ashramic* observances increased, as did his devotion to Ramanama. Ashram was what lived within him, his *Anataryami*, the dweller within that guided him" (*TOI, 2 October, 2019*).

After initiating Satyagraha in South Africa, the Phoenix Ashram was established by him in 1904 but experimented '*ashramic*' features in 1906. A code of conduct was outlined there and all inmates firstly, were aware of the Ashram observances and secondly, were required to strive towards it. The code of conduct was applicable on all including his own good self or his wife. The was place where Gandhi experimented with Truth and any 'Untruth' prevailing in the Ashram was taken by him as his own failing. Mahatma Gandhi said, "From this time onward I looked upon Phoenix deliberately as a religious institution". It was in this very ashram that individual conduct was based on vows or *vratas* and this community of fellow beings strictly abiding by these vows would be a congregation of co-religionists and equality would be permeating feature of all co-inhabitants here. Ahmisa, love, non-stealing, non- acquisition, bread labour, non-violence etc. were introduced here as an experiment in lives of the inmates. In 1925 after fast that he had undertaken was concluded by him, he declared, "It is my best and only creation. The world will judge me by its results".

This ideal community was experimented by the Mahatma at the Tolstoy Farm as well. Later, Mahatma Gandhi founded Satyagraha Ashram, that was subsequently known as *Sabarmati*

Ashram on17 June 1917 to teach the lessons of Satyagraha. This was a haven where his followers implemented his teachings in their lives. Mahatma

Gandhi spent 1520 days in total at the ashram. He left the Ashram after he started Dandi March and did not return back at the place. Infact, Tridip Suhrud, an adherent of the Gandhian School and Former Director of Sabarmati Ashram say that the Dandi March was a 'collective demonstration of the ideals of the Satyagraha Ashram'. He lived for 685 days at a stretch at Sabarmati Ashram from November 1925 to February 1929 during this time the experiments of truth took place on the individual as well as community levels. His book, '*The Story of My Experiments with the Truth*' was written here and discourses on Gita were translated into Gujarati.

When he left Sabarmati Ashram after the call of the Dandi March was answered by enthusiasts, another ashram at *Wardha or Sevagram* was established. Here communal living and spiritual sadhana were the main grounds. "Sevagram was to mark yet another milestone in the secular and spiritual sadhana of Gandhi. Initially, he was of the opinion that Sevagram would work as a centre of his spiritual sadhana and his experiments in village development. Infact, after the withdrawal of the civil disobedience movement, Gandhiji had firmly come to the conclusion that even one ideal satyagrahi could move the country on account of his releasing tremendous spiritual energy" (*Pradhan, Ram Chandra, 2014*). At Sevagram many of his followers settled down leading an ideal life as wished by Gandhi.

Religious Values as a Premise of the Ideal Society

Religion was glorified and Mahatma Gandhi espoused that religion can guide men in all their deeds. He advocated that ***all religions contain Truth*** and should be given ***respect.*** The religious and caste differences were not considered in his opinion. Creating communal harmony and erasing weaknesses like, stratification of the caste system, social injustice, regionalism, ignorance etc. was the aim. Mahatma Gandhi was *critical of degeneration, hypocrisy and ritualism in the practices of Hindu faith* and made ardent efforts to *reform* the same. The life based on the religious precepts is taught by various religions is to be endorsed by one and all. He said, "After long study and experience, I have come to the conclusion that all religions are true; all religions have some error in them; all religions are almost as dear to me as my own Hinduism, in as much as all human beings should be as dear to one as one's own close relatives. My own veneration for other faiths is the same as that for my own faith, therefore no thought of conversion is possible". The medium of human agency is fallible and capable of erring and so, is to be tamed to implement the true values of the religions, which requires a lot of effort and control.

Religion cannot be separated from Politics. Politics and religion were not inseparable and politics itself was a religion. Religion and politics are not two watertight compartments, but are to be seen in continuum. According to him the problems of society like, unemployment, inequality, food, clothing and shelter and exploitation could not be solved without politics. But he was sternly opposed to politicizing religion. Mahatma Gandhi said, 'Everyone has realized that popular awareness could be brought about only through political activity. If such activity was spiritualized it could show the path of *moksha*' (CWMG XIV: p.201).

Politics, in this way, is to be treated as an *instrument for the welfare of people* and lead to creation of a pure society. The problems of the society can be solved if the philosophy of alternative model of social order elucidated by Mahatma is taken into action. The dissensions and non-integration of groups based on religious, caste and other differences can be solved through the equity based order suggested by him. The spiritual foundation based on values like, non-violence, truth, non-stealing, non-possession etc. serves as a check on accumulation and expansionist tendencies of the individuals, thereby maintaining equilibrium in the society.

Some of his ideas like non-violence and brahmacharya took care of the spiritual side of the human life. For the balance in the society, the concepts like, trusteeship, bread-labour, dignity of labour and many other prescriptions were given by Gandhi Ji. A fine balance between the secular and spiritual sides of the human existence was given by him.

Non-violence that was deeply rooted in our traditional religious thought was cultivated as social thought and not only, as a personal virtue. Non-violence coupled with love should be guiding force. Non-violence requires cooperation of *mind, body and speech* and is a weapon in the hands of fearless and strong. ***Ahimsa*** can be taken as deliberate *restraint* and it is distinguished from *non-killing.* Non-violence entails fearlessness and the target of *Hinsa* should not be inflicting pain or used for selfish purposes but used only as a last resort after all other means are exhausted for the righteous purpose. Non-violence empowers the members of the civil society to increase their civic participation. Mahatma Gandhi advocated to harness one's anger through the practice of non-violence and anger if moulded so would have the capability to affect the world. The positive aspect of Ahimsa is manifest in humanitarian values of love, patience, fearlessness etc. This culture is conspicuous by its absence today. The dignity of low class, poor, minorities and even, the small nations is not there. Present times that are marked with confrontations in the minorities and downtrodden and dissensions and war amongst nations; non-violence is path for humanity.

Democracy and non-violence are infact, inseparable from each other. ***Democracy*** if it is *disciplined as well as enlightened, can be converted into the finest thing in the world.* It is collective wisdom that is used to bring out right representation and exhibit public opinion. Democracy is a form of a humane order and the aim of the democratic institutions should be uphold and bring out the humane features inherent in men and society. Interplay between people having conducive mutual relationship is the core of democratic action. Democracy is not mere system of elections but in any good democratic system, the stress should be on *moral thinking and moral judgement.*

Gandhi preached philosophy based on ***Truth*** *and epitomises a life based on Truth* and he combined it with praxis based on Truth. Nowhere did he falter and deviated from the path of Truth in the personal and political space. The wisdom that he acquired during his life laid the foundation of action. *Satyagraha* (Holding on to Truth) was a multi-pronged strategy that was used in political field as well wherein he employed the truth power to change the hearts of the oppressors. "Non-violent methods of conflict resolution have been divided into two major analytical categories termed *Satyagraha* and *Duragraha*. *Satyagraha* means holding on to truth and *Duragraha* means action of a wilfully selfish and prejudiced nature" (*Misra, R.P and Gangrade, K.D., 2005*). Civil disobedience was adapted from Thoreau's writings. Satyagraha was an extension of the non-violent measures to curb the opponent initiated in South Africa.

The principles that were grounds for action in the personal as well as private space are elucidated below.

Ekadash Varata (Eleven Vows): Medium of Gandhi's Spiritual Sadhana for Individual and Collective Upliftment in Secular and Spiritual Domains

The crux of Gandhi's spiritual sadhana is seen in the vows (*vratas*) that a person observes once he has taken a resolve for the same without faltering even in impending difficulties. This is not possible without determination, iron will and unflinching commitment to the cause. These vows have an essential positive *connotations* due to its constructive nature. An individual is geared up to stick to a definite line of action after overcoming allurements in life, which is possible by developing the positive traits of one's character.

During Gandhi's sojourn to England, his unflinching commitment to the vows given to his mother of not succumbing to allurements in life namely, *wine, women and meat* was the testing grounds for the future.

At *Sabarmati Ashram,* a strict daily routine was adhered and morality was the basis of action of all the inmates. The *Ekadash Vrata* or eleven vows were reiterated at the prayer meetings held at the ashram, in the morning and evening. A new way of life was initiated through this daily routine based on strict controlled regime of action. Gandhi elaborated these vows to ashram inmates in his letters written in 1930 from Yervada Mandir or Jail.

1. Truth

Gandhi advocated centrality of Truth or God in life. The umbrella of Truth is the sheet anchor for other ten vows. Truth was equated with God. The earlier statement endorsed Truth as another name of God and he said that ***God is Truth*** *that was later reversed to* ***Truth is God***. Truth is unchanging and constant amid the things that are fluid. Truth has to be observed comprehensively in '*thought, speech and action*' that can be achieved through faith imbued with reasoning and the inner strength. He distinguishes between the ***Absolute Truth*** that is manifestation of God's another name while the ***Relative Truth*** comes to a person during his conduct in the worldly affairs and each one must pursue his own relative truth as a sacred duty. Satyagraha or holding on to Truth was employed as political means to reach the desired goal in the public space.

2. Non-violence (Ahimsa)

The Indian philosophy exhibits the legacy of *Ahimsa* endorsing compassionate living that was stressed by Buddha. Traditionally, non-violence means ***non-physical injury to others***. The concept of *Ahimsa* or non-violence means tolerance and empathy. Tolerating injustice and cruelty is akin to cowardly act and should be challenged and resisted. He defines the concept in a much broader perspective and says, "The principle of ahimsa is hurt by the evil thought, by undue haste, by lying, by hatred, by wishing ill to anybody. Not only that it is also vitiated, may even be violated, by holding or to what world needs' *(Gandhi: Mangal Prabhat).* His conception of non-violence is elaborated in the words, "Man as animal is violent, but as spirit is non-violent.

The moment he awakens to the spirit he cannot remain violent. Either he progresses towards ahimsa or rushes to his doom" (*Murti, V.V. Ranana, 1970*). Ahimsa is soul force and is in turn, depends on spiritual elevation of a person. He says, "We need not be afraid that the method of non-violence is a slow, long drawn out process. It is swiftest the world has seen, for it is surest" (*Young India, April 30, 1925*).

Unjust laws are also a form of violence, which is to be countered by non-violence not violence. Non-violence is a great force. Non-violence is a force "which is more positive than electricity and more powerful than ever ether. Non-violence is a force which is self-acting"

(*Gandhi, M.K., 1948*)."If you resist arrest, you are a coward and a violent man. If you peacefully submit to arrest, you are brave and non-violent" (*Misra, Prof. R.P. and Gangrade, Prof. K.D., 2005*). Non-violence is a positive force and not a passive or inactive method. "Passive resistance is an all-sided sword; it blesses him who uses it and him against whom it is used. Without drawing a drop of blood it produces far-reaching result" (*Gandhi, M.K. edited by Kriplani, Krishna, 1959*).

For Gandhi, there is a close affinity between the principles of truth and non-violence. The concept of Satyagraha that is logical corollary of two principles, Satya and Ahimsa. ***Ahimsa is the means and Truth as the end.*** If the means are taken care, the end could be achieved. So, one should be fully dedicated and adhere to the principle of ahimsa and not be affected by the hitches on the way. This would be testing ground to eliminate any trace of selfishness inherent in a person and prepare him for other *vratras*.

3. Brahmacharya

A *sadhaka/satyagrahi* has to observe Brahmacharya in *thought, speech and deed*. "What is Brahmacharya? It is the way of life which leads us to Brahma-God. It included full control over the process of reproduction. The control must be in thought, word and deed. If the thought is not under control, the other two have no value.....For one whose thought is under control, the other is mere child's play (*Harijan, June 8, 1947*).

The traces of animal passion in a person has to be curbed. The married couples have the duty to take the generation forward but within restraint of mind and act. With the passage of time, the definition of *brahmacharya* underwent a change from 1906 to 1947. 'It had become the *symbol of total dispassion, self-realization and God-realization*'.

4. Non-stealing (Asteya)

The concept of non-stealing has a broad meaning. In ordinary parlance, non-stealing is not to take anything from possession of others without their consent or permission. Many other things falls in the ambit of non-stealing. If one takes away anything under the belief that it does not belong to anyone, also is stealing in one way. Taking this concept a little more further, he adds that if one has taken anything with the permission of its owner, still it would be act of stealing if he has *does not need it* and has taken it. Another logically corollary to it is that one has to *reduce his needs to the bare minimum* and live a simple life. This is actually of real importance in the age of consumerism when people indulge in lavish lifestyles and spend extravagantly. Gandhi was concerned that the a small elite that lives extravagant lifestyle is responsible for this imbalance and creating conditions of poverty and deprivation. A large section is deprived due to this and uneven wealth distribution of the world is result of this. Another thing that Gandhi believes is that if *one's eyes on the possession of others* with envious eyes, one is actually engaging in the act of stealing in one way or another. One more thing that he brings in the ambit of non-stealing is *unnecessary fears and anxieties to fulfil the ever expanding needs of the future.* Lastly, he elaborates this concept and says, if one *borrows the ideas of others* and does not give proper acknowledgment to it, it is an act of stealing. In the present Knowledge Society, when knowledge is the driving force and ideas are the precious possessions of one steering one on the ladder of success, this is of prime importance. The issues of Intellectual Property Rights, Patents, etc. would be resolved amicably if non-stealing principle is adhered to.

5. Non-possession (Aparigraha)

Non-possession and non-stealing are closely connected to each other and non-possession can be taken as self-imposed poverty having unconditional faith in God. Gandhi was aware of the fact that man indulges in accumulation due to his future needs resulting in inequalities in the society. A truth seeker is not troubled by the insecurities of the future and hence, does not aim at grabbing unnecessary possession and leads a simple life. To lead a simple life by only taking things that are necessary for living is the key. He motivated the elite and rich to lead a simple life. For this a key was given by him in very apt words, ***"Earth could provide for every one's needs but not for everyone's greed"***.

The concept of ***Trusteeship*** is closely related to this concept wherein the capitalist are to have possession of the property in their hands that is a trust reposed in them but use it as for the welfare of the needy and take only that is required by them for their personal use. It was an appeal to the wealthy capitalists to give up some of their comforts and was an act of nobility reflecting human values. The principle of Trusteeship is popularly emulated in the corporate world of today solving many a problems arising from greed and accumulation.

This replicates the principles of *Triple Bottomline (TBL) i.e., People, Planet and Profit* endorsed by the modern corporate world and takes into consideration the problems arising from excessive greed and accumulation by the individuals and firms.

6. Control of Palate

The control over one's palate is *an independent vow.* For the human body's sustenance, food is a necessity. However, one should consume anything in the right balance and in appropriate quality and quantity. One should not eat or drink anything for the sake of taste. Even medicine that are prescribed in the right quantity and taken at proper time can cure the illness. The nature cure system experimented in the later part of his life was influenced from this vow. If this vow is followed in the daily routine, many of the lifestyle diseases would be solved. The related problems like, obesity, wastage of food etc. would be solved. The malnourished and poor would get their due share.

7. Fearlessness

Fearlessness is freedom from all bondages of the external fears like of demise, injury, losing one's near and dear ones and losing reputation and so on. This entails a total surrender of one to the Will of God by giving up one's own will. At that time when Mahatma Gandhi gave this call, the masses were dejected and disheartened due to long suffering they had been undergoing under the British regime. It was imperative to reinvigorate the masses and prepare them for the freedom struggle. This vow enthused the people to come out in open against the atrocious regime. This is one of the major contributions of Gandhi Ji in the nationalist struggle and this was acknowledged by Pt. Jawaharlal Nehru as well for the masses that had been dormant from a long time woke from their deep slumber.

8. Elimination of Untouchability

No work is menial and no class is lowly according to Mahatma Gandhi. Untouchability that had creeped in the Hindu society since times immemorial was termed as an *obnoxious system* by Mahatma Gandhi and as 'a blot on the face of *Hindustan*'. Fast unto Death in wake of Communal Award of 1932 and creation of Harijan Sevak Sangh and many other effort were made to eradicate this scourge from the society.

9. Bread-Labour

Bread-labour means that one should put in that much labour in a day that enables one to earn one's bread. Russian author, T.M. Bondarek had coined this concept and later, Tolstoy made it popular. This concept was popularised by Gandhi Ji reinstating the dignity of labour that was declining in the society. At that time the society was segregated into elite and lowly. The people doing mental work were treated as superior than the people doing menial hand work. In order to make all equal, this difference had to be removed and this vow taught that all works are dignified and all people are competent to do any sort of work, mental and physical. Moreover, physical labour employed to earn one's bread is important for keeping the body in fit condition. Bread labour principle would reinforce the rich to be *trustees* of their capital and property. The capitalists should act as trustees of the resources of the society and this would bridge the gap between the rich and poor. Gandhi says, "Obedience to the law of bread-labour will bring about a silent revolution in the structure of society. Men's triumph will consist in substituting the struggle for existence by the struggle for mutual service. The law of the brute will be replaced by the law of man" (*Harijan, June 29, 1935*).

10. Swadeshi

Swadeshi was ***an all-around strategy*** and made a part of the eleven vows. The final aim of *swadeshi* is liberation of physical body from the earthly bondage and emancipation of the human soul. It includes all the dimensions including political, social, economic and health dimensions. *Individual level* swaraj or self-rule is control of one over inner and outer life, *national level* swaraj means self-government for people.

11. Sarva-dharma sama bhava or Equal respect for all religions

The formula for a real conciliation of the secular and the spiritual sides of the human existence is *sarva-dharma sama bhava.* Gandhi advocated this by saying, '(i) *all religions are basically true,* (ii) they are basically *united in their ethical approaches,* and (iii) all religions are *imperfect as they have come through the medium of human agency*'.

No one religion is superior than the other and embracing other religion is not the solution. Aiming at removing weakness and decline in one's religion is one's duty. Hence, *sarva- dharma sama bhava* is more than concept of multi-culturalism of the present times establishing a cordiality between various

release from the bondage of the law of karma was most prominent idea articulated by Mahatma Gandhi although the concept permeated the entire Indian thought since the ancient times. In the four

then one can reach to ultimate aim of release from transmigration of birth, death and rebirth and emancipation. He elucidated *Moksha* not only, as a theoretical concept but also, converted into a praxis making its practice more relevant.

Moksha remained an evolving concept in India. During the Vedic times, ***primarily bhakti & not Mukti***

purging from human impurities and shortcomings. *Tri Ratna* (Three Jewels) i.e., Right Knowledge, Right Faith and Right Conduct can steer one through

Manusmriti, Brahmasutra, the Upanishads and Bhagavad Gita- all six philosophical systems of India, *Sankhya, Nyaya-Vaiesheska, Puva-mimansa and Uttar-Mimansa.* In all these place, the *moksha* stood for being *liberated from the bondage of action as well as from the endless chain of transmigration*".

Although Gandhi's concern for Moksha arose when he was very young. The issue of fundamental questions pertaining to human existence were troubling him even during his stay at South Africa. When he asked 27 questions in his letter to Raichand Bhai, a Jain monk and his spiritual mentor, 6 questions were addressed on it. The answer that he got was that it can be achieved through 'true knowledge, faith and action'. Gandhi enriched the concept by elucidating that matter and spirit are two separate things and the path to human deliverance can be tread only if both are separated. Moksha is not the domain of Yogis but a commoner can achieve it through *right knowledge, right action and detached service.* As he put it, 'As a Hindu, I believe that Moksha is freedom from birth by breaking the bonds of flesh by becoming one with God' (*Young India, 20 November 1924*).

This concept of Moksha was *extended to swaraj or self-rule* as the real foundation for achieving *moksha.* Moksha is not a pursuit to be undertaken at the last stages of one's life or an after-life affair. It has to be integrated in the daily life of a person. It is not reserved for a selected elite of the society but a domain in which all could enter through one's efforts.

Self-purification and self-realization and a society of free individuals is the aim of moksha. The praxis of *moksha* includes morality in the worldly affairs and in the political pursuits. In the worldly affairs people can achieve it through self-control. 'Moksha is liberation from impure thought. Complete extinction of impure thought is impossible without ceaseless penance. There is only one way to achieve this. The moment an impure thought arises confront it with, a pure one. This is possible with God's grace and God's grace comes through ceaseless communion with Him and complete self-surrender' (*Harijan, 22 February 1942*). Gandhi Ji asserts, '*Government over self is the truest Swaraj (self-rule) of individuals. It is synonymous with moksha or salvation*' (*Young India, 8 December 1920*).

It was the ultimate aim of Gandhi's life. The aim of *Swaraj* is not merely accumulation of power and privileges but to promote welfare of country and the entire world. He said, '*I have no desire for the perishable kingdom for earth. I am striving for the kingdom of the Heaven which is moksha*' (*Young India, April 1924*). Politics was imperative for all-round progress of the society. 'Everyone has realized that popular awareness could be brought about only through political activity. If such activity was spiritualized it could show the path of *moksha*' (CWMG XIV:p.201). This aim of a person if realized, would establish Ram Rajya in one's country and when the interest of the country is not in clash with the broader goals of humanity and the countries of the world, this spirit of Moksha will travel at all these destinations and a world society based on cordiality would be made possible. 'And when the interests of one's country are not in conflict with the interests of the world, service in the cause of one's country takes one towards *moksha*'(CWMG XXXII: p. 137)

For Gandhi, Moksha was a prescription for a person to live in this world and yet, be emancipated in the other world. Hence, the concept is a broad concept covering individual, national, international and more importantly, the humane levels.

Gandhi's Call to the Women Reinstating their Dignity

Any society which does not grant a space to the women cannot be considered as an ideal space. At the juncture when there were countless rituals and taboos associated with women and they were leading an isolated life after being confined to their homes behind their veils. He raised his forceful voice against the evil practices rampant in the society including, purdah, child marriage, dowry etc. and championed the rights of the women in very forceful words. Under Gandhi's wide canopy and deep protectionism, women got *confidence.*

Another thing that calls for attention is the *practical measure* adopted by him to grant an equitable and respectable status to women. Mahatma Gandhi gave a call to the ***women*** of those times who *came out of their houses* in thousands and took part in the freedom movement shoulder to shoulder along with the menfolk. Women participated in various *national causes* like, Dandi March and other such calls given by Gandhi Ji from time to time. This is of prime importance if delve into that time period when the women did not have any rights; rather they were disregarded in the society. This call of Mahatma Gandhi elevated the position of women in the society.

The position of women in the society was enhanced from *Abla to Sabla.* Sarojini Naidu, Vijay Lakshmi Pandit, Sarup Rani, Lakshmi Menon, Sushila Nayyar, Aruna Asaf Ali, Kamala Nehru and Rajkumari Amrit Kaur rose to prominence. Along with these, there were another thousands of unsung and unnoticed women of India, who were empowered by the call of Gandhi. They participated with fervour in the freedom struggle attending to the call of Bapu Ji and after independence, they were a part of the democratic franchise that was given instantly after the Constitution came into force.

He referred to marriage as a state of discipline and in Harijan wrote, "Marriage is a natural thing in life and to consider it derogatory in any sense is wrong...The ideal is to look upon marriage as a sacrament and therefore, to lead life of self-restraint in the married state". Whenever, Gandhi went to wedding ceremonies, he would gift a copy of Bhagvad Gita to the newly wedded couple so that their married life is based on spirituality based praxis. The simple message of Gita to focus on karma based praxis and righteousness would be a lesson for life for the couples. His advocacy of a simple marriage ceremony with minimal expenditure is all the more relevant today when spending lavishly on marriages has become an unsaid acceptable social norm irrespective of the fact that one or rich or poor. Moreover, many of such marriages turn into a failed experiment without mental bonding and love and the cases of divorce in the courts are raising at an alarming level.

Attire as a Mode of Dignity amongst Individuals in the Society

Another thing that was employed a mature nationalist tool in the drive of freedom was the emphasis on indigenous clothing, which in turn, would solve economic problems of the society. The British had replaced all our handicrafts and indigenous mode of production that was a major setback to our economy shattering the lives of many. To counter this problem, Mahatma Gandhi initiated Khadi Movement.

Khadi was encouraged by Mahatma Gandhi *as a way of life*. He implored the people to wear Khadi, homespun and handwoven cloth. This was not only as a *setback to the foreign clothes imported* and sold by the Britishers to capture Indian markets but also, as to provide *self- employment* to the local people who had no choice but to work in the factories put by English in India. "Spinning and weaving was elevated to an ideology of *self-reliance and self-government*. Every village shall plant and harvest its own raw materials for yarn, every woman and man shall engage in spinning and every village shall weave whatever is needed for its own use". These factories had resulted in unemployment of a large population who were unfit to work here. Khadi Movement aimed to *eradicate poverty* in the Indian masses living in villages. The target was to end *economic and social discrimination* prevalent in society for the rich, educated and liberal Indians had adopted western style of living and mannerism making them elite section of the society while the poor and live a traditional lifestyle. *Positively, a sense of self-confidence* was inculcated in the minds of the struggling masses who were enthused to challenge the British Empire. Moreover as part of daily routines, he encouraged each Congress member to take out time to spin *Charkha* for some time and he himself did it. This proved as a *connect with the Indian masses and peasants who had always* *remained distanced from the Brahmins* and the educated lot especially the lawyers. Even Motilal Nehru and many other leaders were persuaded by Gandhi who donned Khadi giving up their fine expensive clothing imported from in London. This united the rich as well as the poor for a similar cause and propelled the mass movement that was really the need of the hour without which Independence would not have been possible. So, on the whole Khadi Movement gave an *impetus to the Nationalist Struggle Movement along with propelling an economic movement.*

Today when we are more inclined to synthetic clothing and with reports that when these artificial fabrics are washed in the washing machines, micro plastics are washed into the ground water contaminating it, there is all the more need to resort to Khadi or cotton fabrics. The skin problems that are spread due use of synthetic fibres in the extreme heat is another related issue. Eco-friendly alternative was presented in the form of Khadi popularised by Gandhi Ji.

Village as the Basic Unit of the Society

The heart and soul of India lived in its ***villages***. The richness of wealth of India and its vibrant culture made India as a *Golden Sparrow*. India, right from the its past, had a strong inclination towards the rural mode of living over the urbane one. The villages were not dependent on the cities for survival and growth. The villages of India before the onset of the British Empire were self-sufficient entity. There were craftsmen, farmers, potters, weavers and all other prime professions located in the village itself. Its administration was complete with administrative, judicial and legislative bodies within it. There was no dependence of the villages on the cities but many of our traditional crafts and works were eroded systemically by the British Government to make place for their goods. He was of the opinion that the big cities are a snare and has many problems including the exploitation of rich by poor, robbery etc. But the Gandhian dream of ***Gram Swaraj*** was to revive the grassroots of India that had suffered a harsh blow at the hands of the British.

In Hind Swaraj, Gandhi envisaged the system of rural government based on truth and non- violence that would be true freedom and would give true contentment to the people. This system would make people self-sufficient and enable the people to enjoy true freedom. In a letter written to Pt. Nehru on 5 October 1945, Gandhi wrote, "Village of his conception would be habitat of intelligent people; everyone contributing his/her mite to the commonwealth. Such a village would provide a modicum of cleanliness and healthcare and would be full of activities. No one would remain idle; no one would wallow in luxuries".

Gandhi's dream of Gram Swaraj was to revive the grassroots of India that had suffered a blow at the hands of the British. The administration of the villages must be managed by the village residents themselves. Panchayats or the council of mature and trusted men should be assigned the task of village administration and solve its problems like, disputes, water supply, irrigation, sanitation, construction, maintenance etc. and other policies. His developmental model favoured village-centred planning. The concept of Gram Panchayat and Gram Swaraj was asserted by Gandhi. Yet, the desired dream of Mahatma Gandhi is elusive.

India although initially was a reluctant urbanizer but at present the trend is that our cities are proliferating and expanding tremendously. The accompanying resultant problems including uncleanliness, shortage, robbery, exploitation, corruption, power grabbing, sanitation problems etc. is visible everywhere. The exodus of the rural population to the urban areas has imbalanced both, rural as well as urban areas. The decline in green cover and scarcity of food grains is the result of this. The model of village given by Mahatma Gandhi is truly viable for balancing the rural-urban dichotomy present in present day India. The real democracy would be possible in India if we keep our villages rejuvenated for ***68.84%*** live in villages and pristine condition of India would be possible.

Conclusion

The philosophy Mahatma Gandhi was very wide and embracing, an imperative for an ideal society. After realising the weaknesses in the society like, stratification of the caste system, social injustice, regionalism, ignorance, inequality, absence of dignity, he gave a practical plan of action to meet these. He aimed to establish a society where religious differences are not considered and the mutual confrontation between religions is not there. The malice of man-made caste system was challenged by Gandhi espousing fundamental equality of mankind based on Fatherhood of God. All humans are equal and regardless of castes distinction, they can achieve Truth in this present life. His ideas had a deep impact in the society segregated by the caste divisions and religious differentiations reiterating that all are born from one God. National integration was paramount for him. The values of equality, oneness, righteousness, Truth and Truthful Living, peace and harmony needs to spread to create a positive and social viewpoint to create inter-faith harmony, an imperative that needs to asserted in the modern pluralistic and multi-cultural world.

Gandhi said, "I do not want my house to be walled in on all sides and my windows to be stuffed. I want the culture of all lands to be blown about my house as freely as possible. But I refuse to be blown off my feet by any way". Today when we are living in epoch marked by ideological myopia, this readiness of Gandhi to embrace currents of thoughts from various quarters is to be pondered and emulated (*TOI, 2 October 2019*). In the deteriorating world of today, the impact of materialism and all other allurements in life is discernable in the western as well as the eastern worlds. The peace of mind and *Mukti* have become the key questions and Gandhi addressed these deep philosophical subjects enlightening the humanity.

Gandhi is one of those ***rare social thinkers and a secular and spiritual leader***, who is as much interested in the secular field as in spiritual quest and his thought is combination of it. His communication with the masses was simple and effective that his message went home in the minds instantaneously and would be instrumental in making the world a better place to live in.

As an alternative to the present political system, of both the liberal and the Marxian models, he offered a people-oriented and humane laying foundation for ***participatory democracy***. The grassroots were inter-woven into the political power making possible decentralization till the village level. Economically, the model proposed by him was a critique of the Western model and offered a healthy alternative to consumerism. Gandhi Ji says, "The Socialists and Communists say they can do nothing to bring about economic equality today.... They say, when they get control over the State they will enforce equality. Under my plan the State will be there to carry out the will of the people, not to dictate to them or force them to do its will. I shall bring about economic equality through non-violence, by converting the people to my point of view, by harnessing the forces of love against hatred. I will not wait till I have converted the whole society to my view but will straightway make a beginning with myself. It goes without saying that I cannot hope to bring about economic equality of my conception, if I am the owner of fifty motor cars or even of ten bighas of land. For that I have to reduce myself to the level of the poorest of the poor" (*Harijan, 31 March, 1946*).

Trusteeship and decentralization makes the society more inclusive. It offers the path to sustainability by presenting an overall balanced and ideal society where the marginalized and poor are taken care of. The embracing of voluntary poverty by the elite, addressing the basic needs of the people, decentralized form of economy and so on can be instrumental in solving their problems that remain largely unaddressed even the present scenario despite the village-level being inter-woven into the constitutionally recognised tier for conducting administrative affairs.

The inter-relationship between the humans and other living things in the natural environment is depicted in thought of Gandhi. The resources of Mother Earth are revered and any sort of exploitation of non-renewable natural resources is checked. The cleanliness (*swacchta*) of surroundings and mental outlook was paramount in all dealings of human beings including politics. ***He emphasised on clean habits, balanced diet, strict code of conduct, erasing all impurities of mind and soul and drive towards Moksha and this would create a society where all its components are balanced.***

The spiritual principles experimented by Gandhi can solve many problems of the present day society especially pertaining to religious fundamentalism and frequent outbursts of violence. His political, social, economic and religious ideas were the basis establishing a non-violent society that could lead to real resurgence and regeneration of pure society. When the agenda of politics is personality drawn, Gandhi's style is required all the more.

This inspiring and creative life and equity based sustainable order if emulated today, will be elixir solving ills of the society. The high level of integration of his body, mind and heart is to asserted for wholesome development of mind and society. He ***elevated the level of politics to the highest level imbued with spirituality*** that should be a role model for the youth of the country and the world, if disseminated widely in a proper perspective. If spirituality based on rationality could be ground of his action in the era of turmoil, it can be made a base even today.

An enlightened individual comprise an enlightened society. Inner purification of the hearts is imperative for this enlightened society. The Mahatma was alive to this issue and a well- coordinated composition of the society was his aim. He regarded co-operative and participatory society as the only truly religious society, with enlightened individuals as a prerequisite. A good society cannot be conceived without good individuals who are essential constituent elements of composing an ideal society. He taught the prescription for individuals for attaining fulfilment in life and also, for emancipation. A structured ethics was offered to make, individually and collectively, responsible choices in all individual, personal and political matters. The desired values that should be imbibed by a person in his life were translated into practice especially at Sabarmati Ashram. The principles of moral and rational action laid were akin to the religious and social revolution, the relevance of which is visible in the contemporary world dominated by ever growing materialistic ethos and politics of fragmentation. Integral to him was the awareness of the ills and errors in the society and an ardent concern to remedy these. He presents a *living philosophy* with ideals of faith and spiritual deliverance, human equality and justice, the ideals that are integral to modernity.

Conflict resolution is important in politics and Satyagraha was presented as an alternative to the other methods including the destructive methods. The problem of India and the world at large can be solved by reconciling inequality issues and by encouraging participation of all the shades of opinion in the fabric of the civil society. His message of tolerance and empathy is suitable for the multi-religious and modern pluralistic societies. We should strive for sustainability and creating a healthy environment, both socially and environmentally.

His dream of *clean and enlightened India* both physically and mentally is still a dream, yet to be converted into action plan. Today when the problems are afflicting the society, the futuristic and all-embracing vision of the society are accepted universally to create an ideal and desired society.

References

Biswal, S.K. (2012). Social and Political Thought of Mahatma Gandhi, Arise Publishers and Distributers, New Delhi

Gandhi, M.K., edited by Kriplani, Krishna (1959). All Men are Brother, UNESCO, Paris Gandhi, M.K. (1948). Non-violence in Peace and War, *Navajivan Publishing House*, Ahmedabad, Vol. I

Harijan (1935, June 29)

Harijan (1946, 31 March)

Harijan (1942, 22 February)

Harijan (1947, June 8)

Maslow, Abraham (1997, February). In Rubin, Z., The Love Research, *Human Behaviour* Misra, R.P. and Gangrade, K.D. (2005). Gandhian Alternative: Nonviolence-in-action, *Concept Publishing Company*, New Delhi

Murti, V.V. Ranana (1970). Gandhi's Essential Writings, New Delhi, *Gandhi Peace Foundation*

Pradhan, Ram Chandra (2011). Reading and Reappraising Gandhi, *Macmillan Publisher India*

Ltd. Delhi

Pradhan, Ram Chandra (2014). Integrating Body, Mind and Heart: The Gandhian Way, Trinity, New Delhi

The Times of India (2019, 2 October). Gaurav Dalmia, Gandhi in the 21st Century

Young India (1924, April)

Young India, (1924, November 20)

Young India, (1925, April 30)

Young India, (1924, November 20)

Young India (1920, December 8)

4

The Gandhian Way of Life: An Impeccable Solution to World Environmental Concerns

Rakesh Kumar Gupta ***and Prerna Diwan***

Abstract

"The Earth has enough resources for our need but not for our greed."

This inspiring phrase of Gandhi depicts his concern for nature and environment. Gandhi's consciousness of environment and concerns are clear in the entirety of his works and discourses. Gandhian way of thinking considers human beings and their environment as mutually interlinked, as a feature of an incorporated entirety, and as part of an integrated whole. Gandhi's direction for people to exercise restraint with respect to the utilization of natural resources is significant in the current time frame to fathom the issues emerging with high consumerism lifestyle and high generation of waste.Gandhi's crusade was not against technology driven development, but it was against its misapplication in terms of unsustainable development.

Gandhi, dismissed the present day so called modern method of life and work, and propagated the practice of self-reliance and standing through agriculture, charkha and the village ways for every single person.The application of Gandhian principles and standards can assist usto create a low carbon world by investing in nature-based solutions. Restoring, Rejuvenating and protecting our natural resources including tree covers, soil, seas and the oceans can provide a natural solution to carbon capture. We must reconstruct villages on the principles of reduce, recycle and reuse, where science and culture meets and diminish the movement to urban communities.

Embracing Mahatma Gandhi's way of life can help the world facing the daunting challenge of global warming and climate change. There is a need to focus on principles of sustainability, using natural materials, minimum possessions, need based designs and regulating our lifestyle.

Introduction

"The Solution to Pollution is Dilution". What a good strategy to manage all kinds of pollutants contributed to air, water and soil. This implies that the ill effects of any kind of pollutant entering the environment can be neutralized just by bringing down its concentration by dilution. Indeed, even nature has this capacity to purify itself over the time subject to the pollutant concentration falls in its purification limits. In any case, we need to identify as to what extent it is validin today's world with continuous depletion and exploitation of the natural environments in order to fulfil our incessant needs. The levels of pollution in air, water and soil have crossed the self-purification limits of these natural life line reserves, thereby, challenging the fundamental endurance of living beings on the planet Earth.

The society's greed and insensitivity towards these embodiments of life is taking heavy toll on all types of ecosystems on Earth. Individuals fear sinking urban communities, exhaustion of glaciers, abrupt and extreme changes in weather and climate, rising temperatures, exposure to UV radiations due to the development of Ozone Hole, higher frequency of cancer development due to exposure to xenobiotic compounds or Persistent Organic Pollutants (POPs) used as pesticides, plastics, and so forth. All the Governments universally have demonstrated their interests to save mankind by organising the summits and congregations to settle on agreement choices to cut down the contamination levels and its outcomes.The Stockholm Summit 1972, the Rio Earth Summit 1992, Rio +20 Earth Summit 2012, Paris Climate Accord 2015 are some of the instances of the Global Environment Summits during which major agreements were signed for Sustainable Development, Conservation of Biodiversity, fighting environmental change (Kyoto Protocol), desertification, and so on.

Even people over the world have come up with different fascinating ways of protest against Government's seriousness on this issue. The Earth Day is celebrated each year since 1970 on 22nd April to demonstrate respect for Earth and pledge for support to preserve this only known living Planet in the entires Universe. In the month of September this year, impressed with the youth movement initiated by the Swedish school girl 'Greta Thunberg'demanding the influential people to tackle the global warming, millions of people from all segments of society irrespective of age, cadre and social status across 185 nations came out on streets protesting for this cause. Similarly, major movements to save environment in India were steered by Chandi Prasad Bhatt and Sunder Lal Bahuguna (Chipko Movement), by Baba Amte and MedhaPatkar (Narmada BachaoAndolan), all propelled and inspired from Gandhian thoughts.

Now the question arises who is responsible for this ecological wreckage, the Governments or the people themselves? In the following paragraphs authors have tried to decipher the answers to this burning question from Mahatma Gandhi's thoughts and principles of living.

Population Explosion and Extreme Consumerism

The world population in 2019 is expected to be more than 7.7 billion which implies that all these people will require water, food, cloths, shelter, and so forth for their survival. In India, as per the census of 2011 the population has increased to 1210 million from 361 million in 1951 after independence, a steep hike of 70% (Figure 1). All these people will utilize the natural resources and will continue to generate waste to contaminate air, land and water and therebyincrease the carbon footprints.

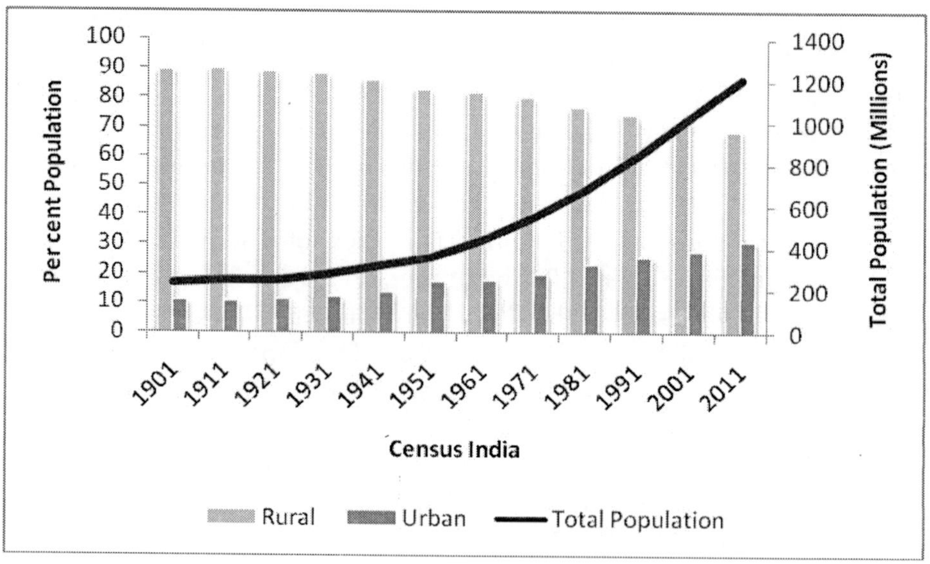

Figure1. Rural and Urban share of population of India since 1901.

Interestingly, the population explosion is still thought to be manageable but the voracityof people to obtainincreasingly more has become the lives and culture of success symbol. There is a drastic difference in the consumption expenditure per capita of developed, developing and. low income group of countries. The household expenditure per capita in United States of America has been estimated to US $ 37922 compared to India where the value is US $1189.In developed countries, per person consumption is about 16 tons on an averageof the four important natural resources:biomass, fuel, minerals and ores per year as compared to an Indian with 4 tons only. Per person consumption in many of these developed countries is as high as 40 tons.One American drains these natural resources equivalent to 35 Indians with very less sense and guilt of sustainability. In India, the consumption of electricity increased 8 times in 2019 from 1970 with only 1/6thshare generated from renewable sources.

Ecological Footprints of one person in developed countries is a lot greater than the ones in developing countries. As per the Global Footprints network's Website, the world's Ecological Footprint (2016) is 2.75 global hectares per person (gha/p) as compared to Australia, USA and India with 6.64, 8.1 and 1.17gha/p, respectively.With this pace of upsurge of population and consumption, one and half planet like Earth is required in today's time in order to sustain all the inhabitants of the Earth. If such ruthless exploitation of this planet known for supporting mankindis not stopped, its environment will be so hostile and aggressive that it could engulf the whole human race.

Village vs Urban Industries

According to the 2011 census of India, about 68.8 % population resides in rural areas which have dropped from 82.7 % as per 1951 census (Figure 1). This sharp exodus of rural people towards urban areas has been attributed to the lesser job opportunities, decline in the farm sector productivity, loss of village based small scale industries, poor health infrastructure, etc. in villages. This has not only overburdened the urban infrastructure and facilities but created a largepool of people living in unhealthy and crowded slums under the abject poverty.

In the year 1950-51, the Agriculture and allied sectors contributed 51.81 % of the total Indian Gross Value Added (GVA) compared to 15.87% in 2018-19. The major share of the agro sector shifted to services sector which rose from 33.25 % (1950-51) to 54.4 % (2018-19) of the total GVA of India. The % GVA contribution of Industries enhanced from 14.16 % (2050-51) to 29.73 % (2018-19). Interestingly, the contribution of Agriculture and allied sectors to the Indian economy is still much higher compared to the global average of 6.4 %. There is still a scope of improvement in other two sectors, Industries and Services to reach to the world level.The increased population burden of cities and urban industrialization have caused havoc on the environment of these ecosystems. In addition, the governments are continuously focusing on increasing their GDPs to grow their economies by pressurizing on the manufacturing sector rather than enhancing the contributions of agriculture sector.

Mr Rao Inderjeet Singh, Minister of State, Ministry of Statistics and Programme Implementation (MOSPI), Government of India, reported in RajyaSabha that per capita income in terms of Net Value Added (NAV) was Rs 98435 for urban household compared to Rs 40,925 for a rural household in the year 2018despite higher labour participation rate and a low employment rate of 5.3% in rural India than urban. There is further disparity between the per capita income of agricultural workers/farmers and non-agricultural workers within villages leading to the dampened spirit in the agricultural services. Though the Indian Government has initiated a number of schemes to bridge the economic gap of rural urban divide, its impact is yet to be realized.

Impact on Environment

In the post-Gandhian era, we face catastrophic global environmental crisis due to large-scale and indiscriminate industrialisation for short-term gains. Investigation and Analysis of the scenario, as to who is responsible for the surfacing environmental concerns, and who is bearing the consequences, it is certain that the burden and implications are shared unequally in developing and developed Nations. There are enormous variations between the major world's economies in terms of CO, emissions measured at the individual level. Measured per person, India's emissions are still very low – at only 1.8 tonnes of CO_2 per capita – which is much lower than 14.95 metric tons for an average American, 6.57 metric tons per person in China and the world average of 4.2 tonnes. This shows that even though the population of India is high still its carbon foot prints are muchlower.

India is highly vulnerable to climate change, notably due to the melting of the Himalayan glaciers and the monsoon changes. The impact of climate change in the form of high temperatures, droughts, floods and other natural calamities are affecting developing nations including India to a much greater extent than developed countries, although the urbanization as cause of all this is more in developed industrialized Nations. Developing nations also suffer more because of absence of the approaches to manage such changes and still relying more on natural resources. They can give us net negative greenhouse emissions at scale, at lower costs and faster speeds than other carbon reduction options. More than 70 per cent of global greenhouse gases are produced from urban areas, which consume 60 to 80 per cent of the world's energy. We need to make a reverse shift that is urban to rural, to reduce the carbon footprint.

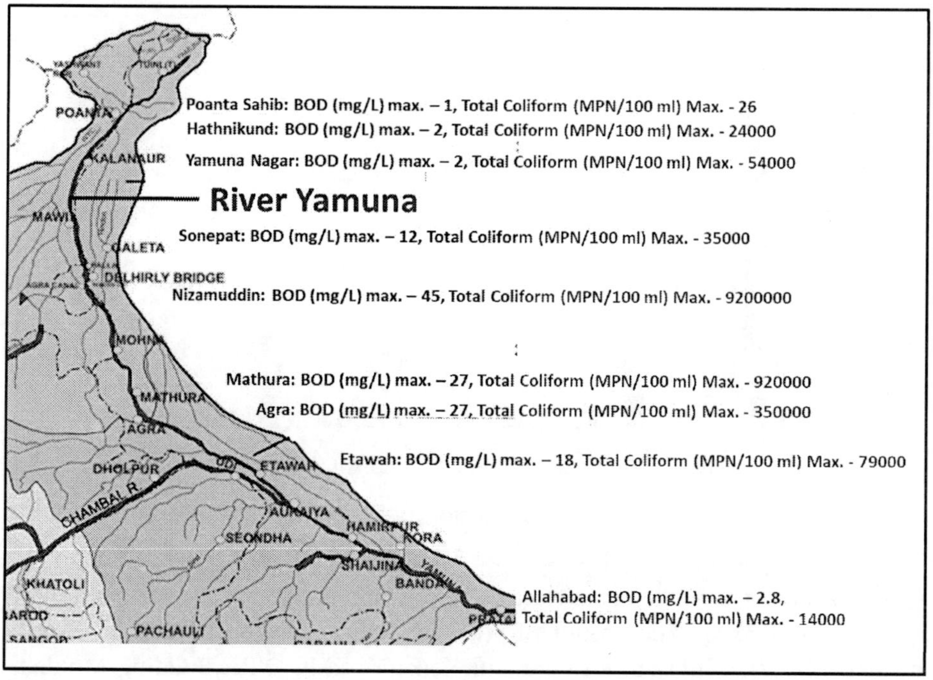

Figure 2. Pollution levels of Yamuna River at various monitoring stations influenced by the number of inhabitants and industries on its route (CPCB 2016)

Map source: http://cwc.gov.in/ybo/about_basin

All the rivers, fresh water reservoirs and wetlands in India are under danger of very high pollution levels due to human activities and industries. Quality of water in rivers from the origin is very good on the basis of the presence of biodegradable organic matter measured as Biological Oxygen Demand (BOD, mg/L).Whenever, the river passes through a high population density urban and industrial area, it gets polluted to such an extent that even a long distance uninterrupted flow is unable to bring the BOD to normal values. As per the water quality data collected by the Central Pollution Control Board from various monitoring centres across the path of the river Yamuna, the water of river Yamuna after Poanta Sahib fails the standards with respect to total coliforms and after Sonepat the values of BOD and total coliforms never come down to normal till it merges at Prayagraj, Allahabad in the river Ganga (Figure 2). At many locations depending on the size and number of industries, the water is, severely contaminated with heavy metals and both biodegradable and non-biodegradable organic matter and is unfitfor any kind of human activity.

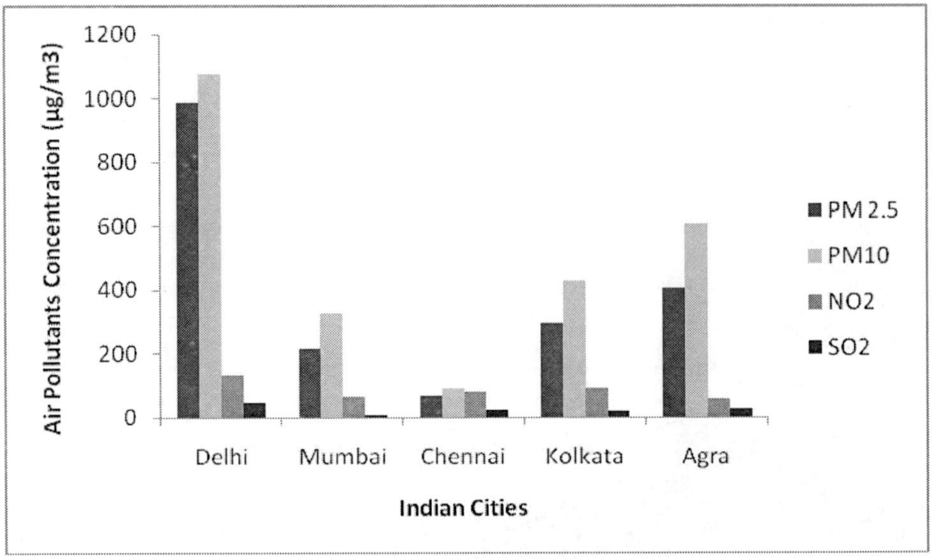

Figure 3. Ambient air pollution at selected cities of India (24 hourly average, maximum values,CPCB 2018). Specific locations in cities are: Delhi – Janakpuri, Mumbai – Worli, Chennai – NEERI, CSIR Campus Taramani, Kolkata – KMC Office Building, Moulali, and Agra– Taj Mahal.

The inhabitants of the Metro cities and industrial towns are gravely affected by the extremely poor ambient air quality. The satisfactory levels of air quality in Delhi in the year 2019 have been observed only on very few days. On most of the days of the year, the $PM_{2.5}$ Air Quality Index (AQI) in the ambient air was more than 100µg/m^{3}i.e. in the range of unhealthy category. A comparison of AQI of various cities on the basis of the CPCB Air Quality Data of the year 2018, the air of Delhi was found to be the most polluted followed by Agra, Kolkata, Mumbai and Chennai (Figure 3). The breathing of high particulate air for a long time results into various health problems related to respiratory and cardiovascular system.

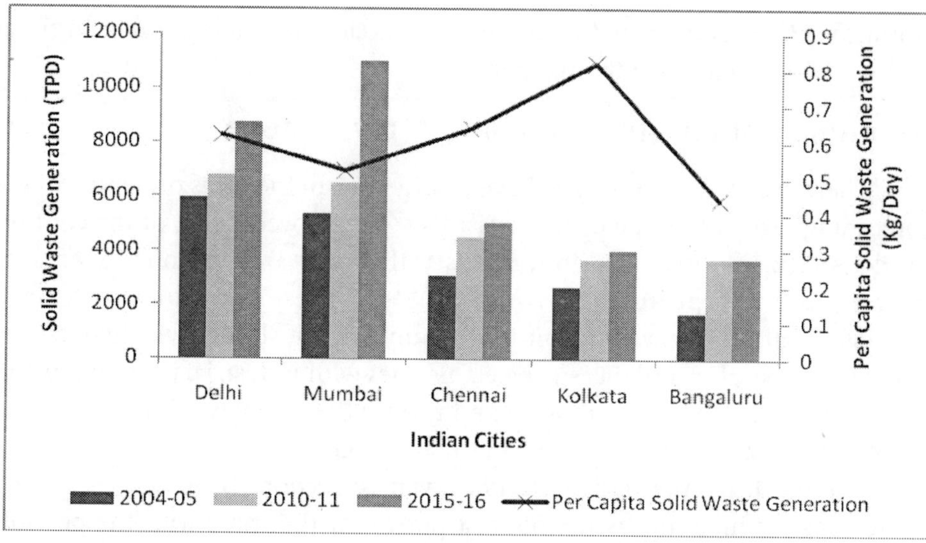

Figure 4. Solid Waste Generation (SWG,Tonnes Per Day, TPD) at selected cities of India in the year 2004-05, 2010-11, 2015-16 and 2015-16. Per Capita Solid Waste Generation (Kg/ Day) has been calculated for the year 2010-11 on the basis of 2011 census of the selected cities.

The competition to acquire more beyond requirement to fulfil our materialistic greed has not only drained our natural reserves but at the same time has created a problem of huge solid waste generation (SWG). The more is the production, the more is the consumption and the more is the solid waste output. The rich countries of the world are utilizing the resources at their maximum, and in turnare also producing solid waste to that magnitude. 34 % of the total world's waste share comes from these countries. Per capita SWG/day by an American is ~2.0 Kg compared to an urban Indian whoproduces only ~0.45 Kg. India produces about 1.5 lakh Metric tonne of solid waste daily with the highest generation by the top highly populated metro cities (Figure 4).

The per capita amount of solid waste generation is directly proportional to the per capita income of the societies. The amount of SW generated from villages is reported to be extremelylow and is nowhere near to what is being produced in cities and towns. In addition, the composition of solid waste generated from villages constitutes mainly biodegradable matter which is either converted into compost or utilizedas fuel. On the other hand only 50% of the solid waste collected from cities is biodegradable and rest is plastic, paper, metal construction material, etc. posing serious challenges before the

Municipal Corporations to find more space and new technology for its disposal in an environment friendly manner.

Gandhian philosophy of living: A ray of hope

There are many factors that have emerged from the ideas presented in the preceding sections on the consumerism, economic well-being of the country and its citizens, urbanisation, industrialization and various extents of environmental pollution. Every one of these variables interface thedeterioration of environment to the human's selfish life style, remorseless material possession and measuring economies with industrial production and consumption. In order to mitigate and reverse the damage, it is imperative to comprehend and follow the life of Mahatama Gandhi.

Gandhi drove the Indian Nation towards freedom from British rule by practicing a simple life as the poorest person of that time with the possible minimum resources. In his books or writings or discussions, historians do not find any direct context to the environment. However, Gandhi's entire life and working principles have left an environmental legacy for all humankind. All the Ashrams that were set up by him were self-reliant, sustainable and environment friendly. While in London, he was once asked whether he is going to follow the same standards of living in India. He answered "It took Britain half the resources of the planet to achieve this prosperity. How many planets will a country like India require?"

Gandhi could anticipate the need for preservation and sustainable development of villages through production of goods at small scale by individuals or by few people together meeting the basic requirements of villagers and surrounding areas i.e. *gram swaraj*. His concerns for mass production at an industrial scale have proved true, looking at the economic condition of villagers with no means of livelihood. He was not against innovation and technology. His own ashram was a lab of experiments where he used to develop new techniques forbetter production of Khadi with minimal resources. He announced a machine challenge in 1929 to develop a machine which could spin yarn at much faster rate than the machines in England.

Gandhi followed the tenets of self-discipline (self-introspection, contentment, cleanliness/sanitation, prayer and freeing of outrage, lust, and greed) and commandments of human behaviour (non-violence, truth, celibacy, non-stealing and non-possessiveness). A significant number of these codes of conduct like non-possessiveness, non-grasping or non-greediness, contentment, non-violence against all living and non-living beingsand self-introspection directlyconnect with the ecological conservation. His simple contention for preservation of biodiversity arising from his faith in non-violence and vegetarianism was *"since a human being had no power to create life, he has, therefore no right to destroy life."*

His concerns for the judicious use of resources and their equal distribution among different sections of the society are reflected in his expression *"man's happiness lies in contentment. He who is discontented, however much he possesses, become a slave to his desires."* That's where the solution to the environmental problems lies. Rather than accusing the Governments, each and every individual needs to self-introspect, avoid eagerness and desire to secure more and be contended with the minimum possible resources. The day, each one of us stops amassing unlimited wealth and merchandise, and displays the desire to share the resources equally and love for nature, Governments which are the extensions of individuals will change their directions of development and parameters of monetary evaluations.We as a whole need to have faith in this statement of Gandhi *"I refuse to buy from anybody anything, however nice or beautiful, if it interferes with my growth or injures those whom nature has made my first care."*

References

1. Barua A. Towards a Philosophy of Sustainability: The Gandhian Way. *Sociology and Anthropology* 3(2): 136-143, 2015.
2. Sasikala A.S. Environmental Thoughts of Gandhi for a Green Future. *Gandhi Marg.* 2012; *34(1)*: 53–68.
3. Khoshoo T. N. Moolakkattu J.S. Mahatma Gandhi and the Environment (Analysing Gandhian environmental thought), 2009.The Energy and Resources Institute (TERI) ISBN 978-81-7993-223-0.
4. Gandhi's Views on Environment- Five Elements of Nature http://www.gandhimanibhawan.org/gandhiphilosophy/philosophy_ environment_ 5elementsnature.html
5. Kaushal R. K., Verghese, G. K. Chabukdhara, M. Municipal Solid Waste Management in India-Current State and Future Challenges: A Review. International *Journal of Engineering Science and Technology*, 2012; 4 (4), 1473-1489.
6. Census of India, 2011. www.censusindia.gov.in
7. Chand R, Srivastava S K and Singh J (2017). Changing Structure of Rural Economy of India Implications for Employment and Growth, National Institution for Transforming India NITI Aayog. Discussion paper https://niti.gov.in/writereaddata/files/document_publication/Rural_Economy_DP_final.pdf
8. Central Pollution Control Board. Water Quality of River Yamuna – 2016. https://cpcb.nic.in/wqm/2016/Water_Quality_data_of_River_2016.pdf
9. Central Pollution Control Board. Trends of Solid waste Journal in 46 cities. https://cpcb.nic.in/

uploads/MSW/trend_46_cities_list.pdf

10. Central Pollution Control Board. National Ambient Air Quality Monitoring Programme (NAMP) Data, 2018.http://www.cpcbenvis.nic.in/air_quality_data.html
11. Myers, N. Consumption in relation to population, environment and development. *The Environmentalist*, 1997; 17, 33-44. https://doi.org/10.1023/a:1018531428876

Online Resources:

12. http://data.footprintnetwork.org/#/compareCountries?cn=all&type=EFCpc&yr=2016
13. http://statisticstimes.com/economy/sectorwise-gdp-contribution-of-india.php
14. https://databank.worldbank.org/source/world-development-indicators
15. Households and NPISHs Final consumption expenditure per capita (constant 2010 US$). https://data.worldbank.org/indicator/NE.CON.PRVT.PC.KD
16. Government of India, Ministry of Statistics and Programme Implementation, http://mospi.nic.in/.

5
The Universalist Called Mahatma Gandhi

Rajdeep Pathak

Mahatma Gandhi was in his lifetime, and remains in death a puzzle to the world. It has been widely accepted that the one thing that can be said with certainty is that Mahatma Gandhi belongs to a small number of great men who cannot be pigeonholed, catalogued, summed up, pinned down or in any way easily explained. He was not a saint. He would say to those who clubbed him in that widely accepted category: "I am not a saint who has strayed into politics. I am politician who is trying to become a saint".

During one of the most violent periods in the most violent century in history, Mahatma Gandhi insisted that "Nonviolence is the law of our species". To those who scoffed, he said, "You say there can be no nonviolent rebellion and there has been none known to history. Well, it is my ambition to provide an instance". And he did.

As George Woodcock in his book "Gandhi" writes: "Gandhi was a political activist, judging his theories by their results. What he thought, he tested in practice. Practice in turn helped to shape his thought, so that he could talk with accuracy of his career as a series of 'experiments with truth'. [1]

He was a natural fighter, but a born peace maker, a socialist whose aim was to make every man a capitalist, a nationalist who refused "to hurt England to serve India". He was a cheerful man who based a movement on humanity's capacity for suffering.

Woodcock further points out that Satyagraha, or truth force, was the name Gandhi gave to the resistance that he and his followers offered to foreign opposition and local tyranny. He writes, "The resistance of people who did not fear to be violent but chose deliberately to be non-violent and to fight by the power of 'Truth', rather than the power of the body".

More than a technique of political action or subject of research, *Satyagraha*, Mahatma Gandhi believed is a way of life. Mahatma Gandhi said that *Satyagraha* wasn't a subject of research, for one must experience it, use it and live by it. R. R. Diwakar writes: "Satyagraha is basically a way of life in which truth and non-violence, the realization of truth through non-violence and loving action, is the idea".[2]

Mahatma Gandhi had said, "Satyagraha is utter self-effacement, greatest humiliation, greatest patience and brightest faith. It is its own reward",[3] adding, "A Satyagrahi will shine the brighter and grow the more courageous the more he is crushed."[4]

Woodcock continues: "Gandhi never sat out to develop a fixed and final doctrine, but emphasized that his practice of *ahimsa* or non-violence was always experimental, that his political struggle like his personal life was part of a continuing quest of Truth as manifested existentially, a quest that could never end because human understanding was incapable of comprehending the Absolute".

"At the height of his struggle with the British", writes Woodcock, "He never lost his admiration for English thinkers and English institutions, and he refused to sever the channels of dialogue with those against whom he fought without bitterness and without envy."[5]

This is how he developed relations. Treating one's enemy as friends was a characteristic that he strongly espoused for. This was because he was firmly attached to his roots. Though Gandhi learnt much in the years he spent outside India and counted Ruskin, Tolstoy and Thoreau among the masters who shaped his outlook, he chose no more that was needed to vitalize his own beliefs, and returned to find again, with the help of western insights, the resources of his own tradition, out of which he drew the strength that made him so responsive to the aspirations of the Indian poor and so imaginative as a leader in the fight for liberation.[6]

It is widely accepted that Mahatma Gandhi had been a product of all that he has read and experienced. He was the product of his ongoing and consistent experiments with truth and non- violence. "Gandhi himself has left us no systematic presentation of his philosophy. It has to be distilled from his autobiography, speeches and extensive writings on various subjects.[7] He would say, "I am not built for academic writings. Action is my domain". Further on he wrote: "What I write or say has not been thought out in conformity with a system. I have only enough strength to enable me to meet every situation as it arises in course of my quest for truth".[8]

This belief came to the 'universalist' Gandhi from his extensive study of people, cultures and traditions. One of the significant facts about the life and vocation of Gandhi, wrote Thomas Merton in his essay, "Gandhi and the One-Eyed Giant", "was his discovery of the East through the West".

For instance, when he went to England to understand the knowledge that made Englishmen powerful, (Mahatma) Gandhi learnt instead his first lessons in the knowledge that had once made Asians wise. He learnt that by the initiative of the European scholars in the nineteenth century ancient Indian history was re-created, the serious study of Sanskrit Literature was begun, and the Indian vernaculars were treated seriously and became literary languages[9].

When for example, he came with the Theosophical Society, the followers of the Theosophist Madame Blavatsky made lasting impression on him and they led him to read for the first time the Indian classic, which in years to come was regarded by Mahatma Gandhi as 'the book *par excellence*' for the knowledge of 'Truth'. This was no other book than the 'Bhagawat Gita', which Gandhi had later made into his own translation after his understanding of the meaning and significance of the epic.

When he read this English translation of Sir Edwin Arnold and read the poem *The Light of Asia*, he learnt for the first time of the life and teaching of the Buddha. He read Tolstoy's "Kingdom of God is Within You" in 1893 and Ruskin's "Unto This Last" in 1904, which in Gandhi's own words had 'captured' him and 'transformed' his life.[10]

If Tolstoy became a guide to Gandhi in developing the theory and practice of non-violent action, which he later called *satyagraha*, it was Ruskin who led him to the conclusion that an unequal social order, divorced from the realities of labour, is likely to make non-violence impossible.[11]

Reflecting on the 'universalist' Gandhi, and the influence he had from Count Leo Tolstoy, V. V. Ramana Murti, in his essay on "Influence of Tolstoy on Gandhi's Political Technique and Thought", writes: "If Tolstoy had the vision of a more civilized law of love, it was Gandhi who translated it into action as non-violence. Gandhi was the Evangelist of Tolstoy. The legacy of Tolstoy was inherited by Gandhi, but the legacy of Gandhi seems to travel again westward. It was Martin Luther King who applied the Gandhian technique in America – that must be regarded as the Evangelist of Gandhi in recent times."[12]

Gandhi's reference to the relationship between the precept and practice in Tolstoy is striking. In fact, it is no less true of Gandhi himself. Gandhi undoubtedly put into practice what he had learnt and understood from his reading of Tolstoy and Ruskin, needless to say that the *Bhagawat Gita* had established the awakening of the spiritual journey within M K Gandhi, who in later years had considerably spoken about it and also transformed his own self. *The Bhagawat Gita* became, as Gandhi had said, his "spiritual dictionary of daily reference."

His study of *The Sermon on the Mount* and *The Bhagawat Gita* led him to the conclusion that the ideal life was one of selfless action in the service of one's fellowmen, and the best method of righting wrongs was to protest non-violently and to suffer lovingly rather than submit to injustice.

In other context, Mahatma Gandhi had confessed, "When doubt haunts me, when disappointment stares me in the face, and when I see one ray of light on the horizon, I turn to *Bhagavadgita* and find a verse to comfort me, and immediately begin to smile in the midst of overwhelming sorrow. My life has been full of external tragedies, and if they have not left any visible and indelible effect on me, I owe it to the teaching of the *Bhagavadgita*.[13]

On the other hand, from his reading of Tolstoy and Ruskin, Gandhi understood that the good of the individual is contained in the good of all; all have the same right of earning their livelihood from their work; and the life of labour is the life worth living.

By founding his first Ashram "Phoenix Settlement" in 1904 on a hundred acre farm 14 miles from Durban, Mahatma Gandhi put his understanding of his reading Ruskin, Tolstoy and others into practice. Further, the establishment of 'Tolstoy Farm' by Gandhi near Johannesburg on May 10, 1910 was another notable event.

One has to also understand that Tolstoy's rejection of violence as the very negation of violence was of great consequence to Mahatma Gandhi. It was of greatest value for him (Gandhi) in his own repudiation of violence.

There is considerable ideological continuity in Mahatma Gandhi claiming Tolstoy as an exponent of non-violence. Whatever Tolstoy preached as a prophet was put into invaluable practice by Mahatma Gandhi in the social order. And his non-violence was positively sustained by Tolstoy's Gospel. His (Gandhi's) *satyagraha* embodies the spirit of Tolstoy's message of 'universal love'.

"The core of Gandhi's philosophy", says Subrata Mukherjee and Sushila Ramaswamy in their edited book "Facets of Mahatma Gandhi – Ethics, Religion and Culture", "Is the application of love, which he described as the 'law of our being, of our species', to all human activities and relationships", adding, "He accepts the notion of the limitlessness of human existence, the basic equality and dignity of all being regardless of their race and status."[14]

In her article, "Gandhi's Contribution to Indian Culture with Special Reference to Liberation" Geeta Mehta writes: "Gandhi found that the nearest approach to God is through love. Love not in the sense of passion but in the sense of *Ahimsa*... He seeks truth and finds it identical with love and non-injury. In Gandhi's philosophy, non-violence and Truth are so intertwined that it is practically impossible to disentangle and separate them. The identity of nonviolence and Truth is so complete that one cannot even suggest the two as twins. They are the faces of the same coin... For Gandhi nonviolence is the universal law of love".[15]

Whenever Gandhi found humanity under duress and injustice, he did not hesitate to take upon himself the imperative obligation to appeal to man's inherent sense of justice and fair play. He refused to be provoked. He led the people to introspection and self-examination, to turn hundred hearts into genuine reciprocity, to stead friends and win over foes against what they mistook for their self-interest, to put heart into those who had been shaken by their suffering, and to bring love where hatred and vindictiveness ruled..."[16]

Gandhi's non-violence was not an end in itself, but had clear consequential dimensions. By weaponising *satyagraha*, or truth force, Gandhi made debate the only available mode for social interaction. He (Gandhi) extended non-violence to verbal acts too because, he believed, angry voices conceal a weak argument and an unwillingness to communicate".[17]

Ray Kurzweil – one of world's leading inventors and futurist in the area of digital technologies and their impact on society and author of best-selling books like "The Age of Spiritual Machines (1998)" and others, says: "Mahatma Gandhi's movement is a very good early example of the power of people coming together, sharing an idea to change an oppressive reality and achieving that purpose nonviolently. He did not have the benefit of the electronic communication. His idea travelled mostly by word of mouth (or through his writings). But he was able to set an inspiring example. Under his leadership, people came together and showed the tremendous power of peaceful collective action".

Mahatma Gandhi's movement was a great example of people inspired by a noble idea organizing themselves and bringing about change. He fought for social justice through constructive collective action. And that example continues to inspire the world even today. His *Satyagraha* for many may be an act of the past today, but one mustn't forget that the power of peaceful collective action for bringing about a positive change is tremendous, for it negates any act of violence which poses a moral question or authority.

The Civil Rights Movement in the United States led by Martin Luther King was directly inspired by Mahatma Gandhi or for that matter the movement led by Nelson Mandela in South Africa was inspired by none other than Mahatma Gandhi.

Dr. Kirti Singh further points out that far off from the Asian and Africa borders, the European communist leaders like Marshal Tito and Alexander Dubcheck tempered communism with democracy and evolved national communism based on the aspiration of the powers, but they put into practice the Gandhian method of passive resistance, *Satyagraha*.[18]

Prof. Mool Chand writes in his book "Nationalism and Internationalism of Gandhi, Nehru and Tagore" on Mahatma Gandhi's love for humanity where he strongly advocated his resentment against strife between nations. He always gave top priority to "The interest of humanity."[19]

The writer elaborates that in spite of the fact that Gandhiji lived and intended to die for the freedom of India, his nationalism was "not exclusive." He asserted that "it is calculated not only to hurt any other nation, but to benefit all in the true sense of the word. India's freedom as conceived by me can never be menace to the world."[20] In reality, the aim of Gandhiji was, through national service to "free my soul from the bondage of flesh… For me the road to salvation lies through incessant toil in the service of my country and there-through of humanity."[21]

"The struggle for India's freedom", said Mahatma Gandhi "was thus part of a larger world movement concerning all mankind.[22] Gandhiji had said, "I want the freedom of my country so that other countries may learn something from this free country of mine. I want freedom of my country so that the resources of my country might be utilized for the benefit of mankind".[23]

Mahatma Gandhi further asserted that 'internationalism' is possible only when 'nationalism' becomes a fact, i.e., when "Peoples belonging to different countries have organized themselves and are able to act as one man". Mahatma Gandhi had a firm belief that "Without being nationalist, none could lay claim to internationalism". Gandhi had said, "Unless a man could serve his family his village and his country he could not serve the world. Internationalism had got no malice, no ill will or contempt, but it had only peace and goodwill in it, and unless a man began to love heartily his neighbours, he could not cultivate the spirit of love for the outside world".[24]

"My patriotism includes the good of mankind in general, therefore, my service of India includes the service of humanity"[25], Mahatma Gandhi had reiterated.

The very reason why Gandhian principles per se and the eternal message of Mahatma Gandhi is valued much more in the world today amidst contemporary crisis is clearly visible from what Pt. Jawarlal Nehru had written in "The Discovery of India".

Pt. Nehru had written: "Gandhi was an intense nationalist. He was also, at the same time a man who felt he had a message not only for India but for the world, and he ardently desired world peace. His nationalism, therefore, had a certain world outlook and was entirely free from any aggressive intent. Describing the independence of India, he had come to believe that a world federation of interdependent states was the only right goal, however distant that might be".[26]

Further elaborating, Pt. Nehru quoted what Gandhiji had said on his 77th birthday: "We must rededicate ourselves over to the great cause of India's freedom and human emancipation for which the Mahatma has stood."[27]

Pt. Nehru could write this with conviction for time and again, Mahatma Gandhi had himself expressed similar sentiments. He said, "For me patriotism is the same as humanity. I am a patriotic because I am human and humane. It is not exclusive... And a patriot is so much the less a patriot if he is a lukewarm humanitarian,"[28] adding, "I want India's rise so that the whole world may benefit".[29]

In the Asian panorama, the influence of Mahatma Gandhi was equally strong. It was Mr. U.Nu, the former Prime Minister of Burma, whose admiration for the Gandhian principle of Sarva Dharma Samambhava (equality of all religions) was followed all across Burma even though many objected to his actions.

Niechidatsu Fuji, the Buddhist Monk who is better known as Fuiji Guriji of Japan associated himself with Gandhiji and his ashram. He sensed in Gandhiji's Civil Disobedience movement an opportunity to actualize the prophecy of *Bodhisattwa Nicheren* about the revival of Buddhism.

Chinese scholars like Dr, Carsun Chang studied Mahatma Gandhi's life and his autobiography. Dr. M Kiriti Sing a cultural anthropologist and journalist says that "the spirit of neo-Buddhism – non violence and self sacrifices – is not only to be found in Gandhism but also in communist China since the foundation of the Chinese Republic in 191130.

The legacy of Mahatma Gandhi continues. Gandhi's ideas of sustainability and mutual coexistence have been the key factors inspiring young and old across the world. Mahatma Gandhi himself was, first and foremost a man of action. While he was indeed a man of deep contemplation, he was also a man of galvanic energy. It is this energy that enabled him to overcome resistance arising from hostility, cynicism, etc. Mahatma Gandhi had emphasized that true economics stands for social justice. From the beginning of his public career to the end of his life, he remained disciplined and close to ordinary people. He used the ordinary messages of common interest and made them extraordinary by people's participation. His message of '*Satyagraha*' is eternally relevant and has transformed many individuals across the world.

There is the Swedish teenage Greta Thunberg, environmental activist on climate change whose campaigning has gained international recognition. Thunberg first became known for her activism in August 2018 when, at age 15, she began spending her school days outside the Swedish parliament to call for stronger action on global warming by holding up a sign saying (in Swedish) "School strike for climate". Soon, other students engaged in similar protests in their own communities. Together, they organised a school climate strike movement under the name Fridays for Future. After Thunberg addressed the 2018 United Nations Climate Change Conference, student strikes took place every week somewhere in the world. In 2019, there were at least two coordinated multi-city protests involving over one million students each. Perhaps after a long time any purely non-violent protest was seen across nations on the issue of climate change. And Greta is continuing.

Further, Burundi ranks as one of the world's poorest nations, with most of its eight million-plus inhabitants surviving on subsistence farming. The average annual income is around $100, and literacy rates are among the lowest in Africa. However, there is a light in Bujambura, Burundi, in a weekly film club… The boys of Bujumbura patrol the streets in third-hand T-shirts and ill-fitting jeans, carrying stacks of DVDs they sell to passing motorists, sidewalk diners and curious passers-by. Rifling through the selections in this busy capital of Burundi and one is likely to find Nigerian crime dramas, Tanzanian romances and Hollywood blockbusters pirated in China. What you won't find are films made in Burundi. For an impoverished country still struggling to emerge from more than a decade of civil war, that might not be surprising. But as peace returns to this troubled African nation, Burundian filmmakers are hoping to finally put their country on the map.

Back in India, the story of many such unsung builders of modern India are stories of transformation and how the Gandhian 'constructive work' is being carried forward.

Shri Harshal Vibhandik from Dhule, Maharashtra, is one such person who quit his job as an Investment Banker in New York to work consistently towards digitalizing all the 1103 government schools in the Tribal district of Dhule, after the launch of Digital India Campaign by Prime Minister Shri Narendra Modi. Harshal got the support of Ram Bhau Mhalgi Prabodhini (RMP), a Mumbai-based organization championing out-of-the-box initiatives for social change. The "Prerna Sabhas" formed as part of this project acted as a medium to bridge the understanding of the project with the students, parents and villagers. The project took final shape in September 2015, and by the end of December 2015, some 45 Zila Parishad (ZP) schools were successfully digitalized. The success of this initial step drew another organization Lupin Foundation towards Harshal, as they (Lupin) offered funds to digitalise all the 1103 ZP schools of Dhule District. With regular intervention with the stakeholders, who were the villagers, parents and students, there generated a feeling of ownership among the villages of the community and digitalization increased. Not only this, 12 schools in Tribal areas under the protected bird sanctuary where any form of construction is banned, and where schools are run in huts, digital infrastructure was provided there and this decreased school dropouts.

Then there is Dr. B M Bharadwaj and his wife Dr. Madhuri, who have sacrificed their married life having committed to not have any children, but serve in their "Apnaghar" to the "Prabhujis" who are mostly destitute and abandoned either by their family or society.

85- year-old Smt. M C Pankaja from Bengaluru who has devoted her life to making psychological help accessible to over a lakh people affected with mental health issues; training 4000 lay counselors who are now ensuring solace to those in stress at the "Prasana Counselling Centre" at Bengaluru speaks volumes of transformative stories.

There is Sunitha Krishnan, who at 15 was gang raped by eight men and her anger at the society trying to prove her responsible turned her into an

Indian social activist and chief functionary and co-founder of *Prajwala*, a non-governmental organization that rescues, rehabilitates and reintegrates sex-trafficked victims into society. Krishnan works in the areas of anti-human trafficking and social policy. To date, *Prajwala* has rescued, rehabilitated, or served over 15,000 survivors of sex trafficking, and the scale of their operations makes them the largest anti- trafficking shelter in the world.

There are many others who are taking forward the baton of hope and transforming lives and making people empowered. They are the real unsung heroes and sheroes who are reliving each word of Mahatma Gandhi's Talisman… "…Recall the face of the poorest and the weakest man whom you may have seen, and ask your-self, if the step you contemplate is going to be on any use to him. Will he gain anything by it? Will it restore him to a control over his own life and destiny? In other words, will it – Lead to *swaraj* for the hungry and spiritually starving millions?"

Mahatma Gandhi's universality is growing day by day. The world has come to recognize that there's no alternative to peace and non-violence. The United Nations has recognized this and thus declared October 2nd the birth anniversary of Mahatma Gandhi to be celebrated as the "International Day of Non-Violence" every year. At a time when the world is hungering for peace, the key concepts such as peace, non-violence, *satyagraha* and sacrifice to the cause of humanity, when applied practically to resolve any form of conflicts can bring peaceful mutual coexistence amongst humankind. These are the eternal concepts that Mahatma Gandhi had spoken about, lived and worked for.

It is apt to quote Gandhi's biographer, Louis Fischer. Fischer said: "I have met Lenin, Churchill, Franklin D. Roosevelt, Wilkie, Stalin, Litvinov, Attlee, Einstein, Lloyd George, Eleanor Roosevelt and may other famous people. I have never met a more remarkable person than Gandhi".

For a man of action, which Mahatma Gandhi always liked to be called and remembered as, it would be quite pertinent to recollect the words of Martin Luther King in conclusion. King compared Gandhi to Christ and said: "For my background, I gained my resulting Christian ideas. From Gandhi, I learned my operational technique."[31] Indeed his technique had earned him the status of a leader, not just within India but across boundaries. Gandhi, the Mahatma lives not just as an idea, but as a practical thinker, a light that illuminated a humble hut and the brightest cities of the world – a light of love, hope and peace that the world unendingly desires.

References

1. George Woodcock; "Gandhi"; Fontana Modern Masters; Editor: Kermode Frank
2. R.R. Diwakar, "The True Spirit of Satyagraha," in *Gandhi: His Relevance*; ed. Ramachandran and Mahadevan, 2nd ed. (New Delhi: Gandhi Peace Foundation, Bombay: Bhartiya Vidya Bhaavn, 1967) p.342.
3. The Collected Works of Mahatma Gandhi, Vol. 26, p.200
4. Ibid.,p257 -3
5. Ibid.,1
6. George Woodcock; "Gandhi"; Fontana Modern Masters; Editor: Kermode Frank
7. The Collected Works of Mahatma Gandhi, (CWMG) 37 :261;MPWNG 1:115
8. CWMG,49 : 256;MPWMG, 1:95
9. Ibid.,4
10. Ibid,4
11. Ibid.,4, p.24
12. C.D. Narasimhaiah; "Gandhi And The West"; Murti Ramana V V, "Influence of Tolstoy on Gandhi's Political Technique and Thought"; University of Mysore, Published by The Department of Post-graduate Studies and Research in English, Manasagangothri, University of Mysore, Printed in India At The Mysore University Printing Press, Mysore.
13. *Speeches and Writings of Mahatma Gandhi* (Madras, 1933), p.126.
14. Subrata Mukherjee, Sushila Ramaswamy, "Facets of Mahatma Gandhi" Vol. 4; published by Deep & Deep Publications, New Delhi, 1994
15. Ibid, Mehta Geeta, "Gandhis Contribution to Indian Culture with Special Reference to Liberation", Chapter 5,p. 47,48.
16. Gyanendra Pandey, *The Ascendancy of the Congress in Uttar Pradesh, 1926-34* (Oxford University Press, New Delhi, 1978), p.116
17. Dipankar Gupta, *The American 'Untouchable'*, The Times of India, New Delhi, April 21, 2018
18. Ibid., 11
19. The Collected Works of Mahatma Gandhi, Vol 33, 169-170.
20. Ibid, p.340
21. Ibid, Vol 23, P.349
22. Ibid, Vol,27, Preface, p.ix
23. Ibid, Vol,28, p. 129
24. Ibid, Vol.28, p. 134
25. Ibid.,p.186
26. Jawaharlal Nehru: *The Discovery of India*, Asia Publishing House, Bombay. (19961),p.445
27. Ibid.,p.249
28. The Collected Works of Mahatma Gandhi, Vol. 19, p.427.
29. Ibid., Vol 26, p. 279
30. M Kirti Singh, "Philosophical Import of Gandhiism"; South Asia Publications, Delhi 1994; (Released on the occasion of 125th Birth Anniversary of Mahatma Gandhi).

31 Martin Luther King, in *Profiles of Gandhi*, p.11

Bibliography

1. Woodcock George; "Gandhi"; Fontana Modern Masters; Editor: Kermode Frank
2. Diwakar R. R., "The True Spirit of Satyagraha," in *Gandhi: His Relevance*; ed. Ramachandran and Mahadevan, 2nd ed. (New Delhi: Gandhi Peace Foundation, Bombay: Bhartiya Vidya Bhaavn, 1967).
3. Gupta Dipankar, The American 'Untouchable', The Times of India, April 21, 2018.
4. Gandhi Mahatma, "The Collected Works", (CWMG)
5. Narasimhaiah C.D.; "Gandhi And The West"; Murti Ramana V V, "Influence of Tolstoy on Gandhi's Political Technique and Thought"; University of Mysore, Published by The Department of Post-graduate Studies and Research in English, Manasagangothri, University of Mysore, Printed in India At The Mysore University Printing Press, Mysore.
6. Mukherjee Subrata, Ramaswamy Sushila, "Facets of Mahatma Gandhi" Vol. 4; published by Deep & Deep Publications, New Delhi, 1994.
7. Singh Kirti M, "Philosophical Import of Gandhiism"; South Asia Publications, Delhi 1994; (Released on the occasion of 125th Birth Anniversary of Mahatma Gandhi).
8. Nehru Jawaharlal: *The Discovery of India*, Asia Publishing House, Bombay. (19961)
9. King Luther Martin, in *Profiles of Gandhi*.

6

Global Peace through People Power: A Gandhian Perspective

Suman Khanna Aggarwal

"Gandhi revealed to the masses a power not of rifles and machine guns, such as their oppressors used, but the power innate in each individual unit of the great mass, a power which this war-haunted world has yet to realize, and which, exploited to the full, can make wars impossible." [1]

Ethel Mannin

Gandhi's Practical Approach

Supported by the Indian Government, **GANDHI – 150 YEARS**[2], the 150th birth anniversary of Mahatma Gandhi, beloved *Bapu,* the Father of the Nation, is being celebrated all over India, for two whole years - from 2 October 2018 to 2 October 2020. During the events, seminars and international conferences to mark the occasion, academicians and lay people alike, are asking an all important question of the practicability of Gandhian values, principles and strategies - like *satyagraha* - today.

This paper is an attempt to see how ordinary people can apply Gandhi in present times; follow Truth through Nonviolence the way Gandhi did!

Gandhi was undoubtedly a man of practice. He is famous for instantaneously translating his ideas into practical reality. For instance, he founded, Phoenix Settlement, his first *ashram,* an experiment in community living, after reading Ruskin's *Unto This Last.*[3] The title of Gandhi's autobiography[4] underlines how Gandhi's whole life was an experiment with Truth, which for him, is synonymous with nonviolence. In his own words:

> "My love for nonviolence is ....equalled only by my love for Truth, which is to me synonymous with nonviolence.[5] When I look for *ahimsa*, Truth says, 'Find it out through me'. When I look for Truth, *ahimsa* says, 'Find it out through me'.[6] *Ahimsa* and Truth are so intertwined that it is practically impossible to disentangle and separate them. They are like the two sides of a coin, or rather of a smooth unstamped metallic disc. Who can say, which is the obverse, and which is the reverse?"[7]

What is Power?

Broadly speaking, power can be conceptualized as:

i. An **ability** or a **competence** to get things done; i.e., **the power to** achieve desired results or goals.
ii. **Control** or **dominance** in relationships; i.e., **to have or to acquire power over** another;
iii. **Self–control** or the acquisition of **power over oneself**, which is to empower oneself to gain success in one's undertakings. In some measure, power in this third sense seems to be a prerequisite to the acquisition of power in the first sense.

The present predominant conception of power as control and dominance is a development of recent decades. The more traditional meaning centered on the idea of ability and strength. Thus, in the old Webster's International Dictionary of 1933,[8] the first definition of power is given as: "Ability, whether physical, mental or moral, to act; the faculty of doing or performing something." The major synonyms for power are given as: "Strength, Vigor, Energy, Force, Ability"

The **present commonly accepted meaning of power figures fourth** in the dictionary: "The possession of sway or controlling influence over others; Control; authority; command; government; influence ascendancy; whether personal, social or political."

It is noteworthy that the terms control, command, sway and dominion do not appear in the 1933 Webster's dictionary as synonyms for power.

It is also significant that Webster's Third New International Dictionary, which was published in 1961,[9] gives as its first meaning the prevalent conception of power in our age: "a position of ascendancy; ability to compel obedience control, dominion... (and as subsequent meanings) ... a military force and its equipment... and... ability to wage war."

People Power – Basis of *Satyagraha*

" 'People Power' is a political term used to denote the populist driving force of any social movement which invokes the authority of grassroots opinion and willpower, usually in opposition to that of conventionally organised corporate or political forces."[10]As is well known, Mahatma Gandhi's *Satyagrahas* - Nonviolent Resistance / Civil Disobedience - changed unjust laws (eg. Champaran *Satyagraha*) and overthrew colonial British rule and made history (eg. Salt *Satyagraha*)The main tools of a Gandhian *Satyagraha* are mass mobilization & use of symbols.

Gandhi not only firmly believes but has also demonstrated the truth of the following: "In this age of democracy.....it is essential that desired results are achieved by the collective effort of the people. (Collective effort) will make the community conscious of its corporate strength.[11]... Anything that millions can do together becomes charged with a unique power."[12] Mahatma Gandhi

Satyagraha vs. Passive Resistance

It is important to note the difference between Passive resistance and *Satyagraha*. In its outward form, passive resistance seems like *Satyagraha*, in so far as there is no active or violent armed resistance in it. But the resemblance ends there. Gandhi awares: "There is a great and fundamental difference between Passive resistance and *Satyagraha*."[13] Passive resistance in its outward form is like *Satyagraha* in that it contains no active or violent armed resistance. But the resemblance ends there. Gandhi deftly brings out the vast difference between the two, in terms of their approaches, underlying philosophies and techniques:[14]

Passive resistance is a weapon of the weak, of the unarmed and helpless. It does not eschew violence as a matter of principle but only because of the lack of the means of violence, or out of steer expediency. It would use arms if and when they are available or when on account of their use there is a reasonable chance of success. Passive resistance may even be preparatory to or go hand in hand with armed resistance. The underlying object is to harass the opponent and then force him into the desired covered of action. Love has no place in it.

It cannot be used against our nearest and dearest because it involves hatred and distrust. There is no place for service of the people or contribution activity in it. Finally it cannot become a philosophy of life. In contrast to passive resistance, *Satyagraha*: Is the law of love, the way of love for all. Eschews violence absolutely as a matter of principle at all stages and in all forms. It can never go hand in hand with any kind of violent activity involving injury to person or property.

The idea behind *Satyagraha* is not to destroy or harm the opponent, but to convert or win him over by sympathy, patience and self-suffering. It brings the opponents around not through coercion but by activating their individual conscience. This accounts for the superiority of *Satyagraha* to other modes of human conduct, for whereas violence generally leaves the defeated smarting under the humiliation of defeat, the end attained through Satyagraha is the cherished healing of hearts, because the wrong-doers have realised their mistake and now want to atone for it.

Satyagraha never fails to distinguish between evil and the evil-doer. While evil is recognised and condemned, the evil-doer is approached through love, with awareness of their ultimate spiritual identity.

The *Satyagrahi* has immense trust in the inherent goodness of human nature. *Satyagraha* can be used even against one's nearest and dearest. A *Satyagrahi* acts out of love and is willing to suffer to any extent for loved ones. When not actually protesting or resisting nonviolently, *Satyagrahis* will enjoin themselves in the Constructive Program chalked out by Gandhi in the spirit of service and sacrifice. In Gandhi's Footsteps : *Satyagraha* for a World Beyond War.

War may be defined as a state of open, armed, often prolonged conflict carried on between nations, states, or parties entailing violence on an extreme and vast scale.

War is synonymous with trauma and suffering. Once a life is lost, nothing can bring it back. The ruinous consequences of war, inter alia, are:

- **Loss of human life**
- **Wounded** and injured soldiers and civilians
- **Loss of vital infrastructure** that countries have to rebuild at huge economic cost
- **Damage to heritage buildings**, and other cultural artefacts
- The acute problem of **refugees** who flee war-torn zones and seek asylum in other countries. Unfortunately, they are often viewed with hostility

and considered a burden on the host nation's exchequer and society.

Presently, nation states have politically legitimised war/violence as a means of conflict resolution, spending USD 3.5 per minute15 on this; i.e., Global Military Expenditure. Given these figures, consider that almost 15,000 children under the age of five die daily16 in our global village due to malnutrition and lack of basic health care.

So, the question is, as mentioned in the beginning of this paper, can citizens living in democracies in our age, mobilize themselves to exercise their collective power to create a global popular movement to politically legitimize Nonviolent Conflict Resolution as a first step to global peace. This will, in due course, outlaw war between nation states; thereby leading to a World Beyond War.

In order to politically legitimize Nonviolent Conflict Resolution, let us petition17 our respective National Govts. & the United Nations for the following:

1. That without abandoning the present Military Defence, a parallel, Nonviolent Defence be instituted in National Defence Systems globally.
2. The Legal Democratic Option to be trained in Nonviolent Defence rather than the present Armed Military System.
3. The Legal Democratic Option for taxpayers to divert their Defence Tax from Military Defence to Nonviolent Defence.

This Petition is in line with UN SDG 16. It draws its legitimacy from the following:

> The Preamble of the United Nations Charter: 'We the people of the UN determined to save succeeding generations from the scourge of war.'

'The right to Freedom of Conscience,' guaranteed to every individual by Article 18 of the UN Convention on Human Rights.

If we believe and live by the Christian commandments: 'Thou shalt not kill; Thou shalt love thy neighbor as thyself' or the Hindu dictum: '*Ahimsa Parmo Dharma* – Nonviolence is the highest religion; *Vasudeva Kutumbh* – The whole world is a family' or the Buddhist doctrine that to kill is wrong, or as atheists believing in the sanctity of human life, we need to make a genuine attempt to evolve to a world beyond war and violence.

Like Gandhi, we have to change unjust structures in our capacity of being citizens of nation states. Says Gandhi:

"In politics, the use of *satyagraha* is based upon the immutable maxim that the government of the people is possible only so long as they consent either consciously or unconsciously to be governed."18

References

1. Sarvepalli Radhakrishnan, ***Mahatma Gandhi, Essays & Reflections,*** Nineteenth Jaico Impression, JAICO Publishing House, Mumbai, 2010, back cover of book, p. 177.
2. https://changlang.nic.in/event/gandhi-jayanti-observed-as-beginning-of-150-years-of-HYPERLINK "https://changlang.nic.in/event/gandhi-jayanti-observed-as-beginning-of-150-years-of-celebrating-the-mahatma/" \h celebrating-the-mahatma/ sourced on 2 December 2019.
3. https://en.m.wikipedia.org/wiki/Unto_This_Last sourced on 2 December 2019.
4. M. K. Gandhi, ***An Autobiography or The Story of My Experiments With Truth,*** Navajivan Publishing House, Ahmedabad, 1959.
5. R. K. Prabhu and U.R. Rao, ***The Mind of Mahatma Gandhi***, Navajivan Publishing House, Ahmedabad, 1969, p. 118.
6. Ibid, p. 24.
7. Shriman Narayan (ed.) ***The Selected Works of Mahatma Gandhi,*** Navajivan Publishing House, Ahmedabad, 1968, Vol. 4, p. 219. Hereafter these works will be referred to as Selected Works.
8. Carroll, Berenice A., ***Peace Research: The Cult of Power,*** in *Journal of Conflict Resolution*, Vol. XVI, No. 4, December 1972.
9. https://en.wikipedia.org/wiki/Webster's_Third_New_International_Dictionary, accessed 28 September, 2019.
10. https://en.wikipedia.org/wiki/People_power, accessed 29 September, 2019.
11. M. K. Gandhi, ***Harijan,*** 8 September 1940; Dhawan, ***The Political Philosophy of Mahatma Gandhi,*** p.166. See also ***Harijan,*** 19 May 1946.
12. M. K. Gandhi, ***Harijan,*** 7 April 1946.
13. M.K. Gandhi, ***Satyagraha in South Africa***, p. 105.
14. ***Ibid.*** Chapter XIII, pp. 103 to 107.
15. Military expenditure in 2018 was USD 1.8 trillion. Source: SIPRI. https://www.sipri.org/research/armament-and-disarmament/arms-transfers-HYPERLINK "https://www.sipri.org/research/armament-and-disarmament/arms-transfers-and-military-spending/military-expenditure" \h and-military-spending/military-expenditure, accessed on 10 August 2019.
16. United Nations Inter-agency Group for Child Mortality Estimation (UN IGME) 2018, https://data.unicef.org/topic/child-survival/under-five-HYPERLINK "https://data.unicef.org/topic/child-survival/under-five-mortality/" \l "status" \h mortality/#status, accessed on 17 September 2019.
17. Sign the Petition for #ChooseNonviolentDefence on change.org https://goo.gl/nqujDe Initiated by Shanti Sahyog Center for Peace & Conflict Resolution, India, website: www.shantisahyog.org
18. M. K. Gandhi, ***Young India,*** 3 November 1927, p. 369.

7

Educational ideas of Gandhi ji and their Importance to Present Education

Rajni Mudgal

Introduction

The importance or need of tolerance, humanism and non-violence values of Mahatma Gandhi is worldwide accepted. His actions and new ways of movements like non- cooperation, padyatras, fasting, Satyagraha and Non-violence means of protesting have taught the world that you could defeat you adversary with firing a shot exactly opposite to the other leaders of his time who were advocating the violent revolution. His ways and thought left undeletable marks on not only on Indians but throughout the world. His services to mankind was numerous. "He is seen as a role model with his universal understanding of peace and tolerance".

His thought and actions are still needed because peace is one of the fundamental universal need for humankind without which the existence of mankind itself is in danger. "There are conflicts in many areas today and individual prefers means of offence with violence sources, instead of listening to the opinions on the other side"(Abdi and Schultz, 2008).

To resolve the problem of violent behavior of today's generation and to defeat the ideologies which promote violence as mean to settle disputes, which they consider an appropriate tool to resolve differences. We must inculcate the teaching of Mahatma Gandhi in our education system strongly.

Once Dr. Martin Luther King Jr. said "when he was in ological school I thought to solve the problem of segregation a armed revolt was need. I thought as a Christian that love was confined to individual relationships. For him, love as too ,to resolve social conflict was un thinkable. Then he read Gandhi's ethic of love and could understood the complex relation between love and social conflict.

We have to tell our generation understand that non-violence is nor a weak reaction neither it is for weeks. The aim of the study is highlight the philosophy of education of Mahatma Gandhi and it's relevance in present educational system.

Methodologyy

The method of the study is documents review based on the educational philosophy of the Gandhi in regard to –

1. adhaytmic element
2. world peace
3. elementary education
4. non-violence

Educational Philosophy of Gandhi

Devi (1987) pointed to "spiritual element in the ideas of Gandhi in educational area". His work was focused on Gandhi's life. Gandhi's view was that that a person should find himself and by doing so he could find the god as well . For Gandhi, Truth is the aim and non – violence is the mean by which he wanted to create a moral, just and spiritual society.

Kour(1992) found " relevance of the educational ideas of Mahatma Gandhi in today"s educational system". He analyzed that when he compare the educational philosophies of Aurobindo and Gandhi. In view of educational curriculum, methods of imparting of education and the role of educator. He found that these ideas are still important relevant in Indian context.

Rana(2006) investigated that " how spiritual depth of Gandhi can be useful".

Sen(1973) study " Mahatma Gandhi 's educational philosophy". The basic concept of the study was to examine the importance of the craft and the correlation between the development of the whole personality of a child and craft Singh (2004) found that "M.K. Gandhi's fundamental concerns was morality" . Gandhi ji consider man as spiritual as well being. He found that Gandhi was mostly concerned with the moral development individual being.

He threw light on the philosophy of morality and how it is related to his ideas and he examined their relevance in the modern times also.

World peace: Educational philosophy of Gandhi

Gigoo (1976) investigated "how world peace can be promoted by implementing gandhian educational ideas". Gigoo examined the spiritual unity as a tool for preserving of new social order and and conflict management. He said "philosophical emphasis on internationalism, which tell teachers that a student is a unity of body. They can teach them of the source of spiritual peace which arises from self realization and lead towards mankind and single humanity."

Bakshi (2006) in his book "Educational Philosophy of Annie Besant and Gandhi" investigated ideas from other angle. He concluded in his research that both Annie Besant and Gandhi want to promote humanism and socialism internationally, through education.

Kamala (1991) in "A comparative study of the Educational Philosophy of Gandhi ji in the world Perspective" examined ideas of Gandhi ji and other educational thinker. Kamala conclude that Gandhi's educational thinking are space and timeless. It is not limited to certain time or for certain region, they are universal, they could be identified with the whole mankind.

Castro and Glance (2010) proved t through their study based on Gandhi's teaching that education for peace can work both as a strategy that achieved peace and an important method to stop violence and minimize conflicts.

Basic educational philosophy of Gandhi

Sen (1973) showed in his study on Mahatma Gandhi's educational philosophy, the influence of basic education on our existence and people's life, The main finding of his study was that that exploitation has no role to play in imparting education.

Rao (1988) studied the "notion of basic education in relation based on Gandhi's view". He tried to find out the relation between the theory and practice In education.

Biswas (2003) in his book "Gandhi as Social Reformer" tried to established that the education should have a social goal.

Akham (2009) studied " the Gandhi's concept of non violence and its importance", he interpreted it in a positive manner and analyzed its importance in modern time including love for human kind.

Bose (1981) in Gandhi's theory of peace, human values take highest pedestal. She studied non – violence and concluded that ashinsa could be used to mange disputes and this way peace could be established.

Surendra(2012) said in his article that "the non - violent protest which were held in India and south Africa by Gandhi ji, have been a major feature of world politics".

Relevance of educationne philosophy of Gandhi to present Time

Rana (2006) studied " the importance of spiritual thought of Gandhi ji in the context of modern time".

Kour (1992) studied "the educational philosophies of Sri Aurobindo and Mahatma Gandhi. He tried to find relevance of their ideas and to modern educational system". He weigh the educational ideas of both with reference to the goal of education, program, ways of teaching and the part of a teacher. The researcher concluded that educational ideas of both are still relevant to new world.

Mahalingam (1992) in "educational ideas of Gandhi ji and their relevance to contemporary education studied the influence of the educational ideas and value of Gandhi and educational system in India".

The review of literature has shown that the area of ideas of education is full of spiritual contents, to find self, truth, compassion and non violance and which filled a person with the qualities like respect for self, concern for the welfare of others etc. True education brings out the spiritual intellectual of a human of the being. According to Gandhi, the goal of education should be to grow inner self. He was of the opinion that mere literacy in itself is not an education. Education fails if it cannot inculcate the spirit of selfless service and sacrifice.

A school it self should be a workshop. The Gandhian veiw of basic education has got the highest consideration. complete development , taking all aspect in mind, were given importance. For a satisfactory system of education the physical, mental and spiritual development are utmost necessary.

Gandhian ideas and his action gave world a new dimension in the field of education, his ideas on truth, love and non – violence brought an important change not only in education but in conflict resolution as well as conflict management. His philosophy is still relevant. our present education system is such that we are simply multiplying thr number of literate youth without any morale value which is very dangerous. These youth with a false pride are becoming increasingly aggressive and becoming problem for society. Gandhi's ideas can surely make a great difference if properly implemented.

References

Akham, H. D. (2009). Gandhi's Concept of Ahinsa and its contemporary relevance. *University News, New Delhi, 48.*

Bakshi, K. (2006). A Comparative Study of Annie Besant, M.K. gandhi and J. Krishnamurti. *University News, New delhi, 45,* 7.

Bose, A. (1981). A Gandhian Perspective on Peace. *Journal of Peace Research, 18,* 159-164. Buch, M. B. (1987). Third Survey of Research in Education. *ncert, New Delhi,* 39.

Cha, M. J. (2013). Ethical Values and Social Change: Mahatma Gandhi, Martin Luther King and Ahn Chang Ho. *Korean Social Science Journal, 40,* 101-111.

Dave, J. P. (2010). Value Education to the Students of Standard Nine in tne History from the Freedom Movements of Gandhi ji. *University News, New Delhi, 48.*

Luther king, M. L. (2019, October 3). His spirit a continual reminder to oppressed people that it is possible to resist evil: king on Mahatma. *Hindustan Times* [jaipur].

Rana, K. (2007). Gandhi ke Adhyatmik Vicharon Kee Prasangikata, vartaman Paripekshya Mein. *University News, New delhi, 45.*

Sen, A. (1973). *Mahatma Gandhi's Education Philosophy.* Bombay: Bombay University.

Singh, N. N. (2014). Morality: Gandhi ji's view and its relevance in the modren times. *International Journal of Humanities and Social Studies, 2,* 75-80.

8

Importance of Gandhian Principles: Its Reflection in the Contemporary Portuguese Polity, Economy and Society in Reference to Antonio Costa ('Gandhi of Lisbon') as Perceived by the Indian Media

Manisha Pal

India (Bharat) has been a point of attraction for all the foreign explorers during 'the age of discovery'. Initially during sixteenth century, the Portuguese marked their presence in order to develop trade and to find Christians on the Indian land. And they entered with the motive to 'Lusitanize' and 'Christianize' the Indian land and its people. To certain extent they succeeded for a certain period of time, due to their polities to create division among indigenous political groups on the west coast of Malabar, and then slowly by bringing changes in their polities over the period of time they explored other peripherals of the West Coast, Kannur, Konkan Coast, Daman, Diu and the Coromandal Coast and then in the East as well. They enjoyed the political power in Goa from 1505 to 1961, i.e. for 456 years approximately. The British Raj stayed in India from 1858 to 1947. During the age of discovery many other Europeans explored and traded in India. The presence of Europeans brought cultural changes in India. Due to trade, their presence affected the language dialects, and slowly with time, socio-cultural changes occurred. Consequently, the European language influences and their presence are very much visible in the twenty first century India. Finally, these European languages in India, slowly over the period of time diluting the original Indian culture, but it is the concreteness of the Indian culture which is still keeping its original identity intact with a continuous struggle. Similarly, presence of Portuguese and English languages brought delusions in the Indian culture and identities. This was the reason Gandhi was against English education, rather he believed that English education with deep rooted Indian values can bring the actual modernity, otherwise it would lead towards a disaster. His own personality besides being the blend of Eastern and Western philosophies, had reflections of the other traditional philosophies as well. He had a strong belief in *Truth, Ahimsa (Non-Violence)* and *Brahmacharya (Celibacy), Asteya (Non-stealing)* and *Aparigraha (Non- possession)* this made him 'Mahatama' i.e. 'A Man of Perfection'[1].

Antonio Luis Santos da Costa, the Prime minister of Portugal (2015-Present), who belongs to the *Partido Sociolista* (Socialist Party) has his roots in the former Portuguese colony Goa in India, where his grandfather Luis Afonso Maria da Costa was born and his father Orlando da Costa, a Portuguese writer of Goan descent spent most of his life in Goa, he wrote essays on Nobel laureate Rabindranath Tagore.[2] Costa was a descendant of Hindu families from the Gaud Saraswati Brahmin community which converted to Catholicism during the Portuguese colonial era.[3] During his interview, with Hindustan Times he said:

> 'I am deeply honoured to attend the Pravasi Bharatiya Divas as a Person of Indian Origin and my speech at the occasion will surely be framed by my roots in Goa, of which I am very proud. I am planning to use the opportunity of travelling of Goa to visit my relatives who still live in Margao, where my father had his house. And I am also very moved by the fact that I will witness the presentation, in Delhi and Goa, of the English translations of two of my father's books.'[4]

Teotonio R. de Souza referred to the term 'Goa Portuguesa' in this regard, and is of importance from the similar point of view while giving an analytical thought to it.[5]

Costa can be considered a good example of socio- cultural changes that occurred in India due to the Portuguese presence in Goa, India for the approximate period of 456 years. Due to the political power in hand the Portuguese were able to bring ethnological changes in Goa, India at the certain level among specified groups and communities. Some escaped with it, but interesting to know that the deep rooted Indian culture is very much visible among the Goan descendants. These ethnological changes can be observed in the regional language of Goa i.e. Konkani, where some words of Portuguese language is already present in the Konkani words and there exist some pronunciations similarities. Besides this Portuguese and Indian both presences i.e. the mix blend of Portuguese and Indian culture can be felt in the structures of the houses, in the food, in the music and the presence of Indo-Portuguese literature which is also known as Goan literature by some is the result of Portuguese colonization in Goa for these many years. The names of the roads and the Christians in Goa are still holding the Portuguese names. Besides this, the dressing sense, we find that among some ladies who are Catholic Christians are usually dressed in western attire quite casually on a daily basis, but their body language, facial expressions, and traditional ties are very much close or linked to the Indian culture ethics.

> 'Goan society is a mosaic woven over the centuries from the social and historical fabric of rare type. Goa proved a melting pot for shaping a synthetic culture which absorbed elements from different sources. Conflicting caste-groups, class-groups, and creed/groups with different ethos mixed and mingled together to evolve a warm, sociable, gay and refined society. Despite the harsh impact that took place on political, social, economic and religion institutions as a result of the grafting of an European power on the placid structure of Goa, the creative cross fertilization of ideas from the west brought about a mighty transformation in the value system of Goan life. The Portuguese had come to India not merely for spices and for evangelical work but also for enculturation, which they did more effectively than any other European power in India. In course of time this region proved more congenial soil for the European renaissance to bloom by sucking the finest elements of Indian traditions into it.'[6]

Goa achieved its freedom from Portuguese colonization in the year 1961, the same year, when Costa was born in Lisbon, Portugal. But he still admires his roots in Margão, Goa, and feels proud to be an Indian-origin identity.7 Therefore, one cannot deny his personality must have some Indian ethnological traits. The paper is making attempt to analyze that how far these ethnological changes can be traced in the personality or character of the Antonio Costa that he is being referred as 'Gandhi of Lisbon' by the Media/Indian Media specifically. Does his Indian-origin identity really justifies him as 'Gandhi of Lisbon' does this comparison with Gandhi is really being reflected in the contemporary Portuguese polity, economy and society?

Gandhi who has been referred as *Mahatama* lived his life on the eleven vows:

> '1). *Satya*- Truth, 2) *Ahimsa*- Non-violence, 3) *Brahmacharya*- Celibacy, 4) *Asteya*- Non-stealing, 5) *Aparigraha* or *Asangraha*- Non-possession, 6) *Sharira- Shrama*; Physical labour, or Bread labour, 7) *Asvada* -Control of Palate, 8) *Abhaya*-Fearlessness, 9) *Sarva Dharma*-Samanatva; Equal respect for all Religions, 10) *Swadeshi*- Duty towards Neighbour and, 11) *Asprishyatanivarana*- Removal of Untouchability.' [8]

According Kurangi Desai- the first five vows are found in most of the religions of the world and are called *Pancha Mahavratas* - the Five great Vows. The remaining six are somewhat new ideas that have been given the importance of vows to fulfill the need of the time.[9] Gandhi was a *Sadhaka* (Yogi) who believed that the human life has its purpose and he must attain salvation or realization of God, i.e. human must devote his life in search of God. He believed in service of man, i.e. selfless service (Concept of *Karma Yoga* of Bhagvat Gita, this will ultimately lead to God. His *Sadhana* (industriousness) as a Yogi did not end with himself.[10] He wanted to include society in his spiritual efforts and so he gave a new dimension to the Five Great Vows and extended them into the remaining six.11

Polity: Many considered Gandhi, a political philosopher who brought Independence to India but he was actually a spiritual person who was a self-willed Man, this, he himself agrees in his *autobiography.*

In case out of the said eleven vows of Gandhi, if at least first five vows: *Truth, Non-Violence, Celibacy, Non-stealing, Non-possession* can be observed in the personality traits of Antonio Costa it will be justified to compare him with Gandhi, specifically *Truth* and *Non-violence.* Antonio Costa is a political leader and do not pretend to merge religion with politics. Whereas, Gandhi never claimed himself as an original thinker rather he always said that the basic concepts of *Truth,* and *Non-violence* are the part of Indian philosophy for many eras. It can be depicted from the reading of his works such as *an autobiography,* a few *pamphlets,* a quite many *articles in Indian Opinion, Young India* and *Harijan, many letters; to different Viceroys, fellow-politicians and disciples; his speeches at the various conferences, congresses and his regular prayer meetings, etc.*[12] that he was a simple, self-will, religiously spiritual human being, who believed that change is possible only if we be the same change what we exactly desire. According to M.Balaji, Gandhji's political philosophy was a mix blend of Eastern and Western philosophical systems. Although, other traditional trends of different philosophies can also be observed in his simple living and high thinking concept. And he never sticks to one. M. Balaji further argues that the theoretical structures of Gandhi are common to philosopher when we look into all of his writings. Besides this his conceptual formulations and practical pursuits are identical through which he can be recognized as a philosopher in the Indian sense. Gandhi unlike other philosophers and political thinkers of the world was not only a man of destiny of the nation but also was the man of the millennium.[13] Antonio Costa due to ethnological process might or might not considered having the influences of Eastern and Western blend of political philosophies. In the public view has mixed opinions about Costa. There are observations that his skin colour has Indian roots and his respect for other religion may be considered a similarity to Gandhian principle.[14] Another opinion is that Costa's Indian roots hardly had any influence on his way of governing.[15] Morris argued that Gandhi, himself was never bothered about constructing a system of political philosophy. His ideas were developed under particular circumstances with experimentation processes.[16] And due to this vary reason his ideas are considered may be impractical but these are universal in nature as practically while experimenting on oneself if his ideas were thrown on different men at different situations will intend to mould men and events, eventually. It seems little difficult to interpret if Antonio Costa also believes in experimenting with oneself and if yes, then till what extend? But this is a fact that in case Costa (different man) wants to experiment with the ideas or principles of Gandhi in the present situations in his own country Portugal (different situation), he must get some interesting results- i.e. the universality of the Gandhian principle actually, which cannot be described in words rather it needs continuous practice consciously, without any divergence.

The instrument of Satyagraha: Gandhi had his methods of discovering the extent of public support – calling of *hartals* (strikes), a means of understanding the mind of India. He wanted Swaraj- the Home Rule- that cannot come by the acquisition of authority by a few but the acquisition of the capacity by all to resist authority when abused. The real home rule is the self rule by the people of its country.[17] Secondly, his instrument *Satyagraha* was a remedy of particular grievances or for the wide purpose of achieving independence.

> 'Satyagraha is a process of self-purification, and ours is a sacred fight, and it seems to me to be in the fitness of things that it should be commenced with an act of self- purification. Let all the people of India, therefore,

suspend their business on that day and observe the day as one of fasting and prayer.'[18]

The Gandhi believed that ideal political state is which can understand the real meaning of human progress and is capable of providing its citizens the basic needs of life along with the economic justice, social equality, political liberty, intellectual growth, and spiritual advancement of all the peoples of the world. To this he referred as *Sarvodaya* i.e. the universal well- being.

Antonio Costa might not be following 'the instrument of Satyagraha' directly, but he seems to be believed in fulfilling his commitments to the public as a political leader. Costa's response to the question by the media:

> **'What accounts for your higher approval ratings after a year in office at a time when other centre-left leaders in Italy and France have fared poorly?**
>
> This is probably due to the fact that we are delivering what we have promised. The citizens' disappointment with the politicians is due, to a large extent, to the fact that citizens believe – sometimes rightly – that politicians, once elected, do not deliver on their campaign promises. We have met all our commitments towards the Portuguese people, as it is our duty, and this reinforces confidence in politicians.

On the other hand, the government's action seems to be supported by a large part of the population. This happens, I believe, because the results confirm that there was in fact an alternative, that it is possible to do politics differently, with a positive impact on people's lives and the economic situation of the country. And it is also understood that the political solution is stable and based on a political line of responsibility and trust, which has stabilized political life through institutional cooperation and social peace.'[19]

It can be perceived from his answer that he believes in delivering to his people, this would help him to gain again. The above statement also demonstrates his thoughtfulness towards the people of his country which is based on the political line of responsibility and trust.

Economy: Naidu, argued that the ideal economy for Gandhism would be the economy that is built upon small scale agriculture and *khadi* industries, based upon indigenous appropriate technology, and tailored to make the village or local community self-sustaining and self- controlled. Such village welfare *(gram uddhar)* should eventually shed the evils of modern industrial economy that are endangering the very existence of Mother Earth and humanity.[20]

In case of Costa, while the question about Portuguese's economic health answers that:

> 'the Portuguese economy is for sure facing important challenges as most other economies are. But as I just told we are addressing those challenges, correcting most structural imbalances and tackling our main bottlenecks. The National Program of Reforms, adopted in April, is based on six pillars intended to transform structurally competitiveness and strengthen social cohesion: 1) capacitation of Portuguese people;
> 2) reinforcement of innovation in processes, processes and products; 3) capitalization of non-financial corporations; 4) valorization and qualification of the territory; 5) modernization of public services; and 6) fighting inequalities. Economic growth is for sure at the centre of our concerns and the most recent results strengthen our confidence that we are moving in the right directions. In the third quarter of 2016 growth almost tripled and Portugal was the Euro-area fastest growing economy. Indicators for the 4th quarter also show signs that growth is gaining momentum.'[21] **He answers the question:**

> 'Have you been able to balance your pledge of running a "socialist programme" with the need to meet international commitments on Portugal's budget and debts? What helped you turn the page on austerity and what more needs to be done?
> During the last year we have proved that it would be possible to follow a different policy, turning the page on austerity and, at the same time, meeting our European commitments. We have managed to obtain the lowest budget deficit in the history of the Portuguese democracy, while pursuing a policy of both restoring families income that had been cut over the last years and stimulating the economy and creating jobs. This policy has enabled us to overcome the crisis we have gone through. This government solution has worked out in a stable manner since the beginning of our mandate and has already made possible the approval of two state budgets, based on policies that promote knowledge and skills as well as their link to the economy. We shall pursue this path, which proved to be not only possible, but also one which allows for better results at all levels: there was an improvement of the living conditions of the Portuguese people, we have today a sustainable economic growth, more and better employment and a controlled budget deficit.'[22]

Costa's focus to improve the economic by following different policy, the use of the term 'Austerity'- which is a political-economical term that refers to the various policies that aim to reduce government budget deficits through spending cuts, tax increases or a combination of both. But it has been in the most macroeconomics models the austerity policies increase unemployment as government spending falls.[23] Keynesian economists argued, in a recession, austerity can be 'self defeating' with spending cuts causing fall in aggregate demand that ultimately leads to lower economic growth. This leads to lower tax revenue and can offset the improvement from spending cuts.[24]

Gandhi's Ideal Society and State : According to M.V. Naidu, Gandhi was a 'practical idealist'. As such he also put forth ideas on what we may call the 'transitional state', the polity that could evolve into the 'ideal political society'. Naidu has discussed about Gandhian ideal typologies of economy (in terms of industry, technology and agriculture), typology of polity (in terms of structures and techniques of democracy) and typology of society (in terms of cultural value and social behaviour). Gandhi's ideal industry rejects massive industrialization. He believes in the small scale basic industry specifically small scale cottage industries, which is dependent on indigenous technology resources, investments, labour and consumers. These industries would be labour-intensive rather than capital and technology intensive. Costa, also believes in skill developments and creating employment but he do not totally rejects massive industrialization. Gandhi rejects technological determinism and its dehumanization. He emphasized *appropriate* technology determined by the native interests and local conditions, and not by the outside experts for considerations of outside or external industry and economy. To some extent Costa agrees to this but being in this era of modernization he cannot afford to completely reject the modern technology. Gandhi emphasized on agriculture, while keeping in mind the agriculture, the local natural conditions, geography, resources available and indigenous technology the economy should be developed. Mass industrialization will steal away the natural skill, and talent from the country. He believed in self sufficient and self regulated village economy should be supported and developed accordingly. Gandhian polity, economic and ideal society philosophy of based on his three main principles Truth, Ahimsa (non-violence), and Prem (love). He believed in actions with the integrity of body, mind and soul- that is a yogic principle. The enough consciousness should be present while performing of *karma* (actions). If the actions are performed consciously it will lead to less or rather no crime finally. Crime to him is being selfish in any regard. If the principle of of *Sarvodaya* followed properly with complete devotion it will lead to the final destination of salvation, to which he referred that life is for search of God i.e. the ultimate Truth, the self realization. While perceiving the Antonio Costa, from his answer during his interview while his visit to Goa in January 2017, it can be perceived, as if he follows the *down to earth* principle which is to some extend similar to Gandhian principle.

'Asked about the demand of some local political outfits that Costa apologise for Portugal colonising Goa for nearly five centuries, Parsekar said, "Goans should feel proud that a person of Goan origin is heading the entire Portugal today." "I don't like to create controversy, particularly when the election is around."In fact, this gentleman (Costa) shows and discloses proudly that his origin is in Goa. In that sense I feel we Goans should feel proud. It is a matter of pride for all of us," he added'[25]

Costa during his interview on his visit to India:

'Do you see more people like yourself - of Goan origin - joining public life and politics in Portugal? Portugal has a tradition of tolerance and openness to the world that is internationally recognised. The ability to interact with people from other origins, cultures and religions is part of our DNA. I am not the first Portuguese of Goan origin to serve in Portuguese politics. Others before me were very active in public life and in politics, like the recently deceased Alfredo Bruto da Costa, the former MP Narana Coissoró, the former Foreign Minister Gonçalves Pereira or the former Secretary of State for Culture Barreto Xavier. And I cannot see any reason why other citizens of Goan origin- or of any other origin – should not join public life and politics in Portugal in future.

The reference of DNA can be various references here and can also be perceived in various senses. The 'tradition of tolerance and openness to the world' is also one of the characteristic traits of the people from Goa. **This is the first PM level visit from Portugal to India since 2007 when then PM Socrates visited Delhi. What are expectations from forthcoming PM trip? What will be big ticket outcome from this trip?** Our countries have a centuries-old relationship based on historical, cultural and personal ties. We want to renew and adapt this relationship to address both present and future challenges. After having normalized our relations, we want to enhance them and extend them to a strategic partnership with ambitious targets in new areas of cooperation.'26

'According to Costa, Portugal and India have a centuries –old relationship which have the responsibility to adapt to the 21st century by building a forward-looking partnership based on historical, cultural and personal ties and by taking advantage of the complementarily of the two countries and economies. He believes that such partnership should be built upon fundamental values that the two countries share, such as **non-violence**, democracy, good governance, rule of law and **respect for human rights**. During his interview he said that India is the world's largest democracy and Portugal has been able to consolidate in the last decades a democratic regime that is considered to be a reference in different parts of the world. This transition to democracy allowed Portugal to renew its ties with India. Having normalized their relations in 1974, and Costa looks forward to deepen, strengthen and diversify this old century's relationship. The following areas: science and technology, infrastructures, renewable energy, start ups, agriculture and food processing, water and waste management, tourism, pharmaceuticals, automotive products and defense, where he found that India and Portugal can really enhance each other's cooperation.'[27]

It has been observed that Antonio Costa, might not be leading exact life as per Gandhian Principal i.e *Truth, Non-Violence, Celibacy, Non-stealing, Non-possession, etc.* but it is being thought that he has uplifted the Portuguese economy since the year 2015, when he became the Prime Minister of Portugal. B.Lana Guggenheim wrote that 'everything is sunny in Lisbon'.[28] Beside this opposite to Gandhian principle, he is definitely leading a normal bourgeois life, and it is believed that he believes that as a democratic state, the politics and the religion are kept at different places, and do not combine with each other, this is also opposite to Gandhian view of state, well Gandhi finds that without religion politics cannot exist, as the religion is the moral support to the politics. But this fact cannot be ignored that it is claimed that Costa does not have any corruption charges[29], this is something uncommon rather rare among political leaders, in case of Portugal as well. In case of development, Costa believes in 'More work means More Money' and has been successful in minimizing the wage differences but could not equalize them. Gandhi preferred agriculture based economy; he had more love for rural based economy, whereas Costa prefers industrial modernized economy and do not show more attachment to the villages in comparison to cities. He believes in harmonious development. This harmonious development has some inclination with Gandhian principle but he is not an ascetic like Gandhi.[30] The fact cannot be denied that a lot many hopes and confidence of the Portuguese People has returned due to his being as a Prime Minister of Portugal. But this comparison might not stand correct as the time in which Gandhi lived was quite different to the present times, seems to be risky and must not exist as its baseless.[31] While others find that comparing Costa with Gandhi is compliment which he does not deserve actually.[32] Being in a democracy the opinions has to be many: in favour and also in oppositions, but it must be visualize that the Gandhian principle do not limit itself to a particular era, to a particular situation or boundary, and do not limit it to particular person as well, rather his principle are much relevant in today's time as well and he himself said that he is thought and will be keep travelling as a thought throughout. Gandhi's motto of life through all his actions (Karmas') was Self-realization, which Antonio Costa might be (due to his roots in Indian ethnology)[33] or might not be [due to his Portuguese (European) upbringing][34] aware of: 'Self-realization is not a melancholy parade, crawling to a pre- destined tomb, but it is a joyous ride to the Palace of Truth, from which man has wandered away in his own ignorance and confusion.'[35]

> 'In the age of social media and instant gratification, there is perhaps no place for ethics, camaraderie, honesty, peace, and non-violence...or is there? Until the day these values continue to mean something to us or matter to our existence, then whether you like it or not, Mahatma Gandhi will remain relevant. He, as a human being, may lose his relevance someday, but his legacy and thoughts can never become irrelevant' [36]

The media in India has been promoting Antonio Costa as *Gandhi of Lisbon*[37] there can be number of reasons attached to it, but reasons which seems more concurrent can be: his Indian roots in Goa, his skin colour that reminds of his ethnological links in India, his daily life habits, respect towards other religion, his 'down to earth' approach in public and political dealings, and his idea and capacities to deal with the economic crisis in Portugal successfully probably compelled Indian media or there might be political reasons behind, to address Antonio Costa as a *Gandhi of Lisbon, Portugal.* Gandhian Principle is universal in nature and very much relevant in present times as well, what utmost needed is: a strong will and a tenacious mind from its initiation towards it culminations.

Note

1. A Man of Perfection is one whose beloved object, the Self can never be apart from him. And

he has no sense of attachment with any other object. Having attained the Self, the inhabitant of his heart, he has such a complete sense of fulfillment that he has no desire for attaining anything. The Self being the All, he has at once attained everything. (http://www.chinmayamission.com/man-of-perfection/, 22 October 2019, 8:30pm).

2. Outlook Web Desk, *Five Things about Portugal's Costa That you Probably Didn't Know*, Outlook : The Fully Loaded Magazine, 26 November 2015. Online available at- https://www.outlookindia.com/blog/story/five- things-about-portugals-costa-that-you-probably-didnt-know/3667.
3. IBTimes India, 16 November 2015, 17:54 IST, 'Antonio Costa, of Goan origin, guns for premiership of Portugal', https://www.ibtimes.co.in/antonio-costa-goan-origin-guns-premiership-portugal-655033, 6 October 2019,11:45 pm and The Economics Times, London, 'Indian-origin politician Antonio Costa in race to become Portugal Prime Minister', By PTI, updated: 30 September, 2014, 03:09 pm IST, https://economictimes.indiatimes.com/nri/nris-in-news/indian-origin-politician-antonio-costa-in-race-to- become-portugal-prime-minister/printarticle/4389..., 9 October 2019, 09 October 2019,1am.
4. Hindustan Times, 'Proud of my roots in Goa': Portugal PM Antonio Costa's Q&A with HT-Portugal PM Antonio Costa is visiting India to attend the Pravasi Bharatiya Divas as a Person of Indian Origin' by Rezaul H Laskar, HT, New Delhi, WORLD, Updated: 06 January, 2017, 07:02 IST.
5. Teotonio R.de Souza, *Goan Ethnography and Colonial Anthropology*, O Herlad, in the 'OPINION' Section, 18 July, 2009, Vol No. CIX No: 199,p.8. online available at www.researchgate.net
6. B.Sheik Ali, in his forward, *Goan Society Through the Ages*, B.S.Shastry (ed.), Asian Publication Services, New Delhi, 1987.
7. Rezaul H Laskar, Hindustan Times, 6 January 2017, 07:02, IST, https://www.hindustantimes.com/world- news/proud-of-my-roots-in-goa-indian-origin-portugal-pm-antonio-costa-s-q-a-with-ht/story- kQVsK5BH10l1fSTaeU4zmK.html,. Downloaded on 10 October 2019, 11:20pm.
8. "Eleven Vows of Gandhi" StudyMode.com. 08 2011. 2011. 08 2011 https://www.studymode.com/essays/Eleven-Vows-Of-Gandhi-753611.html and Kurangi Desai, *The Eleven Vows of Mahatam Gandhi-their Observance and Relevance*, http://www.gandhi-manibhavan.org/activities/essay_elevenvows.htm, 10 October 2019, 4am.
9. Kurangi Desai-http://www.gandhi-manibhavan.org/activities/essay_elevenvows.htm, 10:56am.
10. A.Hemabati Devi, *Gandhi's Concept of Ahimsa: a Spiritual Power*, Bombay Sarvodaya Mandal & Gandhi Research Foundation, online available at - https://www.mkgandhi.org/articles/gconcept.htm, 23 Nov 2019, 2pm.
11. Kurangi Desai-http://www.gandhi-manibhavan.org/activities/essay_elevenvows.htm, 10:56am.
12. MKV Lamani, *A study of the story of my experiments with truth as a literary work*, Karnatak University, 2007, online available at- URI: http://hdl.handle.net/10603/107338 (https://shodhganga.inflibnet.ac.in/handle/10603/107338).
13. M.Balaji, *Philosophy of Political Decentralisation- Gandhi Perspective*, Pondicherry University, http://hdl.handle.net/10603/20921, uploaded on 18-Jul-2004, pp.81-82

14. An opinion: Professor Carmen Frias e Gouveia, Professor of Linguistics at Faculty of Letters, University of Coimbra, Portugal. Interaction on social media dated 1 Nov 2019.
15. An opinion of the Professor Amadeu Carvalho Homem, former professor of History of Portugal at the University of Coimbra, Portugal. During continuous interactions via email dated 21 October- 1 November 2019.
16. W.H. Morris-Jones, "MAHATMA GANDHI – POLITICAL PHILOSOPHER?" *The Indian Journal of Political Science*, vol. 21, no. 3, 1960, pp. 203–224, www.jstor.org/stable/41853840, p.204.
17. M.Balaji, *Philosophy of Political Decentralization*, Pondicherry University, uploaded on 18 July 2014 on Shodhganga,, online available at- http://hdl.handle.net/10603/20921 (https://shodhganga.inflibnet.ac.in/handle/10603/20921).
18. M.K.Gandhi, *An Autobiography or The Story of my experiments with truth*, transalted from the Gujarati by Mahadev Desai, Navajivan Publishing House, Ahmedabad-14, India, p.423.
19. Hindustan Times, 'Proud of my roots in Goa': Portugal PM Antonio Costa's Q&A with HT- Portugal PM Antonio Costa is visiting India to attend the Pravasi Bharatiya Divas as a Person of Indian Origin' by Rezaul H Laskar, HT, New Delhi, WORLD, Updated: 06 January, 2017, 07:02 IST.
20. Naidu, M.V. "THE GANDHIAN VISION OF THE IDEAL SOCIETY AND STATE." *Peace Research*, vol. 38, no. 2, 2006, pp. 23–34. *JSTOR*, www.jstor.org/stable/23607989.
21. Hindustan Times, 'Proud of my roots in Goa': Portugal PM Antonio Costa's Q&A with HT- Portugal PM Antonio Costa is visiting India to attend the Pravasi Bharatiya Divas as a Person of Indian Origin' by Rezaul H Laskar, HT, New Delhi, WORLD, Updated: 06 January, 2017, 07:02 IST and also at https://algarvedailynews.com/politics/10805-proud-of-my-roots-in-goa-portugal-s-pm-interviewed-for-the- hindustan-times, 15 November 2019, 12:55am.
22. Hindustan Times, 'Proud of my roots in Goa': Portugal PM Antonio Costa's Q&A with HT- Portugal PM Antonio Costa is visiting India to attend the Pravasi Bharatiya Divas as a Person of Indian Origin' by Rezaul H Laskar, HT, New Delhi, WORLD, Updated: 06 January, 2017, 07:02 IST.
23. Auster 'Asituation in which there is not much money and it is spent only on things that are necessary', The Economist, https://www.economist.com/buttonwoods-notebook/2015/05/20/what-is-austerity, 21 October 2019, 4pm.
24. Tejvan Pettinger, *Austerity – Pros and Cons*, https://www.economicshelp.org/blog/5366/economics/austerity- pros-and-cons/, 22 October 2019, 8:30pm.
25. By PTI, https://www.dnaindia.com/india/report-goans-should-be-proud-that-a-person-of-goan-origin-is- portugal-pm-laxmikant-parsekar-2291439, 22 October 2019, 9pm
26. By Dipanjan Roy,, Ishani Duttagupta, https://economictimes.indiatimes.com/opinion/interviews/portugal- will-always-be-a-strong-advocate-of-india-in-europe-pm- antnio-costa/articleshow/56383080.cms, 22 October 2019, 5pm.
27. By Vikas Shah MBE/ @MR Vikas, https://thoughteconomics.com/interview-with-antonio-costa-pm- portugal/, 4 January, 2017.
28. By B.Lana Guggenheim, *Everything's Sunny in Lisbon*', 5 September, 2019, https://www.southeusummit.com/europe/portugal/everythings-sunny-in-lisbon/, downloaded on 5 November 2019, 3am.
29. B.Lana Guggenheim, in *the Socialists Cruise to Victory in Portugal,* wrote that a series of

scandals may have also eroded Costa's overall popularity, and likely cost him the outright majority that pre-election polling had suggested was within his reach, https://www.southeusummit.com/europe/portugal/the-socialists-cruise-to- victory-in-portugal/, 9 Ocotber 2019, 4am.

30. An opinion of the Professor Amadeu Carvalho Homem, former professor of History of Portugal at the University of Coimbra, Portugal. During continuous interactions via email dated 21 October- 1 November 2019.
31. Prof. Amadeu Carvalho Homem, a former Professor of Contemporary Portugal (18th '19th centuries), Faculty of Letters, University of Coimbra, Portugal. During continuous interactions via email dated 21 October- 1 November 2019.
32. An opinion: Professor Carmen Frias e Gouveia, Professor of Linguistics at Faculty of Letters, University of Coimbra, Portugal. Interaction on social media dated 1 Nov 2019.
33. Because in India is the country where most of the people specifically the people who belong to Hindu religion are consciously striving for Salvation 'Moksha'. Jaggi Vasudev 'Sadguru' has refered in one of his videos that one must go and visit Allahabad, U.P during *Kumbh Snan*, where one can find that millions of people are performing the snan (baths) as an conscious effort to achieve salvation 'Moksha' (https://www.youtube.com/watch?v=MLVsk_j3whk, 112,060 views, 3 February 2019).
34. Deals with materialistic world of senses i.e. pleasure, sadness, happiness, love, hatred, jealousy, and enjoyment, etc.
35. http://www.chinmayamission.com/man-of-perfection/, 22 October 2019, 8:30pm.
36. Rahul Srivastava, *Bapu's way: the Relevance of Gandhi in Modern India and the World*, https://www.onetravel.com/going-places/the-relevance-of-gandhi-in-modern-india-and-the-world/, 10 October 2019, 3pm.
37. Correio de manhã (e-mail in the morning, Portuguese newspaper), *Indian newspaper call António Costa 'Ghandi of Lisbon'*, the mayor of Lisbon has Indian roots, 1 October 2014,00:29. Excerpts from Hindustan times, Author- Prasun Sonwalkar, *Indian-origin Costa is Portugal's next PM candidate*, London, 24 September, 2014. Downloaded on 31 October 2019, 1:21am.

References

Articles and books

1. Antonio Costa Pinto, 'Contemporary Portugal: politics, society and culture' 2nd Edition. Columbia University Press, New York., 2011
2. *Antonio Costa speaks of 'Victory of responsibility'* 10 May 2019, https: //www.youtube.com/watch?v=X7af87n8Jd0, watched on 11 October 2019, 3:00pm.
3. https://shodhganga.inflibnet.ac.in/bitstream/10603/127925/18/09_chapter%204.pdf, Gandhi and ambedkar polity- 21 Oct 2019, 8:29am.pp. 1-31
4. https://shodhganga.inflibnet.ac.in/bitstream/10603/20921/7/08_chapter%203.pdf, 9 October 2019, 9:00pm. Gandhi's political philosophy – shodhganga
5. https://shodhganga.inflibnet.ac.in/bitstream/10603/69562/7/07_chapter%202.pdf, 9 October 2019, 8:45pm. Philosophical foundations of Gandhi- shodganga
6. List of important personalities and their contribution, https://www. jagranjosh.com/general-

knowledge/list-of-important-personalities-and-their-HYPERLINK "https://www.jagranjosh.com/general-knowledge/list-of-important-personalities-and-their-contribution-in-indian-history-1466673956-1" \h contribution-in-indian-history-1466673956-1, 20 October 2019, 10:51am.

7. M.K. Gandhi, *An Autobiograpphy or The Story of my experiments with truth*,Navajivan Trust, Ahmedabad, India.
8. Morris-Jones, W. H. "MAHATMA GANDHI – POLITICAL PHILOSOPHER ?" *The Indian Journal of Political Science*, vol. 21, no. 3, 1960, pp. 203–224., www.jstor.org/stable/41853840, p.214s.
9. Naidu, M.V. "THE GANDHIAN VISION OF THE IDEAL SOCIETY AND STATE." *Peace Research*, vol. 38, no. 2, 2006, pp. 23–34. *JSTOR*, www.jstor.org/stable/23607989., https://www.jstor.org/stable/23607989?seq=1#metadata_info_tab_contents, 3:35pm, 21 Oct 2019.
10. Pedro Lains, 'The Portuguese Economy in the Twentieth Century: Growth and Structural Changes'.
11. Reply of Prime Minister Antonio Costa To Mr. Nuno Magalhaes, https://www.youtube.com/watch?v=qxHHflmJhf8, watched on 12 October 2019, 1:20am.

Article from the Newspapers Online

1. Ana Peixoto Fernandes, 28 Setembro 2019 at 17:52 https://www.jn.pt/nacional/canal/legislativas-2019/antonio-costa-foi-assistido-como- qualquer-cidadao-no-hospital-de-viana-11349867.html, downloaded on 30 October 2019, 12:15am.
2. B.Lana Guggenheim, in *the Socialists Cruise to Victory in Portugal*, https://www.southeusummit.com/europe/portugal/the-socialists-cruise-to-victory-in-HYPERLINK"https://www.southeusummit.com/europe/portugal/the-socialists-cruise-to-victory-in-portugal/" \h portugal/, 9 Ocotber 2019.
3. https://www.cmjornal.pt/cm-ao-minuto/detalhe/antonio-costa-recebido-como-filho-em-HYPERLINK "https://www.cmjornal.pt/cm-ao-minuto/detalhe/antonio-costa-recebido-como-filho-em-visita-de-estado-a-india?ref=Pesquisa_Destaques" \h visita-de-estado-a-india?ref=Pesquisa_Destaques, son of the state, downloaded on 31 October 2019, 1. 25am
4. https://www.cmjornal.pt/politica/detalhe/costa-recebe-primeiro-ministro-indiano-para-HYPERLINK "https://www.cmjornal.pt/politica/detalhe/costa-recebe-primeiro-ministro-indiano-para-consolidar-parceria-economica?ref=Pesquisa_Destaques" \h consolidar-parceria-economica?ref=Pesquisa_Destaques, downloaded on 31 October 2019, 1:27am
5. https://www.cmjornal.pt/politica/detalhe/jornal_indiano_chama_antonio_costa_de_ghand HYPERLINK "https://www.cmjornal.pt/politica/detalhe/jornal_indiano_chama_antonio_costa_de_ghandi_de_lisboa?ref=Pesquisa_Destaques" \h i_de_lisboa?ref=Pesquisa_Destaques, downloaded on 31 October 2019, 1:21am- Indian newspaper calls Antonio Costa Gandhi of Lisbon.

9

Gandhi's Thought: A Powerful Tool to Control the Mind of the Youth

Rajeev Ranjan

Gandhiji, one of the greatest thinkers of the modern world, who experimented all the thoughts that came into his mind and only then he either advised others to follow or gave his own words to those thoughts in written form. Gandhiji believes that everything is present in our natural surrounding (may be biotic or abiotic components) that can not only prevent us from all the diseases but also cure from different diseases. He was never in favour of any chemical and western medicine. Today's youths usually do not believe on any restriction or boundary. They live in present without caring future or learning from past. They believe only in scientific explanation of everything. The paper tries to emphasize scientifically about the importance of vegetarian diet, importance of traditional medicine (Naturopathy), importance of *bramcharya* (celibacy), and the most important one is the power of chanting *Ram Naam*. Gandhiji realizes and experiences all these at his own level.

Vegetarian Food Habits

Gandhiji was one of the biggest supporters of vegetarian food. He advocated its numerous benefits at larger extent. According to him, "My experiments in England were conducted from the point of view of economy and hygiene. Vegetarian diet is the least expensive. The real seat of taste was not the tongue but the mind. One should eat only articles that sustained the body. Man eats not for enjoyment but to live."[1] "I have always been in favour of pure vegetarian diet. Vegetarian diet must include milk and milk products to keep perfectly fit. Milk and banana make a perfect meal. Alcohol ruins one physically, morally, intellectually and economically".[2]"A man can secure enough nourishment both for the tissues and the nerves from fruits like grapes and nuts like almonds. Restrain from the sexual and other passions becomes easy for a man who lives on such food. Indian proverb is much true that as a man eats, so shall he become."[3]

These are number of thoughts that Gandhiji put in favour of vegetarian diet. Different scientific evidences also prove the suitability of vegetarian diet for Homo sapiens (modern human). Some are:

a) **Biomagnification:** 'It is the process through which some harmful chemicals (Pesticides, Insecticides, weedicides, etc.) enter our bodies through the food chain. As these chemicals are not degradable, these get accumulated progressively at each trophic level (Each step or level of food chain.) As human beings occupy the top level in any food chain, the maximum concentration of these chemicals get accumulated in our bodies.'[4]
If one is vegetarian, he/she is at lower or often at second trophic level, while one who is non-vegetarian is comparatively at higher tropic level and thus who is at higher trophic level in an ecosystem (the sustainable zone where biotic and non- biotic components interact together.) consumes much, those harmful chemicals used in field. "DDT (Dichloro Diphenyl Trichoroethane) is stored in the fat of animals and takes many years to break down, as the fat is consumed by predators, the amount of DDT bio-magnify. DDT is now banned substance in many parts of the world."[5]

b) **Animal Fats Vs Vegetable Fats :** "Avoid the trans-fats, limit the saturated fats and replace with essential poly- unsaturated fats."[6]
"Plant fats are healthier than animal fats. People who ate lots of fats had 16% lower risk of dying compared to those with lower intakes, while those who ate lots of animal fats had 21% higher risks, compared to those who didn't eat many of these foods." 7 Simply,animals fats are saturated that need much energy to convert it in to simpler form(Fatty acids) during its digestion in alimentary canal in comparison to plants fats those are usually unsaturated.

c) **Anatomical Evidences:** "Human are naturally plant-eaters", 8 the comparative anatomy of eating by Milton R. Mills MD supports vegetarian habits of human. i.e. the carnivorous animals do not contain salivary enzymes. Teeth (canines) of carnivores are long, sharp and curved, while human has short and blunted as herbivores have. Today's youths love to eat fast food, and non-veg. food. If one has to lead a healthy life, one must go for vegetarian habit of food as upper scientific explanation support it.

Naturopathy

"With the growing simplicity of my life, my dislike for medicines steadily increased. 'Return of Nature' was one of that, based on earth treatment and advocated fresh fruit and nuts as the natural diet."[9]

"Though I have had two serious illnesses in my life, I believe that man has little need to drug himself. 999 cases out of a thousand can be brought round by means of a well regulated diet, water and earth treatment and similar household remedies.

He who seems to the Doctor, *Vaidya* or *Hakim* for every little ailment, and swallows all kinds of vegetable and mineral drugs, not only curtails his life, but, by becoming the slave of his body instead of remaining its master, loses self-control, and ceases to be a man."[10]

"I know the reason of my three illnesses. I am fully conscious that I alone am responsible for them, and it is because of that consciousness that I have not lost patience. Infect have thanked God for them as lessons and successfully resisted the temptation of taking numerous drugs."[11]

Upper mentioned few thoughts tell the great faith of Gandhiji on naturopathy or household remedies.

Now adays Medical field has become a lucrative field of business. Billions and billions of investments are being done in this field. People especially poor are the easiest victim, who are easily trapped by the so called developed society. They consume chemical medicines blindly and many of them lost their life due to side effect of so called modern medicines. Now some sensible medical practioners as well as experts believe that most of the allopathic medicines especially antibiotic have side effects that may be fatal.

"Antibiotic resistance is one of the most urgent threats to public's health. Each year in U.S., at least two million people get infected with antibiotic resistance bacteria and at least 23000 people die as a result." About 30% of antibiotics or 47 million prescriptions are prescribed unnecessarily in doctor's offices."[12]

The solution to overcome from this mega problem is to incorporate 'the importance of house hold medicines' in school syllabus and bring awareness among people specially among youths.

Bramcharya (Celebacy)

In Gandhiji words "Brahmacharya means control of the senses in thought, word and deed."[13] "The knowledge that a perfect observance of Brahmacharya means realization of Brahman (God) that realization is impossible without practicing self- restrain. Self-restrain means restrain of all the senses. But ordinarily Brahmacharya is understood to mean control over the sexual organs and prevention of seminal discharge through complete control over the sexual instinct and the sexual organs. Mere abstention from sexual intercourse, cannot be term Brahmacharya. So long as the desire for intercourse is there, one cannot be said to have attended Brahmacharya. Full-fledged Brahmachari's speech, thoughts, and his actions, all be speak possession of vital force. For him distinction between men and women almost disappears. The cultivated impotency of the man, whose sexualsecreation are being converted into vital force, is wholly different. It is true that such a Brahmachari is rare to find."[14]

Today's science has proved that reproduction is not an essential life process for individual. It helps only to maintain the continuity of generations. This is the life process that needs maximum energy. Its use for pleasure (only the animal that is human) affects various aspects of life badly. Some of researches confirm it.

"A species investing heavily in reproduction early in life should have relatively short life expectancy than that of the species that invests little in reproduction."[15]

The researchers used the Australian cricket, Teleogrullusoceanicus to prove that the production of quality of sperm is expensive and males are about strategic about investing energy in biological process.

So for a healthy nation, healthy new generation are needed and that is possible only by purposeful planned reproduction and follow the rules of Brahmacharya, as Gandhiji states.

Ram Naam (Realizing God)

"The existence of God within makes even control of the mind possible. Let no one think that it is impossible because it is difficult. It is highest goal and it is no wonder that the highest effort should be necessary to attain it."[16]

"Supplication, worship, prayer are no superstition, they are act more real than the act of eating, drinking sitting or walking. It is no exaggeration to say that they alone are real, all else is unreal. I have not the slightest doubt that prayer is an unfailing means of cleaning the heart of passions. But it must be combined with the utmost humility."[17]

"Those who desire to observe Brahmacharya with a view of realizing God need not despair provided their faith in God is equal to their confidence in their own effort."[18]

विषयाविविर्तन्तेविराहारस्यदेविह
रसिरजूरसोऽपूयस्यपर
दृष्टव्य ॥59॥

viṣhayāvinivartantenirāhārasyadehinaḥ
rasa-varjaṁraso 'pyasyaparaṁdṛiṣhṭvānivartate

BG 2.59: Aspirants may restrain the senses from their objects of enjoyment, but the taste for the sense objects remains. However, even this taste ceases for those who realizes the Supreme.(BG 2.59, refers Bhagwat Geeta 2nd chapter, 59th verse) "Therefore His name and his grace are the last resource of the aspirant after moksha. This truth came to me only after my return to india."18There are number of researches conclude that despite all the comforts and lot of wealth many people end their lives by committing suicide. Rate of suicide increases many folds irrespective of age, in recent years despite development in almost all arena of life. One of the mainreasons of this is'there is no mental peace and no philosophy of life.'

"Researchers concluded after Mindfulness Meditation (MM) that favourable structure changes occurred in the brain that helps in number of emotional balance".[19]

In this well-equipped modern fast growing era, busy schedule of people specially youths, their food habits and without any philosophy of their life, Gandhiji's thoughts very much relevant and are the most powerful tool to control the mind of youth across the boundaries.

Refrences

1. An Autobiography by M.K.Gandhi- page 52
2. Key to health by M.K.Gandhi- page 12 (www.mkgandhi.org)
3. An Autobiography by M.K.Gandhi- page 250
4. NCERT Science class-10 (2015 publication) page 261

5. U.S. Environmental protection agency (31-12-1972) Archived, Wikipedia.org
6. Harvard Health Publishing, Harvard Medical School (Feb.- 2015)
7. TIME magazine by Jamie Ducharme (21-03-2018)
8. Human are naturally plant eaters by Michael Bluejay- June 2002, uploaded Dec.- 2015, (vegetarian Guide)
   (http//michaelbluejay.com/veg/natural.html)
9. An Autobiography by M.K.Gandhi- page 247
10. An Autobiography by M.K.Gandhi- page 249
11. An Autobiography by M.K.Gandhi- page 249
12. www.cdc.gov/features/antibioticuse/index.htm , (9-11-2018)
13. An Autobiography by M.K.Gandhi- page 194 (Brahmcharya-II)
14. Key to health, by M.K.Gandhi- Page 29.
15. Reproduction and life story, Laurie J. vitt.,Janelee P. Caldwell in Herpetology (IV edition-2014)
16. An Autobiography by M.K.Gandhi- page 194
17. An Autobiography by M.K.Gandhi- page 67
18. An Autobiography by M.K.Gandhi- page 195

10

Gandhian Values on Contemporary Global Peace

Shakti P. Rout

"Nonviolence is the weapon of the strong"
Mohandas Karamchand Gandhi

In the Galaxy of world leaders Mahatma Gandhi shines as Pole star depicting the symbol of non-violence, peace and truth. His stature as the most influential philosopher lies in his experimentation with truth; truth based on practicality of existing values and resources where he values human being as supreme creation of God -'Vaishanava Jana to' . So, his idea stands for values of moral idealism. Though he had not developed a structural theory of state and established any blue print of it like Savarkar and Ambedkar. But his understanding of power and politics flows in four levels like- Personal level(self-rule); Level of Community (Gram Swaraj); National level(Swaraj); International Level(Comity of equal nations). His method Satyagraha supports the most practical notion of non-violent collective resistance and to establish collective tolerance and inter-faith dialogue which are the most prominent need of the hour.

In recent years, a strong trend has become evident for conflict and war. To many of us, the world seems more war prone and violent space. The factual details can be recollected from war ravaged Afghanistan to rubrics of Iraq civilization. The wars in Darfur (Sudan); between Ethiopia and Eritrea; Uganda indicates the misery of human civilization. These destructive wars and uncontrollable situation need not to be final destination of human civilization. Gandhi being a philosopher of eminence had foreseen the genesis of war and conflict lies in human nature; this human nature has proliferating impact on social and political life.

Like all other political philosophers Gandhi realised power is an inescapable feature of human social life and structure. With the use of power, human being influence each other and tries to control others life or resources. Being a pacifist, he was always against any type of war and violence. According to him the supreme human endeavour should be the pursuit of Satya. He applied many Hindu philosophical traditions to eliminate contemporary social injustice and worldwide domination of European powers like Great Britain, Portugal, France and Germany. His idea of **Satyagraha is an approach of conflict resolution by using soul force**. His Satyagraha is inspired by boundless love and compassion. The use of 'Satyagraha lies in its self-limiting character as a form of political action that seeks to constrain the negative consequences of politics; while working towards progressive social and political reforms. So, Gandhian nonviolence points out towards using **non conservative, moral or spiritual and cultural power as its instrument of conflict resolution**. However, non violence as an instrument of negotiation, mediation or conflict resolution can be used in primary stage of conflict resolution even contemporary situation.

Mahatma Gandhi believed **in decentralization of power as fundamental aspect of power. He has emphasized that Indian independence must have bottom up approach and villages should be considered as republic and should be bestowed with full power**. His idea of 'gram Swaraj' has its genesis in home-rule tradition of Anne Besant and combination of anarchism along with the faith on religion. In contrary to coercion and use of weapon Gandhi elevated negation or conflict resolution to a higher stage of morality and compassion. Empowered by soul force a *Satyagrahi* always appeals to the opponent to be kind; in the same time a *Satyagrahi* do not harm his or her opponent. A *Satyagrahi* does not passively wait for transformation of opponent, he boldly takes the course that enlightens the opponent and changes his heart. That he fight the enemy with patience and sympathy and still he pursues truth.

Gandhi was essentially a pacifist. He emphasised **the purity of means would definitely lead to noble ends**. He considered that long lasting peace in the world can be attainable through non violence and mediation and abstaining from any type of war and hatred. According to him, violence produces counter violence and leads to instability. So, he never justified any type of war including the World War I and World War II. Peace through violence at best may be truce, but it cannot be a lasting peace. Violence and war end in colossal destruction of human life and property. As Gandhi asserted that, an eye for eye only ends of making the whole world blind. In the age of nuclear age either we follow non-violence and mutual respect or we will nonexistence as nations.

Being a true champion of truth and nonviolence Gandhi strongly stood for peace and non- violence. His conception of Swaraj goes hand in hand with his idea of humanism and universal brotherhood. In the midst of scientific discoveries, establishment of modern civilization he suggested of **courage to strengthen the 'soul force'- the *Aatmic Shakti*, to enhance peace and stability in the world**. His idea of peace is not of related to any kind of competitive or antagonistic in nature. His idea of peace is an integrated human being in social, political and spiritual level. He mainly 'spiritualized politics' to create ethical and fearless human being who will contribute to the nation in all form. His idea of Purna Swaraj is not isolated independence of India from British colonialism but, he aspired for a healthy and dignified interdependence of other nations. He had envisioned synthetic nationalism like his predecessor Sri Aurobindo and Shri Ravindra Nath Tagore. He envisaged an international league, only when all nations, big and small, composing it was fully independent. In the midst of his fight for independent nationhood of India he visions a world order base on truth and nonviolence.

Gandhian model of global **peace is one of the viable alternatives to realistic model** based on war and conflict. He prescribed moral and ethical means to settle national and international disputes. His ideas are being experimented throughout the world. He himself made his experiment in South Africa during 1915 which had proliferating impact in Ghana in the leadership by Nukrumah; President Keenth Kaunda in Zambia; Nyerere in Tanzania; in America during Martin Luther King Jr; later in South Africa in the leadership of Nelson Mandela. For example President Kenneth Kaunda who had led Zambia to freedom through campaign of non-violence and had hither to have been a leading advocate of Gandhian politics dedicated a moral rather than physical force.

Gandhi along with all these leaders espoused a peaceful and non-violent change, to establish social equality with self-sufficiency, and harmony against all forms of racial and ethical discrimination or racial subjugation prevalent during that time. He stood for **non-violent society**; the smallest nation to him should have its own self respect and should stand as tall as the tallest. The idea of superior nation and the inferior one was to be completely obliterated. However, in certain ways, the situation in South Africa was comparable to that of India, where the combination of different groups committed to violence and non-violence produced an effective dialectical instrument of counter hegemony. Mandela also succeeded because he refused to adopt violence. He was completely committed to non-violence as fundamental principle to achieve independence. In Gandhi's theory of peace, human values take a great prominence. Nonviolence (ahimsa) is a way of life rather than a strategy; is a means to reach the truth. It inculcates strength to bear the truth 'satya' ki 'agraha' (holding on the truth with moral strength or spiritual courage).

Gandhi laid down the principles for ideal international organisations which can be attainable through non-violence, freedom from colonialism, equal representation of all nations, complete disarmament and a small international police force to maintain order if violence occurs. Gandhiji explains his concept of nationalism along with internationalism beautifully in the words, "just as the cult of patriotism teaches us today that the individual has to die for the family, the family for the village and the village for district, the district for the province and the province for the country, even so a country has to be free in order that it may die if necessary for the benefit of the world. My idea therefore of nationalism is that our country may become free from that if need be, the whole country may die so that the human race may live". Thus, it can be calculated that Gandhi's nationalism is not opposed to internationalism. Rather, it is the foundation of the latter. The very concept of the Swaraj meant healthy and dignified interdependence, a federation of friendly interdependent states.

According to his scheme, his **ideal nations should absent from use of brute force for settling disputes among themselves**. They should adopt methods like **negotiation, mediation and arbitration** for resolving their disputes. The world federation may maintain an international non-violent policy of the non-violent state for the purpose to resolve conflict between the states, but soldiers of this force will bear no arms. Gandhi wanted to train these soldiers with nonviolence and moral courage to resolve the dispute between the states. Though he conceived that such a new world order will take time to evolve, yet he has faith in the inherent goodness of man. Even if in the age of nuclear weapons and scientific inventions we still aspire to live with harmony with other nations. Policy makers all over the world prefer to use mediation and arbitration in the place of war. However, nonviolence technique seems to be the only solution to the world armed with nuclear weapons.

His thoughts are relevant as it influenced decision making of many world leaders. According to Gandhian principle, a leader in contemporary scenario must be honest, inspiring and competent to hold the path of peace. A leader must be truthful and honest in order to be followed by his people. He should have moral strength in his character to uphold truth in any form. Gandhi assumed, "politics without ethics is a death trap". For Gandhi politics and political power is dangerous without moral understanding and ethical values.

In contemporary times also Gandhi's theory of peace, human values takes great prominence. Nobel peace prize winners in the current decades like Mr. Martti Ahtisaari(2008), Mr. Muhammed Yunus (2006), Ms. Waangari Maathai (2004) and Ms. Shirin Ebadi (2003) have effectively changed their parts of world to maintain amity and bring peace in the midst of trouble. On the other hand, it must also be viewed how political leaders like Mr. Jimmy Carter(2002), Mr.Al Gore (2007) , Mr. Barack Obama(2009) and very recently Mr. Abiy Ahmed(2019) had played a crucial role for understanding the global conflict through the perspective of peace.

Gandhian perspective on peace has given way out to many international, national conflicts. It has inspired thousands of political leadership who used truth and nonviolence as biggest attribute. His method Satyagraha is being used nationally and internationally for resolution of conflict. Gandhian philosophy of truth and nonviolence will remain relevant to generation to come.

Bibliography

- Chakrabarty(2006), Socio-Political Thought of Mahatma Gandhi, Routledge: New Delhi
- Chakrabarty & Pandey(2015), Modern Indian Thought: Text and Context, SAGE Publications India Pvt. Ltd: New Delhi
- Desai, Mahadev (translated)(2009), An Autobiography or The story of My Experiments with Truth, General Book depot: New Delhi
- Flak, Richard (2003) Politically Engaged Spirituality in an Emerging Global Civil society, *Revision,* spring, vol.25. Issue.4, pp2-10
- Fischer, Louis(2012), The Life of Mahatma Gandhi, Harper Collins Publishers: India
- Mantena, Karuna(2012), Another Realism: The Politics of Gandhian Nonviolence, *American Political Science Review* 106,(2), Cambridge University Press, pp. 455-470
- Mehta, V.R.(2016), Foundations of Indian Political Thought, Monohar Publishers: New Delhi
- Pandey, Upasana(2010), Postmodernism and Gandhi, Rawat Publications: New Delhi
- Prabhath, S.V.(2010) Gandhi Today, Serials Publications: New Delhi

11

Truth as the Supreme Goal of Mahatma Gandhi and Its Relevance in 21st Century

Krishan Gopal Tyagi

I have nothing new to teach the humankind. Truth (Satya) and Non-violence are as old as the hills (Mahatma Gandhi).The Truth is the highest goal of Gandhi ji and also it is the means to understand God. Mahatma Gandhi does not draw any line of difference between Truth and God. Until 1931 he said, "God is Truth" but later on he said, "Truth is God". He says, "I have no God to serve but Truth". Truth is articulated through the inner voice. It is the call of conscience. It should pervade the whole life. He believed in the practical application of truth in our daily behaviour and in our dealings with not only the human being but all creation of creator. Truth should be the guiding norm of human conduct. This truth is the ultimate reality (God) which must conquest over evil and animosity." His recommendation was to realize that "Truth is life". The way to attain the goal of Truth is Ahimsa or Nonviolence and knowledge. To him, "Ahimsa and Truth are so interweaved that it is practically impossible to extricate and separate them." They are the two sides of a coin, or rather a smooth metallic disc, where it is not possible to say "which is the obverse and which is the reverse"? Ahimsa is not a negative approach; it is a positive approach of tolerance, patience, perseverance, self-sacrifice, self-suffering, humility, charity, self-control, rise above attachment and hatred. He said that it is only through love that one can attain truth. To see the universal and all-prevailing essence of truth face to face, one must be able to love the nearest of creation as oneself as our Vedic quotation "अहम ब्रह्मास्मम" . One can conquer the enemies and heartless evil forces not by becoming evil but through love. Just as God is truth, God is also Love and bliss (सतचिदानंद). In the words of Mahatma Gandhi about God **"instead of being in the temple, church and mosque, is to be found in the temple of humanity."** The idea of Ramrajya is truly the image of his idea of Truth, Ahimsa and Love. These three central values are identical in nature.

In cultural tradition of India truth is the only mean to attain moksha which is liberation from rebirth. According to Indian knowledge system Satya is the only way to realize self and God. Satya or Truth which is immortal and one can attain it only through knowledge. Whole spiritual system is based on Satya. Great saint Ram Krishan Paramhans master of Swami Vivekananda emphasizes to know the Satya which exists in our body and also in the Universe. Satya is the base of everything material or spiritual.

Following the Gita, which he took as his torch bearer in these profounder matters, he believed in the pursuit of Truth required 'selflessness'; he would often interpret the Gita as recommending a life of Nishkam Karma, that is, action that was indifferent to the personal gain (or pain) that might grow from it. The face of Truth is hidden behind the golden cover of maya, says the Upanishad. The quotation was from the Isawasya Upanishad, which became a favorite of Gandhi's life and was used regularly in his ashram at morning prayers. The full verse reads as "The face of reality is surrounded by the golden cover. O Provider of the world uncovers the shining face that the Truth seeker can have a glimpse of the light of reality". The beauty of the golden cover is nothing compared to the beautiful face it secretes, but it is appealing nonetheless. Much of Gandhi's own struggle was against the temptations of natural affection and desire, which, though not evil in them, obscured his vision of reality and weakened his resolve to realize the Truth.

We need to follow Gandhi's ideas in our daily life and in our ever changing and fast moving world. And while doing so, there is a need to understand that without firm willpower and loyalty, no solid result will be possible. Only by doing so, the significance and importance of Gandhi's ideas can be perceived. Ahimsa is the basis in Gandhian ideas. Therefore, adoption of non-violent means is compulsory in Gandhism. Gandhism calls one to Truth; it appeals to accept the real state of affairs, and without renouncing self-respect, it urges readiness to compromise. There is no space for elimination of evil-doers but evils. It believes end of evil not of the evil doer. It recommends a win-win situation for all the parties concerned, and not only for one party in dispute. It integrates high morality in it and talks of good, healthy and welfaristic human behaviours.

Let us consider the situation of the new world. These are the days of globalization. Today, not any country of the world, whether it is weak or powerful, can think of its existence in a state of isolation. When it cannot think of existence in a state of isolation, how it can think of its development? In such a condition if a country exploits the people of another country or snatches its freedom, or oppresses it, then bearing the wide interest of the people in mind and with care, if other countries of the world take the way of non-cooperation with that country, it is not possible for it to tolerate such an action.

Non-cooperation was one of Gandhian methods. It was an important part of India's freedom struggle. But it needs extra care during its implication in the international sphere. Moreover, it demands all sincerity. Therefore, if under the leadership and guidance of the United Nations, a symbol of the Indian concept of "Vasudhaiva Kutumbakam" at the international level is taken, it will definitely substantiate to be effective.

Gandhi put emphasis on non-violence, consequently in all situations non-violence must be used. But when all such means fail for protection of freedom and justice, if least possible violent means are applied in the larger public interest, it is not contempt to the Gandhian method. Freedom and justice were supreme objectives for Mahatma Gandhi. Therefore, he always advised to keep them if possible by non-violent means. Violence must not be accepted in any way against the rival. Gandhi's brief statement, 'intent behind the act' should remain the focus during the course of indulging in momentary violence.

Mahatma Gandhi is an Indian-born world's mentor. Great Indian values, particularly the supreme value of Truth and Ahimsa were basis of his ideas. Practically, he wanted solutions for all problems through the means of non-violence and truth. His ideas based on non- violence are completely important in the new world. They are absolutely relevant for today and will remain so in future as well to attain the peace of heaven.

References

M. K. Gandhi, *The Story of My Experiments with Truth*, 2nd edn (Ahmedabad: Navajivan Press, 1940) See the discussion of this in G. Ashe, *Gandhi: A Study in Revolution* (London: Heinemann, 1968)

Erik Erikson, *Gandhi's Truth* (London: Faber, 1970.

Leo Tolstoy, *The Kingdom of God and Peace Essays* (London: OUP, 1936)

Raghavan Iyer, *The Moral and Political Thought of Mahatma Gandhi* (New York: OUP, 1973)

Young India, February 1930, in *In Search of the Supreme*, vol. 1, p. 257. Cf. Joan Bondurant's remark in her *Conquest of Violence* (Los Angeles: University of California Press, rev. 1965)

John S. Dunne, The Way of All the Earth (London: Sheldon Press, 1972

Margaret Chatterjee's *Gandhi's Religious Thought* (London: Macmillan, 1983) Gora, An Atheist with Gandhi (Ahmedabad: Navajivan Press, 1951)

Gwilym Beckerlegge, World religions reader, 2001

Guha, Ramachandra , Gandhi before India. Allen Lane, 2013 Gandhi, MK (26 October 1907). Indian Opinion: 438.

12

Emerging Opportunities and Challenges in Indian Cottage Industries: A Special Reference to Khadi Village Industries

Rajinder Singh

Abstract

Indian economy is rural dominated economy because more than 65 percent population is residing in rural areas. The cottage industries are not a new concept as its history is long back (ancient time) in which most of the peoples were engaged in rural employment i.e. started from home with less capital required. Mahatama Gandhi was not only a thinker, leader and freedom fighter but a great economic reformer of the society also. The country was facing the problem of poverty, illiteracy and some other social evils at the time of freedom. Gandhi Ji wanted to make rural people self-employed without depending on others. Then, he started "Sarvodya" movement to end poverty through cottage industries. Mahatma Gandhi presented khadi as a symbol of nationalism, equality and self-reliance through promoting the concept of "Swadeshi" and, "Swaraj".

Cottage industries (includes handloom, pottery, handicrafts, coir, silk weaving and leather) in India have a great contribution (about 40% share in total exports) to Indian economy and also known as household industries. The production activities are carried on in the house where the individual along with their family member involve themselves in production process. These cottage industries are playing very pivotal role to strengthening the economy and help to reduce the migration from rural to urban areas as it is providing the employment opportunities especially to weaker section. Even after almost seven decades of independence the cottage industry in rural India is still to gather the required momentum to get a suitable place in industrial sector.

The main objective of this paper is to highlight the opportunities and challenges ahead cottage industries with large scale industries in form of technological, managerial ability, shortage of raw materials, marketing, competition and many more which decline the production of cottage industries.

Keywords: Cottage industries, Employment generation, Opportunities and challenges, KVIS.

Introduction

India is well known for its large numbers of traditional cottage industries like silk weaving, handicrafts, cotton weaving, pottery, khadi etc. The cottage industry term used when products manufactured at small level but since the industrialization development cottage industries are declined due to some problems. However, government is taking initiatives to revive these traditional industries to get their contribution in development of the economy. Generally, cottage industries are fall in small scale industries and considered unorganized sector. These kinds of industries originate where unemployment and under employment are widespread in country and help to engage the rural people with household production activities for their livelihood thus called as household industries.

Though, there are many potential sectors in economy and cottage industries are facing tremendous threats and challenges of technological as well as competition from the modern market in which it becomes difficult to survive in economy. One important benefit of these industries is where it can be started with low capital and traditional tools for the production process. The output produced by these industries is generally sold in the local markets.

Gandhi ji stressed on economic self-sufficiency by an individual who helped in nation's economic development and growth and gave direction to develop cottage industries to achieve universal well-being which help to eradicate the poverty of rural people. Thus, economic model of Gandhi ji was based on rural development and he used to weave khaddar by moving charkha which was the first foundation laid stone to cottage industries.

Presently, Khadi and village industries commission (KVIC) has been promoted khadi as a global fabric as it helps to generate employment across the country. More advanced production techniques and younger designer are appointed from National Institute of Fashion Technology (NIFT) to sounding the success of khadi. According to MSME Ministry Data, sales have grown 30% in last four years against 6.7 previously. Government has planned to increase turnover to Rs. 5000 crore which was Rs. 3215 in 2018-19.

Review of Literature

Some of the major studies selected for review have been discussed below:

1. **The National Planning Commission (1962)** constituted a high level rural industries planning committee to review the progress of rural industries and to chalk out programs for the intensive development of village and small-scale industries in rural areas and stated that the artisans were not involved while preparing plans. They suggested that the artisans should also be involved right from the beginning.
2. **The Government of Kerala (1964)** appointed a working group to study the organizational and functional aspects of Khadi and village industries in Kerala and observed that the organizational and technical deficiencies hindered the growth of this sector and also tried to identify the various steps to be taken to overcome these deficiencies. They suggested to focus on the problem of raw materials and marketing accessibility to artisans and suggest to exempt the village industries product from the levy of Sales Tax.
3. **Kripalani (1967)** in his book 'The Gandhian Way' analyzed the relevance of rural industrialization. He viewed that adoption of large-scale industrialization to reduce dependence on agriculture was inappropriate. Even in industrialized countries there existed the problem of poverty and unemployment. He also discussed the relevance of spinning wheel.
4. **Arunachalam (1977)** in his article 'The Livery of Freedom- Before and After Independence' asserted that after independence, Khadi production has increased but the entire program is being undertaken on a commercial basis. If Khadi is to be symbol of instruments of **Purna Swaraj,** it had to give up commercial aspects and it must become a way of life. Spinning and weaving are more important to achieve economic and moral freedom.

5. **Rao (1979)** in his article 'Small Scale Industries and Planned Economy' highlights the problems and prospects of these industries and stated that marketing channels is the main problem of village industries which can be removed with the help of KVIC which playing a very key role to distribute the finished products through its wider network of distribution channels.
6. **Ramachandran (1984**) in his article 'Some Thoughts on Reorganization of Khadi and Village Industries Programs' noted that the value attached to Khadi has undergone change as it stands more as a relief measure than to destroy the evil of poverty and unemployment. The Charkha increases income and improves working condition of artisans and also stated that use of power in Charkha will further improve the income earning capacity of the artisans.
7. **Pande (1991)** in his report 'Origin of Training Program and its Gradual Transformation under KVIC' reviewed the need for trained personnel to become an effective salesman in the Khadi and Village Industries sector. He found that the KVIC has taken some measures to make its training program effective to create high skill among the artisans.
8. **Damayanthi (1992)** in her article 'Employment and Income Generation through Khadi and Village Industries in Kerala' emphasized that the Khadi and village industries in Kerala play a significant role in solving the problem of unemployment in rural areas by generating large scale employment opportunities.
9. **Rajendran (1993)** in his study titled 'Training in Khadi and Village Industries 'A futuristic Approach' stressed the need for training in Khadi and Village Industries and he pointed out that training occupies a prominent place in the efficient management of any developmental program and also suggested that KVIC should work seriously about strengthening the training program to meet the future requirements.
10. **Solanki S.S. and Quershi M.A. (1998)** in their study 'Village Pottery Industry' aimed at exploring the scope of up gradation of village pottery industry. They concluded that adoption of modern technology by pottery units is unsatisfactory. They stated that about 70 per cent of the potters used traditional raw materials and also revealed that village pottery industry has failed to grow because of its inability to get adequate finance facilities.

11. **Das (2001)** in his article 'Khadi and Village Industries Program: An Employment Evaluation' examined whether there existed any significant relationship between generation of employment and resource allocation and he concluded that there was no significant relationship between resource allocation and employment generation either in Khadi or Village Industries.
12. **Veena Mazumdar (2001)** in her article 'Implication of Naya Margh' has analyzed the performance of KVIC with special reference to Khadi and the role of women as equal partners, participants and beneficiaries in the program as propounded by Gandhi ji. Case study of Amreli and Mehasana districts of Gujarat was undertaken. Performance and administrative structure of KVIC is less satisfactory as 70 per cent of time is spent on administrative procedures and she pointed out that KVIC is not following labour laws for the artisans and not giving maternity and other benefits to the rural women. She pointed out that KVIC does not have any specific target group like government's anti-poverty program. Gandhi ji's concept of self-sufficiency was not applied.
13. **Brahmananda, Narayanan and Kallappa (2002)** in their book 'Dimensions of Rural Development of India' has identified the shortcomings of the village industries sector as traditional skills, inaccessibility to institutions and markets, inadequate information of market and marketing channels, resistance to change, inadequacies of credit, technology and lack of proper entrepreneurship training and skill.
14. **Vinod Deepak (2003)** in his article 'Development Through Khadi and Village Industries' argued that khadi and village industries opened a novel way of self-employment, using local resources, traditional but improved techniques and tapping the market for such products locally as well as from nearby towns. To achieve this objective, the successive Central Governments had initiated several schemes and programs since independence.
15. **Mada swami (2004)** in his article 'Creating More Employment in the Rural Areas' pointed out that village and cottage industries provide immediate large-scale employment and offer a method of ensuring a more equitable distribution of national income and facilitate effective mobilization of capital resource and skill. The principle of self-

employment is motivated by offering various promotional schemes by both the Central and State Governments.

16. **Kulwant Singh Pathania and Surrender Singh Metha (2009)** in their book 'Status, Problems and Challenges of Khadi Village Industries' have attempted to study the working performance and other issues of KVI sector in Himachal Pradesh. They opined that shortage of finance forces entrepreneurs to use second hand machines, inferior methods of production and ineffective techniques of production which leads to lower productivities.

Objectives Of The Study

Present study is undertaken with the following objectives:

- To know the present position of cottage and small industries
- To study the role of cottage industries in employment generation
- To study the problems and future prospectus of cottage industries
- To make appropriate suggestions and measures on problems of cottage industries

Research Methodology

Research methodology is the systematic way to find out the given problems. Different sources are followed to collect the data of cottage industries. The study is based on secondary sources which are collected from articles, books, research papers, magazines, reports, and websites etc. Opinions obtained towards the origin of cottage industries in India were reviewed.

Opportunities For Cottage Industries In India

Cottage Industry has significant potential for employment generation in cottage industries and the person getting employment regarded as self-employed. It is evident that women are also getting self-independence in this sector and contributes in economic development of the economy. As women are the members of the self-help group and they can easily get the financial assistance at low interest as comparatively other financial institutions. Government also time to time provides the financial support to cottage industries and launched the different schemes for the upliftment of this sector. Cottage industries are the part of small scale industries hence it is the second largest industrial sector after agriculture. Following significant roles are played by the khadi industries in India and some of them are:

1. Production and sales of khadi (2015-2019)

Years	2015-16	2016-17	2017-18	2018-19
Production of khadi (Amount in crore)	1065.6	1401.84	1626.66	1963.30
Sales of khadi (Amount in crore)	1510	2007.61	2510.21	3215.13

Source: Annual report, Government of India, Micro, Small and Medium Enterprises (2015-2019)

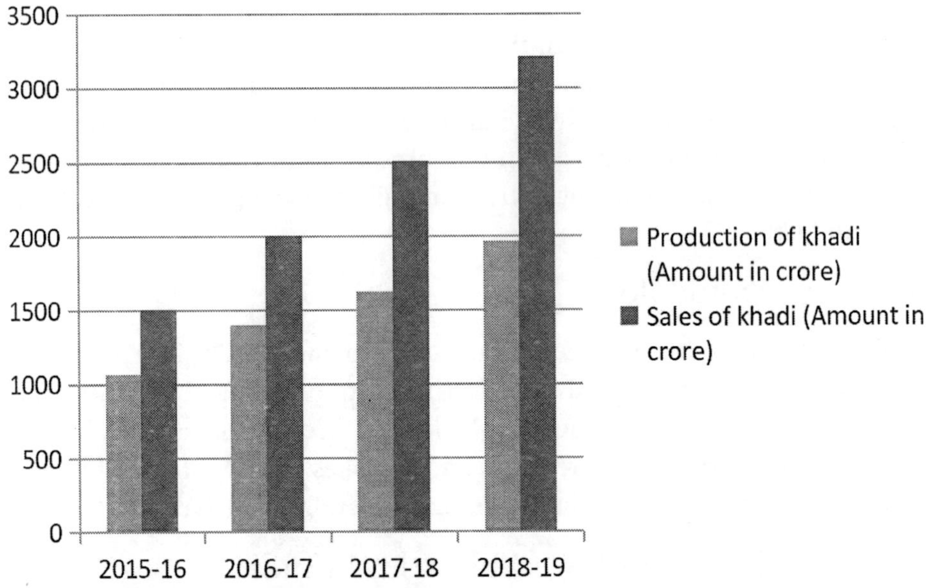

Interpretation of data: The above table shows that production and sales of khadi's are increased consistently over the past five years which means that demand of khadi has generated year by year.

2. Employment in khadi and village industries

Years	2015-16	2016-17	2017-18	2018-19
Employment (In lakh)	137.83	136.40	137.79	146.98

Source: Annual report, Government of India, Micro, Small and Medium Enterprises (2015-2019)

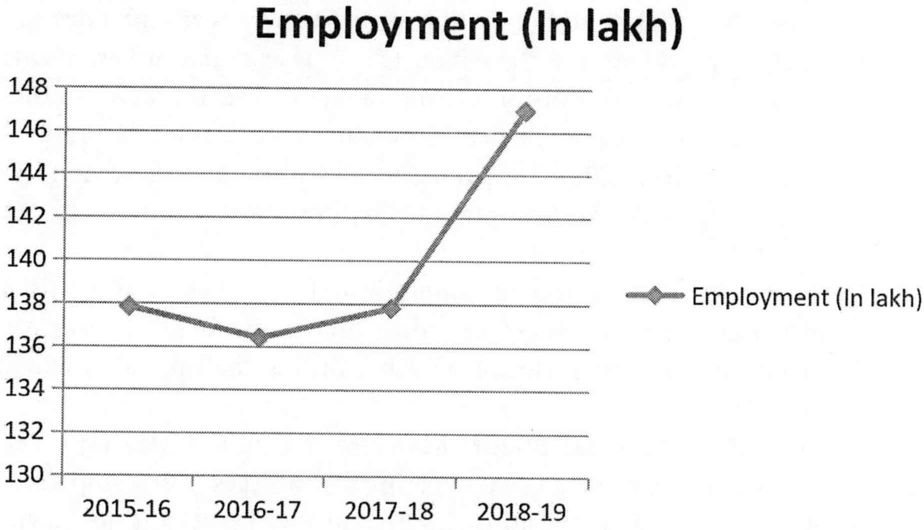

Interpretation of data: The above figure reveals that employment in khadi industries constant during the period of 2015-2018 but in 2018-19 showed increase in employment.

Challenges Ahead Cottage Industries

It is worthy to note that employment opportunities in cottage industries over the years have increased but income level as comparatively not much due to the involvement of middlemen who offer them low prices to the artisans but make heavy profits from the buyers. Handicrafts and handloom weavers are facing the competitions from power looms industries. Even having unbeatable traditional skill still they are not succeed to find a suitable place.

Government of India is taking initiative to provide required materials at subsidies rates at initial stage still the cottage industries are fighting against unfavorable conditions like marketing channels, insurance against risk, inadequate market information and access over the required capital to carry on the business activates smoothly. Major challenges ahead cottage industries are:

1. **Problem of finance:** To get cheap and easy finance is not available to these industries due to the complex procedures and formalities to avail the financial assistance from government institutions and banks.
2. **Problem of raw materials:** Due to the inadequacy of the financial resources, the owner is not able to buy the raw material in bulk. That

is why they are bound to buy low quality materials at high rates.

3. **Marketing problem:** As these industries only exist and survive in rural areas and faced the problems of transport and market facilities. Therefore, they are not able to find the suitable markets for the products.
4. **Lack of credit facility:** Sometimes small scale industries are not able to get credit facility which restrict to continue the production activities smoothly.
5. **Increment in sales and remuneration:** To remunerate the artisans and increment in wages can only be maintained if sales and remuneration increase steadily which is the big challenge ahead khadi industries.
6. **Lack of managerial talent:** Managerial talent is playing a very significant role to take the competitive advantages over competitors. But cottage and small industries are run by the person not having proper managerial training. Thus, how they survive in the market before organized large scale industries.
7. **Advanced technological threats:** Khadi and village industries always face the technological threats from large industrial house.
8. **Inadequate Infrastructure:** Inadequate infrastructure is a major problem for the cottage industries which leads to underutilization of capacity. Moreover machines and equipment employed for production are outdated which reduce the productivity.
9. **Competition with large scale industries:** The main problem before these industries is that they are not able to compete with large-scale industries which prevent them to take economic advantages.

Initiatives Undertaken By The Government To Overcome On Problems

Khadi and Village Industries Commission (KVIC) which is well known organization working with the objectives of providing employment in rural areas and creating self-reliance amongst people and building up a strong community spirit. Cottage industry is a statutory organization established under Khadi and Village Industries Commission Act, 1956 under the aegis of Ministry of MSME. Following recent initiatives are undertaken by KVIC:

- Direct Benefit Transfer (DBT) system has been made operational for fund transfer to Khadi Institute and Artisans. These institutions and artisans uploading their data and filing their claims under MDA and ISEC in the DBT portal of KVIC and incentives directly transferred tin the accounts of khadi artisans.

- KVIC signed MOUs with Giants Textiles Corporate like Raymond, Arvind Mills, Birla Fashion and Retail Ltd. (ABFRL) for developing and promoting sales of Khadi in India and abroad through their modern outlets.
- Signed MOU with National Institute and Fashion Technology (NIFT) for designing design in khadi garments and to promote fashion fabric of India.
- KVIC launched exclusive online application for registration of new Khadi Institution to undertake Khadi activities through Khadi Institution Registration and Certificate Sewa (KIRCS) to enlist more khadi institution.
- Introduced Solar Charkha and Solar Looms for enhancing productivity and income of Khadi artisans.
- KVIC launched honey mission 2017-18 to create the momentum in generating employment opportunities to trained beekeepers.
- Establishment of Khadi Lounges in Delhi, Mumbai, Jaipur and Bhopal for selling premium khadi products.
- Khadi fabrics and other products are supplied to PMO, Air India, Health Ministry, Defense Ministry, ONGC, IOCL, PSUs and other Govt. Departments.
- KVIC has established "KHADI HAAT" (with co-operation of NDMC in 2018) and KHADI KORNER (with M/S APNA BAZAR and M/S COTTON BAZAR) which are already operational in NOIDA, Ahmadabad, Mumbai and Varanasi.
- In order to expand the network of Khadi zero capital investment franchise schemes has been launched in Delhi, Pune, Kolkata, Aligarh, Kerala and Mumbai.
- KVIC has developed an exclusive Mobile App for the customer to locate the nearest khadi store.

Schemes Implemented By KVIC For The Khadi Industries

Sr. No.s	*Schemes*	*Activiteis Undertaken By Kvic*
1.	Work-shed Scheme for Khadi	In 2008 – 09, KVIC launched the Work-shed Scheme for Khadi Artisans belonging to BPL Group. Under this Scheme financial assistance given up to Rs. 60,000 to individual Artisans. Duringthe year 2018 – 19 around 1,179 Khadi Artisans were benefited.
2.	Strengthening of Infrastructure of Existing Weak Khadi Institutions and Assistance for Marketing Infrastructure	This scheme is the combination of two schemes namely strengthening of infrastructure of weak existing khadi institution and assistance for marketing infrastructure. Rs. 9.90 lakh are provided to weak khadi institution to bring back their activities in to normalcy and Rs. 25 lakh also provided for assistance of marketing infrastructure.
3.	Khadi Reform and Development Program (KRDP)	KRDP was introduced and supported by the Government of India by availing the loan amounting US $ 105 million from ASD. These assistance are provided to Khadi (400 Khadi Industries) and Village Industries (7 V.I). Till March, 2019 around 24,951 artisansbenefitted.
4.	Interest Subsidy Eligibility Certificate (ISEC) Scheme	This scheme is introduced to provide the financial support to khadi industries through bank @ 4 percent per annum on actual lending rate and minus to be paid by the KVIS. In 2018-19 around 1065 khadi institutions are subsidies assisted under khadi andpolyvstra program.
5.	Aam Admi Bima Yojana (AABY)	This is social security measures scheme which is specially designed by the LICI for the khadi artisans. Under this scheme following monetary benefits are

		provided: Natural death (Rs. 30,000), Total Permanent Disability (Rs.75,000), Partial Permanent Disability (Rs. 37,500). Around 200974 Khadi Artisanswere enrolled in 2018-19.
6.	Science &Technology (S&T)	Khadi and Village Industries Commission has been functioning with the vision of boosting and injecting innovation, qualityand productivity to make the Khadi products globally competitive and also to enable rural industries to get its due to marketdemand.
7.	Capacity Building	KVIS conduct training program through 40 Departmental and Non- Departmental Training Centers impart need based training under various disciplines, viz., Soap and Detergent making, Food Items, Bakery Products, Ready Made Garments, Beekeeping, Agarbatti making, Candle making, Motor Binding, etc. Under this Scheme, 76,683 Nos. of persons were trained during the year2018 – 19.
8.	Honey Mission	Our Hon'ble Prime Minister announced a Statement "Sweet Revolution is needed along with White Revolution." inspired of his vision, Ministry of MSME accorded approval for Honey Mission.Under this Scheme, 95,726 Bee Hives (Boxes) with Bee Colonies have been distributed to 9,636 beneficiaries during the year2018 – 19.
9.	Kumbhar Shasktikaran	Khadi & Village Industries Commission (KVIC) for strengthening Potter families engaged in Pottery were distributed Pottery Wheels along with other tools & equipment.Under this program, 25,820 of Pottery Artisans werebenefited during the year 2018 – 19

Conclusions

Cottage and village industries are playing a very significant role to raise the economic level of rural people engaged in traditional and cultural activities. As our country is developing country and a large portion of population living in rural area which help country to fight with the unemployment of economy only by developing the cottage industries. Khadi business has great opportunities which can be achieved only with the initiatives and endless support of government by providing the financial as well as other assistance to small artisans without any unnecessary hurdles but to achieve the common goals of economy, joint efforts of small artisans are required to get better output. Awareness programs must initiate to aware the artisans about the schemes introduced by the government through social media and other means of communication. Concisely, development of the cottage industries should be the prime concern of government to tackle the unemployment problems and open up the self- employment avenues for the rural artisans. Government is introducing new schemes and policy for the cottage industries time to time still there is a long way to go to achieve the desired goals.

Refrences

1. Bhattacharya Dhritiman (2014): Cottage Industries Clusters in India In Improving r Rural Livelihood an overviews International Journal of Humanities & Social Science of India, ISSN, 2349- 6959 (Online), ISSN: 2349-6711 (Print), Volume-1, Issue-1, July, 2014, Page, 59-64
2. Thanga Joy Merlin, Kanmelba R. (2013): Emerging Opportunities and Challenges for Cottage Industries in India, International Journal Scientific and Research Publications, Volume-3, Issue-3, March, 2013, ISSN: 2250-3153, Page 2-4
3. Srivastva Abhinav, Prasad Anjana (2018): A Study on Contribution Khadi and 'KVIC' in the Economic Development and Employment Generation for Rural Chhattisgarh, IJARIIT(ISSN: 2454-132X), Page, 379-383
4. M.K Gandhi, Khadi, Why, and How, Edition Bhartan Kumarappa, Navjivan. Publishing, Ahmedabad, 1955
5. Subhamoy Banik (2018): Small Scale Industries in India: Opportunities and Challenges, IJCRT, Volume 6, Issue-1, and January, 2018, ISSN: 2320-2882, Page, 337-441
6. Pandey ,Vivekanand (2013): Trends, Opportunities & Challenges in Small Scale and Cottage Industries in Uttar Pradesh, Asian Journal of Technology & Management Research [ISSN: 2249 –0892] Vol. 03 – Issue: 02, Jul – Dec, 2013
7. Pandey, Suresh Kumar (2015): Emerging Opportunities and Challenges in Indian Carpet Industry, Asian Journal of Multidisciplinary Studies, ISSN: 2321-8819 (Online) Volume 3, Issue 1, January 2015, 2348-7186 (Print), Page, 20-23
8. Biswas Swatee, Giri Arunagushu, Biswas Debasis (2017): The impact of issues and challenges

on cottage industries in Rural West Bengal: An Empirical Study, Int. J. HIT. TRANSC:ECCN.Vol.3: Issue 1A (2017) Page 21-28 ISSN: 0973-6875

9. Annual report, Government of India, Micro, Small and Medium Enterprises (2015-2019)
10. h ttps://msme.gov.in
11. h ttps://rbi.gov.in
12. www.kvic.org.in

13

Gandhian Philosophy as a Driver of Sustainable Development

Swagata Karmakar, Radhey Shyam Sharma and Vandana Mishra

Gandhian philosophy, though simple, not only provides solutions to the complex problems humanity is facing but also serves as a foundation principle for designing sustainable earth. Environmentalists, social scientists, and economists have adopted the Gandhian way of achieving sustainable development through protecting the environment while ensuring social equity and securing economic development. Gandhi's speeches, writings, and actions have been the guiding principles for individuals, communities and nations for (i) ensuring environmental justice to the poorest of the poor; (ii) respecting different life forms, accepting pluralism and conserving nature; (iii) advocating access to natural resources like water, land and forests by all irrespective of race, caste, and religion; and (iv) practicing minimalism and reducing ecological footprints by human being to maintain sustainability of economy and to ensure good quality of life.

As per some of the historians, Gandhi is considered as "early environmentalist." Through his voluminous writings, he provided better insights into the critical linkages between the environment and humans. His remarks, for example, on irreversible damage to humanity due to over-exploitation of nature, and his idea of minimizing materialism and consumerism favoured human responsibility towards nature. While promoting the handloom industry and suggesting an individual to practice weaving cotton, his philosophy sensitizes individuals to experience life-cycle of an economical product developed from natural resources so that we reduce our impact on nature via rejecting the idea of consumerism and materialism. Unlike the western model of industrialization, he favoured a model of industrialization that respects the mother earth and the natural resources and leads to a low ecological footprint of individuals. He was a vociferous critic of the greed of accumulating natural resources to overpower the deprived individuals, society, and nations. Though not visible, Gandhi spread the message of conservation of biodiversity silently while supporting the idea of using the traditional system of maintaining health, especially the medicinal plants. Spirit of Gandhian philosophy of 'Satyagraha' has been widely used by several renowned environmentalists and local communities as a tool for several environmental movements like 'Chipko Movement' for protecting natural resources in India and the outside world. To further elaborate, it is believed that Gandhian philosophy had an influence on the Norwegian philosopher Arne Naess while developing the concept of 'Deep Ecology', which has been widely used by ecologists to conserve the ecosystems and biodiversity. Deep ecology, simply, emphasizes that rather the cost-benefit-analysis of using or conserving the biodiversity or treating pollution (shallow approach or an anthropocentric economic framework), we must protect the ecosystem due to the critical linkages among man, other living organisms and environment (ecological view or web of life framework). Gandhian thoughts had an influence on several great writing on the link between environmental protection and economic security such as *Small is Beautiful* by E.F. Schumacher, *Limits to Growth* by Dennis Meadows and *Economy of Permanence* by J.C. Kumarappa. In *Economy of Permanence* J.C. Kumarappa disscussed on matters related to environmental pollution and conservation of natural resources.

Social equity i.e., equal access to natural resources by a human being without any bias of gender, caste, and religion, has been one of the facets of Gandhian philosophy. As a visionary, he realizes that promoting social equity based on access to natural resources will help in maintaining peace and harmony among communities, states, countries, and continents. In fact, the past seven decades have witnessed an emergence of conflicts between the societies, states, and countries primarily due to establishing power and natural resources and reducing access to the poorer or less empowered ones.

Gandhi used the principle of human ecology to promote the idea of sustainable development. He emphasized that the sustainable development should be centre point of economic development which ensures harmonious co-existence of human with the nature. He believed that modifying human behaviours towards nature acts as a driver of a good quality of life and a sustainable economy. Use of natural resources should be in such a way that the future generations can also sustain themselves very well. He promoted deploying cultural practices for conserving the environment among large sections of society. He advocated the developing and relying on indigenous and low-technologies for economic development as they not only provide jobs to the native people but also remain safe to the environment. Also, such technologies, though local, bear a high potential to be successful as they are developed while considering the local resources, and environmental conditions. Currently, many developed and fastest-growing countries like Germany, the UK, and China have also focused on adopting the concept of low-technologies. He also believed that the country's economic reliance also depends on protecting the domestic industries and flag-ship industrial products like handloom cottage industries in India. Our experience of 70 years substantiated his philosophy of protecting the domestic industries, and natural resources provide insurance to the country while the rest of the world may experience an economic crisis.

To summarize, Gandhian philosophy accepts technological solutions to the problems of humanity, provided the technologies to take into account the principles of ethics, sociology, and the environmental sciences. Ideological, economic, and technological structures based on Gandhian philosophy would lay a deep foundation of the concept of present-day sustainable development. His idea of realizing conservation as a practice in day-to-day life would pave a '*yellow brick road*' for a happy, healthy, and prosperous nation.

References

- Mahatma Gandhi – An Environmentalist With A Difference, http://www.mkgandhi.org/environment/jha.htm
- Environmental Toughts of Gandhi for a Green Future, http://www.mkgandhi.org/articles/green_future.htm
- T N Khoshoo, Mahatma Gandhi: An Apostle of Applied Human ecology (New Delhi: TERI, 1995), p.9.
- Gandhian Environmentalism (New Delhi: Global Vision, 2003), p.45.
- Gandhian relevance to environmental sustainability https://www.mkgandhi.org/articles/gandhian-relevance-to-environmental-HYPERLINK "https://www.mkgandhi.org/articles/gandhian-relevance-to-environmental-sustainability.html" \h sustainability.html

14

Gandhi and Global Peace

Beena

At the present time international arrangement is based on the concept of nation state and national interest which is far away from the concept of global peace. The idea of global peace revolves around the ideal of freedom, peace and happiness among and within all the nations and among their people. The real sense of global peace is actually based on the idea of Gandhi's philosophy of non-violence. Gandhi states, the entire world is considered as a mankind and it would be achieved by the philosophy of non-violence. This mankind is beyond to international boundaries and territories and it framed the whole world into a single picture of mankind.

The political idea of Gandhi is based on the peace which is achieved through the non- violence not only established on the morality of an individual but also international manner and behavior. According to Gandhi, through weapon we can only get external independence but not the real independence which is the core of mankind. If we do not have a new method of combating imperialism then the only solution of resolving our problem is violence and we will leave the world where an eye for an eye makes the entire world blind and there is no look forward to the oppressed races of the earth.

Gandhi's way of life founded on ethical social order and mindful of what reality is and walked behind a pathway of humanism. Humanism is measured as originator of Greek humanism as Protagoras stated 'Man is the most important of all belongings'. Humanism is invented in second half of 14th century and reach all over the Europe. The time of Vedas and Upanishads, 'India has announced the inside superiority of primeval cosmic inspirational completely factual existence which is (Chit) itself. The Buddha, Gita, Patanjali, Bhagavata Purana and Gandhi stated ethical principles'. Since Gandhi learned these values from his childhood by her mother Putlibai who was religious woman and he also learned non-violence which is the uppermost form of religion. Along with this he was also inspired by the knowledge of Gita which made unfathomable consciousness on him of non-violence and truth. As well he had also deeply inspired by Ruskin, Tolstoy, Romaine Rolland and several other persons. Ruskin wrote his renowned work 'Unto this last' and Gandhi admitted: 'acquired immense motivation from 'Unto this last' by Ruskin and his idea that good quality human being is contained in the good of all. The ideas of Sarvodaya and Antyodaya were the invention of this influence. Albert Einstein believed, the trust that it is probable to attain safety throughout weapons on a national level is, in the present state of armed technology, a devastating misapprehension.

Although Gandhi did not formulate much effort concerning international dealings is statement in domestic background. He said that international order is fundamentally based on culture of peace. His idea of non-military struggle and the peaceful co-existence have resolved international matters. Gandhi's philosophy of *Ahimsa* and *Dharma* planned independent refusal of violence in any form of human affairs and he showed strengthen of non-violence in the case of Hitler where England not fight with weapons against him. He suggested that Satygraha as strategy for dealing with international relationships. Gandhi in his book of 'Young India' assured that India's freedom through harmony or peace will be the major contributions in the direction of global peace. He believed that violence could not be removed by violence. It could be only removed by non-violence. Gandhi always emphasised that there is no enemy, simply there can be competitors who could be succeeded by essence strength not by evil power. Gandhi stated that the great Ashoka the ruler of Kalinga converted into the Dharma Ashoka after adopted the Buddhist values and principles in his life. He realized that the actual conquer is- conquer the people's heart not the land of the people who are living there. And after the Kalinga episode, he realised that the world exist in the power of peace not in the war and later on, he followed Buddha's principles and values in giving up wars rest of his life. After that Buddhism has started spreading all over the world and became the most important power to conquer the other countries. Along with this Gandhi also mentioned Lord Mahavir and Jesus Christ who advocated the significance of feel affection, forgiveness and peace.

At some stage in the twentieth century, Gandhi expressed the effectiveness of non-violence against violence. He advocated moral means to resolve international disputes. Gandhi also implemented his idea of non-violence in South Africa and India in the hope that the experiments he implemented would motivate the entire world. Gandhi's conception of India's independence had global relevance in the sense that he wanted free India to be instrument for human welfare and global peace.

According to Gandhi the journey of freedom was incomplete and inseparable without peace and nonviolence. In fact deeply rooted on India civilization values Gandhi channelized the timeless philosophy of peace for the realities of the contemporary world. Truth was means and desires for him. Satyagraha was the cornerstone of Gandhi's philosophy. The truth for Gandhi was threading together of the principle of Sarvodaya of holistic development for all. Picking up a handful of salt as an act of device or creating the political metaphor of the chair.

The humble hand is symbols of India's freedom embodied not to lead the team moral strength of peaceful resistance but also the vision of sustainability of an economy with human dimensions. Nothing ever happened in isolation with starting clarity Gandhi saw how the crisis of the modern world affect all of us and how the transition from the conflict to cooperation needs a global response guided by a shared sense of humanity. His life was his message walking together on the blonde road to peace and sustainability.

Gandhi's role of global peace has witnessed during 1947 Partition of India when Muslim league demanded separation of Muslim majority provinces from India and he went on fast till death instead using violence against Muslim. This is proved his philosophy of world peace during any kind of ethnic and religious conflict. Post II World War the world has witnessed the conflict among nations on the grounds of ethnic, religious, energy and boundary disputes. The existing character of Nation States considers non-interference of internal issues of other sovereign countries that which Gandhi has advocated in India's foreign policy. Gandhian principles and beliefs maintains the non- alignment movement as an aim of India's Foreign Policy for which Nehru practised it in the case of Palestine. Gandhi also spoke like Hindu for Hindustan and Palestine for Arabs and rejected the formation of Israel in the Palestinian state.

Gandhian philosophy still has their own importance and relevance in the contemporary time when UN Chief Antonio Guterres, during the International Day of Non-Violence on October 2nd 2019, had spoke to the world to remember the Gandhi's idea of transformational change in the society while he was talking about Gandhi's vision of peace and sustainable development. He recalled Mahatma Gandhi for his idea of non-violence. He said that today humanity is struggling with global warming, ecological deprivation, that extended all over the globe due to violent behavior originated by overpopulation, armed clashes and poverty.

He said that Gandhi's idea continues to boom crossways the globe, including during the work of the UN for mutual understanding, equal opportunity, continuous development, and empowerment of young people and peaceful declaration of disagreements. He also discussed about the 'Climate Action: Gandhian Ways'.

Apart from this, President Mohammed Bande in the 74th session of UN assembly, was also talked about Gandhi's ideas and principles and said that 'It is not easy to speak something innovative concerning with Gandhi. I do not identify any school child anyplace in the globe, who has not been motivated by the determination of Gandhi, the thought that the furthermost courage is actually to be non-violence. He also emphasized that there is a strong relationship of Gandhian way in every sphere of life'.

In today's time, we used to believe in the concept that peace can only be achieved after the war; peace can only be achieved after violence because for us violence is synonymous with a method as a method of getting peace. Gandhi during his 40 years showed us that violence is not a way to achieving peace because whatever peace we achieved through violence is only temporary that peace is a child of violence and it will eventually show it's true colours. Global peace is broad term having many dimensions. A nation of starving people needs all the help that requires but what about the war hungry nation. A war hungry nation needs nothing it only wants to create war. Gandhi once said that if we have no charity and no tolerance then we will never settle our differences and conflicts. Many of today's conflict management techniques and resolution processes have a clear shadow of what Gandhi had seen as an interrelation on international issues at this time. Peace can never be achieved by one dimension and unilateral talks. Throughout his lifetime he showed us a multitude of ways through which peace can be achieved because unfortunately in today's world the power bring about peace is in the hand of few powerful nations and we always get one side of the story because we only get peace that the powerful wants us to have. Gandhi always had this point to make peace live in the soul and consciously demanding him to take on fast, no matter where he was in the country. Thus peace for him became universal and internal. Therefore, we need to ask our own spirits whether sitting in a room talking about world peace is actually breaking world peace. The concept of world peace after the League of Nations and the United Nations still remain a big dream for many of us because of the fact that we do not have a mechanism, a panacea to achieve global peace.

Today, the entire world measured their security on the bases of warheads nuclear and chemical weapons they have and they feel secure. The sense of superiority increase with a number of weapons they have. But in reality, national security for a country should be in its political stability, economic strength and diplomatic relations. Global peace remains a concept because the countries that have the power to bring out a change still rely on armament and the use of violence to achieve peace in the society.

Though Gandhi was not the originator and messenger of global peace who talked about particularly on the matters which are related to international peace and order, but his ideology of non-violence is to be proved as a solution provider and conflict breaker for which he is known for the peace activist. Balamurali Balaji (2017) said that we need to rethink on the ideas suggested by the Gandhi and their relevance in today's time. If we see the concept of global peace then it has seen in the minutest thing but this concept itself unfolds into broader dimensions. There is a big dilemma at the international order where a civilian government struggling with their own rebel citizens to establish peace in a country. Unfortunately, today we are living in an extremely cultured, democratized state where states are struggling with their neighbours on cross-border issues to sustain peace in the region. Therefore, the solution we left behind is the peace where peace would become everyone and everything in the world. Even at present time, a well planned economic reach into the bigger pressure, creating economic conflict that disturbs peaceful existing.

References

Balamurali Balaji (2017), *Relevance of Gandhi: Ideas and Issues*, Publisher: Lulu.com.

Business Standard (2019), UN leaders recall Gandhi's power to bring transformational change through non-violence, URL: https://www.business-standard.com/article/pti-stories/un-leaders-recall-gandhi-s-power-to-bring-transformational-change-through-non-violence-119100201136_1.html

15

Changing Trends of Student Politics and the Relevance of Gandhian Values in Modern Bangladesh

Hoimanti Barua

Background of the Study

The most salient bequest of India to the coeval world is the message of non-violence and global peace. The message was promulgated by Mohandas Karamchand Gandhi, popularly known as the *Mahatma Gandhi,* with a vision to achieve societal, national and global peace idiosyncratic in its own ways. Gandhi's intellection behind his ideology was an upshot of his execrable experience in South Africa against the practice of apartheid. Established on coherent premises that the only way to bring peace in society is by practicing peace, his socio-political doctrines are rather multifaceted.

He practiced the technique of Satyagraha or Non-violence that believed, violence of any degree used as a medium of interaction by people forbids one from seeing the larger prospects brought by truth and acceptance. Singh (2014:117) precisely outlines, "Gandhi's concept of Ramarajya or the Kingdom of righteousness on earth stands for an egalitarian and non-violent democratic social order; The law of 'Dharma or righteousness' and the morality of the individuals bind together the members of the society; Dharma or social ethics exerts strong moral pressure on the individuals and sustains social cohesion". In the first instance, his expositions on such complex concerns related to peace, non-violence and education may come across as quite simplistic to many. Underneath the facet of the oversimplified philosophical affirmations, nonetheless, one frequently unveils complex and antithetical characteristics of his ideology.

The Mahatma's philosophy acts as a catalyst directing us to ponder on our understanding on non- violence, violence, education and peace. As the world grapples with the threats of religious intolerance, fascist political leaders, terrorism, persecution, politically induced violence at domestic as well as regional levels, and various other challenging issues so forth; the situation desperately generates the necessity of retrospective interpretation of the relevance Gandhi's philosophy's in the contemporary times. In the context of the study, the Indian subcontinent that was not long ago colonised by the British, the collective conscience nurtured the aspirations to gain freedom from the foreign rulers. Gandhian principles played crucial roles in the attainment of freedom of India and later during the liberation struggle of Bangladesh. Not even a century has been completed and glimpse of vehement forces of intolerance, atrocities are experienced; this time by no colonisers but fellow countrymen. At the wake of Liberation, Bangladeshi political environment turned into a brutal one that saw a series of deadly coup d'états replacing the democracy with military rule. Throughout the period of volatile political paradigmatic shift, it was sadly ironic how Gandhi's credo of non-violence did not fully manifest in Bangladesh's political practices during its formative years. The political structure of Bangladesh was changing and concurrently, student activists, members, supporters and the vanguards of the liberation war continued their responsibility of challenging the totalitarian military government till it's ousting in 1990. The onset of twentieth century re-democratized Bangladesh but since then not only the politics of Bangladesh is defined by confrontation, monopolization, political violence and terrorism also the nature of student politics changed drastically. At this juncture, Gandhi's teachings of truth, compassion, non-violence and self-realisation only grew feeble with time.

Student Politics in Bangladesh: Historical Glance

Student politics commonly holds the centre-stage in the political scenarios of the third world countries. According to Klemeni and Park (2018:1),

"The concept of student politics refers to the activities related to the power

> relations between students and other social actors in and out of the higher education systems; more specifically, it pertains to the relationships between students and university authorities, as well as the interactions between students and state officials".

That is to say, these are typically political activities carried out by students enrolled in higher educational institutes. The nature of politics within student community has transformed with time in many countries that were former colonies, notably after obtaining independence; a scenario Bangladesh is not devoid of. The activities vary from inconsequential disturbances to major pandemonium in the political history of a nation-state (Munshi, 2014).

Historically, higher education sector has played pivotal part in the formation of Bangladesh. Universities have been used by the state to operate as nation-building mechanisms; by the teachers and students for resistance movements against oppressive rulers (Kabir and Greenwood, 2017). Bangladeshi student politics has a renowned history associated with sacrifice for the sake of freedom struggle and national cause. In fact, the birth of Bangladesh is an outcome of a constructive student's politics played at the time. East Bengal (now Bangladesh), was the eastern extension of the great Bengal of the then Indian subcontinent and remained so until the colonial rulers executed the historic partition leading to the birth of two countries, namely India and Pakistan in 1947. East Bengal became and remained East Pakistan, until attaining freedom from Pakistan in 1971 to finally become a free Bangladesh. The student community throughout (whether against the British while being a part India or against Pakistan) played important role in the fight for freedom.

In Bangladesh, like other developing countries, student activism continued after independence but underwent a metamorphosis in its nature and essence. The changes are conspicuous in the changing power dynamics, interactions and relationship among students, state, politically active student representative and other social actors (Klemeni and Park, 2018). The disconcertments now are prone to be localized that addresses political conflicts, rather than focusing on university issues or on national or broader ideological discourses. The diegesis presents political contestations in and outside the campuses spawning antagonism, erratically belligerent enough to raise trepidations among both civil and civic society (op.cit).

The Britishers built the University of Dhaka in East Bengal, to restraint the socio-political turmoil and to ameliorate the overall condition of the Muslim majority populace of Bengal (Rahman, 2009; Chowdhury and Kabir, 2014). Later, the university, continued as a catalyst to attain political goals during the Pakistani regime. Quddus and Rashid (2000) argues, from 1947-71, the university has been the plinth for resistance movements carried out by students, teachers and intellectuals towards the founding of liberty and democracy of the country. Bangladesh Chhatra League and Bangladesh Chhatra Union introduced in 1948 and 1952 respectively were in the forefront of these struggles. Possibly, the most significantly indelible of all was the fight to conserve 'Bangla' language in 1952. Few other noteworthy events comprise- Education movement in 1962, the Six Point Movement in 1966, the mass upsurge in 1969, the Liberation War in 1971.

The freedom movement was not completely devoid of violence and atrocities but has prominent reflections of Gandhi's principles of non-violence, civil disobedience and *Swadeshi* movement. Since the formation of Pakistan on August 14, 1947, the Bengalis on very many occasions adopted civil resistance and peaceful methods to fight for their emancipation. From 1948-52, a number of prominent individuals, academicians, intellectuals, students of schools and colleges joined the language movement under the headship of Sheikh Mujibur Rahman set in motion the non-violence non-cooperation movement. The students of Dhaka University expressed fulmination in the form of strikes, demonstrations, slogans, posters and pamphlets throughout the city in non-violent display of force. The people-driven Bengali language movement was phenomenally victorious considering the degrees of coercive actions employed against it by the Pak-military. Furthermore, various others factors like economic disproportion between West and East Pakistan, social discrimination, demand for political autonomy etc from 1951-71 'reinforced the collective consciousness' of Bengalis raising aspirations to have a free country. This phase observed complete rejection of Pakistani links with economic goods, educational institutes, and government offices. Eventually, with the West Pakistani army's acquiesce to the Indian army, the revolutionizing of subjugated people into a nation happened, through collective acts of nonviolent resistance (Hossain, 2012).

Changing Nature of Bangladeshi Student Politics

Since the nineties, indoctrination of neoliberalism not only radically changed the higher education sector in general but also the nature of campus violence. What must be contemplated is that how the typically nation centric ethos of student politics gradually reshaped its raison d'être, functioning and attributes since the onset of the twenty-first century. In various universities, across the country, a number of incidents occurring in the educational institutes has divergent context juxtaposing the previous student activism. The resistance movements in the past were meant to contribute to the nationalist movement to bring down oppression and autocratic rulers. Antithetical to the rationale behind exercising the activities in the past whether it is Gandhi's non-violence, civil disobedience and Swadeshi practices, student politics has lost its original essence after getting embedded within the power system accompanied by political parties and monetary agendas (op.cit, 2017). The tradition of student activism has reduced to mere political agendas turning in to a more insidious form of campus politics with coercive forces.

The student leaders, members and sympathizers are systematically affiliated to a mainstream political party. That is, every licit political party has an annexing student organisation as their extended political bodies. Alam et al, (2011:6045) explains, there are four major national political parties in Bangladesh, namely Bangladesh Awami League (BAL), Bangladesh Nationalist Party (BNP), Jatio Party (JP) and Jamaat-e-Islami Bangladesh (JIB). Their affiliated political student organizations are: Bangladesh Chhatra league (BCL) under BAL, Jatiotabadi Chatro Dal (JCD) under BNP, and Bangladesh Islami Chhatra Shibir (BICS) under JIB and Jatiyo Chhatra Samaj for (JP). According to Alam and Shahjalal (2008), the coupling of the teachers and the students with the mainstream political parties has highly politicized public universities.

A fundamental shift is observed in student politics in recent times. The circumstances that had arisen under British, Pakistani and later martial rule, students were at the forefront of independence struggle, as people's representatives, the nation builders, campaigners of social change and the challengers of irrational governmental activities. The recent upsurge in student politics is different. They are used as political tools by national political parties. Bangladesh characteristically suffers from an unstable, patrimonial and confrontational internal politics, habitual *hartalization* and parliamentary boycotts, political killings and violence and lack of democracy within party-politics (Kamruzzaman, et al, 2016; Osman, 2010). Osman (2010:311) posits that winning party monopolizes the system and often exhibits a 'winners take all' attitude. Similar functional attributes strongly reflects on their student organisations whereby many members (if not all) do not feel accountable to the rule of law for their lawlessness, hooliganism and criminal activities. Since 1971, as noted by Rashid (2011) not only activists but ·also innocent students in large number and ordinary citizens have been killed or harassed by the student politicians.

Conclusion

Mahatma Gandhi repeatedly expounded and urged that violence in any form- social, psychological, physical, economic only leads to more violence, and the society is enmeshed in a perpetual viscid cycle of parochialism, intolerance and hatred. Mahatma Gandhi's philosophy is exceedingly apposite in the contemporary society of Bangladesh as well as the world for upholding harmony and peace where we are experiencing a growing tendency of people use violence as means to address their problems and dissensions. Increasing pressure due to decreasing resources, employment, economic challenges, climate change etc. are pushing people towards becoming more competitive each day resulting in lack of forbearance, endurance and empathy towards fellow humans. Gandhian righteousness of self-restraint is essential in this desire driven materialistic world. The desire is not only materialist but also for power and dominance. Societal virtue and human value has degraded to the level that one does not vacillate before killing someone to fulfill their requirement. Bangladesh is considered a medium development country that has shown noteworthy improve in economy, education, health, poverty reduction and also set an example by accommodating thousands of refugees. This indicates this small nation has the potential to improve its societal and human value. At this juncture, political violence should not be the way to practice power dynamics. Gandhiji's ideal society is based on the ethical evolution of mankind. If humans unhypocritically observe non-violence and learn to cooperate, then the society will automatically be culturally uplifted. Pomposity, selfishness, hatred, anger derived from power are counter-productive and not the path to progress. Bangladesh's political culture needs to remember the fundamental Gandhian values to be able to convert in to a non-violent social order that will benefit both their national and international goals.

Reference

Singh, J (2014), "Gandhian Jurisprudence of Non-Violence and Global Peace", *Indian Journal of Public Administration*, Vol. LX (1): 117-125

Klemeni, M and Park, B.Y. (2018), "Student Politics: Between Representation and Activism", in Brendan Cantwell, Hamish Coates and Roger King (eds.) *Handbook on the Politics of Higher Education*, United Kingdom, Edward Elgar Publishing

Kabir, A.H. and Greenwood, J. (2017), "Neoliberalism, Non-Violence and Student Resistance in the Higher Education Sector in Bangladesh", *Society and Culture in South Asia*, Vol.3 (1): 68-91

Munshi, S. (2014), "Student Politics: A Game-Theoretic Exploration", Indira Gandhi Institute of Development Research, Mumbai, India.

Hossain, I. (2012), "Bangladesh: Civil Resistance in the Struggle for Independence, 1948-1971", in Maciej J. Bartkowski *Recovering Non-Violent History: Civil Resistance in Liberation Struggles*, Lynne Rienner Publisher, London.

Alam, G.M et al. (2011), "National Development and Students Politics in Bangladesh", *African Journal of Business Management*, Vol. 5(15): 6044-6057.

Kamruzzaman, M and Khan, B.U. (2016), "Extrajudicial Killings: The Violation of Human Rights in Bangladesh", *International Journal of Environmental Planning and Management*, Vol. 2(4): 20-28

Osman, F.A. (2010), "Bangladesh Politics: Confrontation, Monopoly and Crisis in Governance", *Asian Journal of Political Science*, Vol. 18(3): 310-333

Bala, S. (2014), "Student Demonstration: The Case of 2007 Demonstration in Dhaka University, Bangladesh", *IOSR Journal of Humanities and Social Science*, Vol. 19(5): 24-31

Bose, S. (2005), "Anatomy of Violence: Analysis of Civil War in East Pakistan in 1971", *Economic and Political Weekly*, Vol. 40(41): 4463-4471

16

Gandhian Philosophy: A Practical Approach for Finding Solution

Utsav Krishan Murari and Chandan Kumar

Abstract

Indian as in the history of humanity for reconstruction of society and polity based on non violence. Gandhi's thought is based on the concept of Satya (Truth), Ahimsa (Non-violence) and Satyagraha (as Gandhi loosely translated: holding on to truth, which in fact is the philosophy and practice of the non-violent resistance). According to the Gandhian idea the courage is most importantly required to fight against of the problem or find the solution of the problem. Gandhain idea is a combination of truth, sacrifice, non-voilence, self less service and cooperation. ." According to Gandhi's thoughts, nonviolence is ultimate solution of every kind of problem in the world. In present day it has been seen that the concept of Gandhi's based on truth, non violence, satyagrah still exist and many of the problem get solved by using the idea of Gandhi's tool. Ghandhian strategy. Mahatma Gandhi was against any form of exploitation and injustice. According to him, evils must be opposed at any cost. But he insisted that the weapons must be non violent and moral ones. This paper is an attempt to analyse the idea of Gandhian philosophy and the further it will reveals the relevance of the Gandhian philosophy in present day context.

Keywords: Humanity, Satya (Truth), Ahimsa (non-violence), Satyagraha, Injustice

Introduction

"My life is my message."

M. K. Gandhi

Mohandas Karamchand Gandhi is a most influential personality of the 21st century as his idea of attaining the victory is very much influential in terms of humanism. The concept of influencing and the work get done is based on the pious path defined by Gandhi i.e Satya, Ahimsa, and Satyagrah. The Gandhian massage is based on spirituality and the heritage still has its actuality and relevance. "[T]he force which is born of Truth and Love or nonviolence", which in fact is the philosophy and practice of the nonviolent resistance)– should have or must have an important role in dealing with the real problems of our globalized world.[1] Gandhian thought on non violence is a positive aspect of proving and solving the problem and find the solution of any kind of problem. Gandhi idea of the non-violence is an active weapon against the British rule. Gandhi initiated non violence activities like Quit India Movement and Non- cooperation movement. Gandhi's ideology of political and social philosophy is an approach towards serving humanity by following the path of Truth, Non-voilence and Satyagrah, could be the starting phase of the regeneration of non-violent or less violent cultures and societies. The whole non-violent philosophy of the Mahatma, based on the two core concepts of the Gandhian heritage, is not a new proposition. Gandhi himself says that "I have nothing new to teach the World.[2] Gandhian philosophy about society and its people based on love, truth and nonviolence must look and function and he tried to realize it as much as possible in the real life. His attempts and results in making this operable have had echoes and followers all around the world. For example, Edward Thompson wrote in his paper, *Gandhi: A Character Study*: "he will be remembered as one of the very few who have set the stamps of an idea on an epoch. That idea is 'Non-violence' which has drawn out powerfully the sympathy of other lands."[3]

Gandhian Philosophy

The fundamental concepts of the Gandhian thought should be considered the milestone in every practical aspect of life as it comprises of the experimental aspect of life a fully based on the idea of Satya or Truth. He considered where ever there truth prevails God exists and there is no chance of failing. The importance of Satya is underlined, too, by the fact that the Mahatma's

Autobiography was entitled by himself "The story of my experiments with Truth", which let us deduce the importance of Truth in his everyday life. There should be Truth in thought, Truth in speech and Truth in action." [4] As we can conclude from this quotation, for Gandhi, the concept of Truth has a much deeper sense than it is understood by the majority in the everyday life.

Gandhi's thinking about mobilising the youth in positive direction is an important aspect because he thought that to provide strength to any country it is more important to strengthen the youth population of the country resulting the whole country will follow them. And the most important he focused on the spirituality, said religion and the religious activities provide strength to your ideas and working. As we could find in his writings – especially in his *Autobiography* – Gandhi, except for a short period of his youth, was deeply religious. In his *Autobiography*, he states: "What I want to achieve—what I have been striving and pining to achieve these thirty years—is self-realization, to see God face to face, to attain Moksha."[5] Mahatma Gandhi also focused on religious ideas as he simply simplified the religion as a tool of attaining something best out of religion. During his studies in England and his work in South Africa, he continuously and thoroughly studied the major religions of the World, such as Jainism, Christianity, Buddhism or Islam. Quoting Lord Bhikhu Parekh's words: "Although he was profoundly influenced by Hinduism, Christianity and Jainism, his religious thought cut across all of them and was in a class by itself. Belief in God was obviously its basis."[6] His religiosity, according to Akeel Bilgrami, was "eclectic and individual",[7] Due to these influences, his religiosity became a very maverick mix, and that is why he was considered very often Christian or even Jain among the Hindus. The Mahatma himself makes a statement regarding his open-minded and open-hearted interest shown in other religions than Hinduism. He says that "My religion enables me, obliges me, to imbibe all that is good in all the great religions of the earth."[8] The concept of Gandhi's Ahimsa is based on ethical values in which there is no space of hatred among the beings. According to this religious tradition, the Mahatma considers that the Truth must be more than a moral idea or an ethical demand. He states that God is Truth: "My religion is based on truth and non-violence. Truth is my God. Non-violence is the means of realizing Him."[9] In later years Gandhi's experiment with truth, re analysis his own views and later further elaborated and said it sis much more and correct to say that it is much exact and established concept that Truth is God than God is Truth.

Few years later, due to his experiments with truth, the Mahatma reconsiders his view and he decides that it is much more exact and correct to say that Truth is God than God is Truth. Passion for discovering Truth, they have not hesitated even to deny the very existence of God—from their own point of view rightly. And it was because of their reasoning that I saw that I was not going to say 'God is Truth', but 'Truth is God.' "[10]

Gandhi repeatedly said that who sow violence, will reap violence, but who sows peace and non-violence, will reap peace. As in the case of the Satya, the roots of the Gandhian concept of Ahimsa could be found in the religious tradition of India, being "a cardinal virtue of the Hinduism through the centuries". [11] In addition to Satya, the Ahimsa can be considered the second fundamental category of the Gandhian philosophy.

As we can say that, the Gandhian concept of Satya and Ahimsa gets a positive sense and it is understood as a "universal law acting under all circumstances" [12], as "one of the world's great principles which no power on earth can wipe out". [13] It is considered by the Mahatma as a new weapon in politics, which is in the process of evolution.

Conclusion

Before concluding my paper I want to quote the words of Dr. Sarvepalli Radhakrishnan, he said in his book that "since Buddha, Gandiji was the greatest moral force in Indian history. For the accomplishment of liberty, justice and peace, he rediscovered the old techniques of Ahmisa and Satyagraha. He revealed to the masses a power not of rifles and machine guns, but the power innate in each individual, a power which this war-haunted world can exploit fully in making wars impossible." (Radhakrishnan 2010)

Lastly In my perception the message of the Gandhian heritage could be considered universal, irrespective of time, geographical space and cultural background, thus relevant even in the 21st century because it is based on such values as Truth (Satya), Nonviolence (Ahimsa), human dignity and respect and the love of our fellow beings.

References

1. Gandhi, M. Karamchand (1999a), Satyagraha in South Africa. In: *The Collected Works of Mahatma Gandhi (vol. 1–98)*, vol. 34, 1–278. Electronic Book on http://www.gandhiserve.org/cwmg/cwmg.html
2. Gandhi, M. Karamchand (1960), *My Non-Violence*. Navajivan Publishing House, Ahmedabad.

3. Thompson, Edward (2010), Gandhi: A Character Study. In: Sarvepalli Radhakrishnan (ed.): *Mahatma Gandhi. Essays & Refl ections on His Life and Work.* Jaico Publishing House, Mumbai.
4. Gandhi, M. Karamchand (1999b), Letter to Narandas Gandhi. In: *The Collected Works of Mahatma Gandhi (vol. 1–98)*, vol. 49, 381–384. Electronic Book on http://www.gandhiserve.org/cwmg/cwmg.html
5. Gandhi, M. Karamchand (1999c), An Autobiography or The Story of My Experiments with Truth. In: *The Collected Works of Mahatma Gandhi (vol. 1–98)*, vol. 44, 88–470. Electronic Book on http://www.gandhiserve.org/cwmg/ cwmg.html
6. Parekh, C. Bhikhu (1997), *Gandhi (Past Masters Series)*. Oxford University Press.
7. Bilgrami, Akeel (2011), Gandhi's religion and its relation to his politics. In: Brown, Judith M. and Parel, Anthony (ed.): *The Cambridge Companion to Gandhi.* Cambridge University Press, 93–116.
8. Gandhi, M. Karamchand (1999d), Am I a Messenger of God? In: *The Collected Works of Mahatma Gandhi (vol. 1–98)*, vol. 77, 26–28. Electronic Book on http://www.gandhiserve.org/cwmg/cwmg.html
9. Gandhi, M. Karamchand (1999f), Presidential Address at Kathiawar Political Conference, Bhavanagar. In: *The Collected Works of Mahatma Gandhi (vol. 1–98)*, vol. 30, 53–67. Electronic Book on http://www.gandhiserve.org/cwmg/ cwmg.html
10. Gandhi, M. Karamchand (1999g), Speech at Meeting in Lausanne. In: *The Collected Works of Mahatma Gandhi (vol. 1–98)*, vol. 54, 267–276. Electronic Book on_http://www.gandhiserve.org/cwmg/cwmg.html
11. Rynne, J. Terrence (2009), *Gandhi & Jesus. The Saving Power of Nonviolence.* Orbis Books, New York.
12. Gandhi, M. Karamchand (1999l), To the Princess. In: *The Collected Works of Mahatma Gandhi (vol. 1–98)*, vol. 76, 92–95. Electronic Book onhttp://www. gandhiserve.org/cwmg/cwmg.html
13. Gandhi, M. Karamchand (1999m), How Can Violence Be Stopped? In: *The Collected Works of Mahatma Gandhi (vol. 1–98)*, vol. 90, 374

17

Relevance of Gandhi's Economic Ideas in the Modern Era

N. Shradha Varma

Abstract

Economic Inclusion has always been the prime focus of the economists across the world and over the time. It refers to the growth and development aspects associated with every segment of the society. And this very idea took a shape of 'School of thought' by the great Indian leader, Mahatma Gandhi. His focus was on the development of every right holder of the society irrespective of gender, caste, creed etc.This paper focusses on illuminating the economic ideas of Gandhi, highlighting his thoughts and discussing the relevance of his viewpoints in today's era of modern consumerism and it's been observed that his long back ideas of equitable economic growth are still prevalent and proven to be necessary time and again.

Keywords: Economic inclusion, Policy, Economic growth, Equal Opportunities.

Economic Inclusion

The idea of economic inclusiveness brings in the concept of development of all, equal opportunities for all for their growth, it is to provide the same level of chances and advantages to all so that everyone can participate in the economic life of their country as consumers, producers, investors, entrepreneurs etc., in every possible role. The integral idea of Economic

Inclusion is opening up of all available economic, socio-economic and financial opportunities for all, especially for the undeserved sections of the society.The idea of inclusive growth not just involves the provision of economic opportunities for all but also allowing every individual to get engaged in decision making activities which can improve the effectiveness of their economic potential.

Gandhi's Economic Views

Mahatma Gandhi has been one of the greatest influencers of his times and of modern times as well,whose ideas and views are widely accepted by the social beings even in the contemporary era. From being a strong believer of non-violence to being the determined promoter of self-reliance, his beliefs are undoubtedly worth enduring. He has also elaborated his views on the functioning of an economy and his thoughts have taken the shape of a "School of thought" which has laid its foundations on the spiritual, social and moral principles where the idea of a rational consumer seeking maximum utility is condemned and a consumer fulfilling his needs ethically is promoted rigidly. His economic ideas always rejected Rationalism for its materialistic approach, and he aimed to promote spiritual development and harmony, based on moral values. Gandhian Economics does not distinction between economics and ethics, rather these two go hand in hand. According to him, Economics that hurts the well-being of an individual or nation is immoral and unethical, thus sinful. So, Supreme consideration has to be given to 'man' rather than to 'money'. He never emphasized for the economic dependence based on external or foreign market forces which mainly weakens the village community. Gandhiji was very much influenced by Ruskin's heterodox doctrine that the wealth of a nation is, not in its production or consumption of goods, but in its people. (Chavan, 2013). He was a strong promoter of village-based production activities because of the fact that the villages are self-sufficient in the sense that these have enough natural raw materials and resources which can lead to production of almost all kinds of consumer and producer goods. These geographical regions have access to every natural element and that too in the purest form available in nature. So, according to him, villages are totally independent and self-reliant which can fulfill their own needs. He encouraged indigenous industries like small scale, cottage industry of khadi, handloom spinning and weaving mills which purely involves manual labour so that employment generation is the key feature of such manufacturing units.Rural based industries focusing on local available capital, labour and techniques would achieve what is called sustainable and equitable growth.

Relevance of His Views

There is no doubt about the fact that the views of Gandhi are quite relevant in the modern era where capitalism and materialism have taken the special place in the decision-making process of economicpolicies. Gandhiji's principles of his economic thoughts are three: first he emphasizes on "Standard of life" which, according to him, could be attained only if, along with material advancement, there was a serious attempt to imbibe cultural and spiritual values and qualities in one's activity. His second idea was the production through small scale and locally oriented, using local resources and meeting local needs self-sufficiently. This would provide employment opportunities everywhere, promoting the idea of Sarvodaya- the welfare of all. His emphasize was on the labour using techniques for the production task rather than labour saving methods, thus his economic thought aims at increasing employment options and such ways of producing goods which should not be labour displacing. Ironically, Gandhiji was never the opposer of machine-based technology or new innovations, in fact, he cited the example of the coming of Singer sewing machine in India as a welcoming step. His main objective was to hold on the dignity of labour by criticizing the society's contemptuous attitude towards manual labour. Third principle of his economic thought is the crucial one as it requires the social responsibility of individuals towards the welfare of the society. It is claimed by him, that the part of the population which has the sole objective of creating new economic enterprises for their living and which accumulates surplus wealth more than what is necessary for their needs and wants should be held as 'trustee' for the equitable welfare of others especially poor and vulnerable sections of the society.So, all these three principles of Gandhian economics focus on relevant contemporary issues which have been challenging the modern economists and experts for a very long time. He was the founder of the idea of "Swadeshi" which consisted of stimulating and enhancing the small-scale production, that can satisfy local consumer and producer needs, at cottage and village-based industries. This was initiated to make villages and non-urban areas self-reliant and self-dependent and could lead onto the path of production and marketing on their own.In current India, the provision of independent ministry for medium and small-scale industries and for local manufacturing units and the proper flow of funds towards their working and betterment in all the financial union budgets is the sign of the relevance of Gandhian thought which has been the key focus of MSME (Ministry of Micro, Small and Medium Enterprises).

Conclusion

Every human in this world has the basic right to lead his/her life with dignity and respect and has complete authority over his actions and work but these courses of actions require certain sense of responsibility towards the environment and the society in which the living beings reside and this has been the core ideas of Gandhi. He has, time and again, emphasized on equity of opportunities and treatment and equality among the core groups of humans.

References

1. Koshal, R. K. and Koshal, M. (1973) "Gandhian Economic Philosophy", American Journal of Economics and Sociology, Vol. 32, No. 2, April, 1973, pp. 191-209.
2. Chavan, S. (2013). "Economic Ideas of Mahatma Gandhi" Indian Streams Research
3. Journal. vol 3(9): pp 1. Available online at www.isrj.net .
4. Chavan, S. (2013). "Economic Ideas ofMahatma Gandhi" Indian Streams ResearchJournal. vol 3(9): Pp 1. Available online at www.isrj.net.
5. Pani, N. (2002). "Inclusive Economics: GandhianMethod and Contemporary Policy". Sage Publications, New Delhi.
6. Ishii, K. (1994)."The Socio-Economic Philosophy of Mahatma Gandhi: with a Particular Focus on his Theory of Trusteeship". The Economic Review. 154(1). Pp: 72-91.
7. Rivett. K. (1959) "The Economic Thought of Mahatma Gandhi". The British Journal of Sociology. Vol. 10(1), pp. 1-15.
8. Iyengar, S. (2005). "Gandhi's Economic Thought and Modern Economic Development: Some Reflections". Working Paper. Centre for Social Studies (CSS), Surat.

18

भविष्य के भारत के लिए महात्मा गांधी के विचार : स्वदेशी परम्पराओं की भूमिका

सुधीर कुमार गढ़वाल

महात्मा गांधी की अहिंसात्मक, सहिष्णु, शांतिवादी और मानवतावादी शैली विश्व स्तर पर एक मान्यता प्राप्त तथ्य है। यूनेस्को द्वारा शांति और सतत विकास के लिए महात्मा गांधी शिक्षा संस्थान की नींव रखना इस तथ्य का समर्थन करने वाले सबसे अच्छे उदाहरणों में से एक माना जा सकता है। महात्मा गांधी अपने व्यक्तित्व में कई सार्वभौमिक मूल्यों को समायोजित किये हुए थे जैसे कि इंसान मात्र के प्रति प्यार, न्याय, शांति, अहिंसा, सहिष्णुता, और स्वतंत्रता। गांधी जी को जब कभी भी विपरीत परिस्थितियों का सामना करना पड़ा, तब भी उन्होंने वही दृष्टिकोण अपनाये जो इन मूल्यों पर आधारित और उनके सिद्धांतों के अनुकूल थे। इस लेख में गांधी जी के आर्थिक विचारों, राजनीतिक धारणाओं और सामाजिक विचारों की अभिव्यक्ति के लिए कुछ हद तक हिंद स्वराज, और उनके कुछ अन्य एकत्रित ग्रंथों का व्यापक रूप से परिक्षण करने का प्रयास किया गया है। इस लेख में गांधी जी की स्वदेशी, स्वराज, सत्याग्रह, और सर्वोदय की रचनात्मक दृष्टि को समझाने का भी प्रयास किया गया है। इसी रचनात्मक दृष्टि को उन्होंने जीवित अर्थव्यवस्थाओं और लोकतंत्रों के निर्माण के लिए अनुकूलित करने में प्रयोग किया।

भारत का सबसे तात्कालिक कार्य सामाजिक-आर्थिक या राजनीतिक परिवर्तन का लक्ष्य रखने से पहले स्वराज की प्राप्ति करना था। इसके लिए सरकार पर स्व-शासन के साथ साथ व्यक्ति के मन और भावनाओं पर स्व-शासन दोनों की आवश्यकता थी। गांधी जी अपनी पुस्तक 'हिंद स्वराज' में लिखते हैं कि ब्रिटिश शासन खत्म होने के बाद भारत को सिर्फ नाममात्र का 'स्वशासन' प्राप्त होगा, लेकिन तब तक वास्तविक स्वशासन नहीं मिलेगा जब तक भारत अपना

आध्यात्मिक उत्थान नहीं कर ले। गाँधी जी के अनुसार आत्मा और अन्तः मन की दोष निवृत्ति ही भविष्य के भारतीय राज्य की पूर्व शर्त है। इस तरह से भारतीय समाज में आध्यात्मिक नवीकरण हो जाने से सरकार जैसी नियामक संस्था की आवश्यकता नहीं होगी। गांधी जी के अनुसार, नागरिक सरकार के ताम-झाम जरूरत से ज्यादा हैं और इसके अभाव में भी आनंद का जीवन संभव है। उनका मानना था कि सत्याग्रह (अहिंसात्मक आध्यात्मिक प्रतिरोध) की मदद से, भारतीय अपने पूर्वजों के आध्यात्मिक रूप से प्रबुद्ध जीवन को जी सकते हैं।

गाँधी जी का मानना था कि सरकार व्यक्ति के नैतिक अस्तित्व की प्राप्ति के लिए एक वाहक के रूप में कार्य करने के बजाय एक बाधा के रूप में कार्य करती है। गांधी जी ने सरकार नामक संस्था का विचार आधुनिक सभ्यता से संबंधित होने के कारण इसे भविष्य में अतीत के प्रबुद्ध भारत के लिए अनुपयुक्त माना है। उनका मानना था कि पाश्चात्य सरकारों का स्वरूप सांस्कृतिक और नैतिक दोनों रूपों से आक्रामक हैं। गांधी जी हिंद स्वराज में लिखते हैं, 'भारत के दुर्भाग्य के लिए अंग्रेज ही जिम्मेदार नहीं हैं, बल्कि हम ही इस आधुनिक सभ्यता के आगे झुक गए हैं।"[1] आधुनिक सभ्यता ने भौतिकवाद को बढ़ावा दिया, योग्यता और धन के झूठे आदर्शों को प्रेरित किया, और हिंसा और प्रतिस्पर्धा का नेतृत्व किया। इसके विपरीत, गांधी जी ने कहा, सत्याग्रह सादगी का जीवन लाएगा जिसमें लोग प्रत्यक्ष उपभोग के लिए नहीं बल्कि अपनी जरूरी आवश्यकताओं की पूर्ति के लिए काम करेंगे। भारत केवल अपनी ही परंपराओं में उपलब्ध नैतिक संसाधनों के माध्यम से एक स्वतंत्र राष्ट्र के रूप में एक नया जीवन शुरू कर सकता है।

गांधी जी के आदर्श राज्य की आर्थिक रूपरेखा

गांधी जी ने जिस तरीके से एक नए भारत की परिकल्पना की थी, उसमें अर्थशास्त्र पर एक नया दृष्टिकोण शामिल था-एक ऐसा दृष्टिकोण जिसमें पूंजीवाद को इसकी शोषणकारी ज्यादतियों के लिए और समाजवाद को इसके औद्योगीकरण के साथ संबंध के लिए खारिज किया। गांधी जी की दलील थी कि भारत को अब माल और पूंजी के स्वतंत्र विनिमय पर आधारित वैश्विक बाजार पर भरोसा नहीं करना चाहिए। न ही समाजवाद अब सहनीय रहा था। 1940 के एक साक्षात्कार में, गांधी जी ने स्पष्ट रूप से समाजवाद पर अपनी आपत्ति जताई :

> "पंडित नेहरू औद्योगिकीकरण चाहते हैं क्योंकि उन्हें लगता है कि, अगर इसका समाजीकरण किया जाता है, तो यह पूंजीवाद की बुराइयों से मुक्त हो जायेगा। मेरा अपना विचार है कि बुराइयाँ उद्योगवाद में अंतर्निहित हैं, और समाजीकरण की कोई भी मात्रा उन्हें मिटा नहीं सकती है।"[2]

ऐसा लगता है कि गांधी जी एक ऐसा आत्मनिर्भर राष्ट्र चाहते थे जिसमें सांप्रदायिक सहयोग

और शारीरिक श्रम को अपनाया जाये। यह गांधी जी के संग्रहित ग्रंथों (कलेक्टेड वर्क्स) में निहित है, जिसमें उनका तर्क है कि खादी (हाथ से काता कपास) के उत्पादन को अधिकतम करने के लिए समाज को संगठित किया जाना चाहिए।[3]

गांधी जी ने सार्वजनिक स्वामित्व के पक्ष में निजी संपत्ति की अस्वीकृति की वकालत की; इस व्यवस्था में सम्पत्ति के मालिक सामान्य हित में प्रबंधित सार्वजनिक संपत्ति के न्यासी (ट्रस्टी) मात्र होंगे। तदनुसार, इस खादी आधारित आर्थिक व्यवस्था के अंतर्गत प्रत्येक व्यक्ति को एक विशेष प्रकार से उसके कार्य के अनुरूप 'भुगतान' किया जाएगा। उदाहरण के लिए-एक लोहार को उपकरणों को तराशने के बदले में भोजन या अनाज के रूप में भुगतान किया जाएगा, जबकि किसानों को बीज बोने के लिए आवश्यक उपकरणों के रूप में भुगतान किया जाएगा, और इसी तरह अन्य को।[4]

गांधी जी मशीनीकरण का विरोध करते थे। उनका मानना था कि मशीनरी ने उपभोक्ताओं की इच्छाओं को इस हद तक बढ़ा दिया है कि यह अनिवार्य रूप से शोषण, बेरोजगारी और अंततः भुखमरी पैदा करेगी। गांधी जी को उम्मीद थी कि परंपराओं को अधिक महत्व देने के लिए उल्लेखनीय होने के कारण आने वाले समय में उनकी मातृभूमि एक पूर्व-आधुनिक मार्ग का अनुसरण करेगी।

गांधी के भारतीय राज्य का राजनीतिक भविष्य

गांधी जी द्वारा आधुनिक अर्थव्यवस्था (पूंजीवाद, समाजवाद और औद्योगिकीकरण) की निंदा ने आधुनिक राजनीतिक मामलों के बारे में उनके महत्वपूर्ण दृष्टिकोण को प्रतिबिंबित किया।गांधी जी समकालीन राजनीतिक व्यवस्थाओं की आलोचना करने में विशेष रूप से मुखर थे। उन्होंने विशेष रूप से पश्चिमी लोकतंत्र को निशाना बनाया। गांधी वेस्टमिंस्टर की कमियों के बारे में भावुक होकर कहते हैं : "यदि भारत इंग्लैंड की नकल करता है, तो यह मेरा दृढ़ विश्वास है कि वह बर्बाद हो जाएगा। उनकी हालत जानवरों से भी बदतर है।"[5] यहाँ गांधीजी ने अंग्रेजी सभ्यता को उसकी भौतिकवादी सोच की वजह से उसकी स्थिति जानवरों से भी बदतर बतायी है। गांधी जी ने इसी क्रम में साम्यवाद को भी नापसंद किया। उन्हें मार्क्सवाद के कुछ पहलू सिद्धांतिक रूप में स्वीकार्य थे, लेकिन उन्होंने इसके उस व्यवहार को सिरे से अस्वीकार कर दिया, जिसमें इसके द्वारा इसे थोपा जाना और नास्तिकता का प्रचार करना था। उनके शब्दों में,

> "...जब तक यह हिंसा और ईश्वर को मानने से इंकार पर आधारित है, यह मुझे प्रतिकर्षित करता है।"[6]

गांधी जी ने इसलिए भारत से पश्चिमी लोकतंत्र और साम्यवाद दोनों से दूरी बनाने की मांग की। ऐसा प्रतीत होता है कि उन्होंने एक ऐसे राजनीतिक विकल्प का समर्थन किया है, जो

राजनीतिक संस्थाओं और राजनीतिक नेतृत्व दोनों की अनुपस्थिति को पूरी तरह से प्रोत्साहित करता है। आशा के साथ, उन्होंने कहा, "आने वाले समय में देश की स्थिति ऐसी होगी जिसमें प्रत्येक व्यक्ति अपना स्वयं का शासक बन जाएगा। वह स्वयं को इस तरह से संचालित करेगा कि उसके व्यवहार से उसके पड़ोसियों की भलाई में कोई बाधा न आए।"[7] इस सिद्धांत ने गांधी जी की विनम्र विश्व दृष्टि को प्रभावी ढंग से परिभाषित किया। गांधी जी को लगता था कि अराजनैतिक और आत्मनिर्भर गाँवों से संपन्न राज्य राजनीतिक शोषण की संभावनाओं को कम करेंगे और अनियमित व्यक्तिगत स्वतंत्रता के लिए अवसरों को बढ़ाएंगे।

गांधीजी का मानना था कि संघीय सरकार की दमनकारी सत्ता को खत्म करके, विकेंद्रीकरण से भारत के गांवों को कई तरह से लाभ होगा। यह गाँवों को आर्थिक रूप से आत्मनिर्भर बनाने और खादी के विस्तार के लिए भी सकारात्मक भूमिका निभाएगा। गांधी जी ने 1944 में प्रकाशित एक लेख में इस ग्राम केंद्रित सिद्धांत पर विस्तार से बताया :

> "स्वतंत्रता की शुरुआत स्थानीय स्तर से होनी चाहिए। इस प्रकार, प्रत्येक गाँव एक गणतंत्र होगा जिसके पास पूरी शक्ति होगी। इसलिए, प्रत्येक गांव को आत्मनिर्भर होना होगा साथ ही साथ अपने मामलों का प्रबंधन करने में और यहाँ तक कि पूरी दुनिया के सामने अपने आप को स्थापित करने में भी सक्षम होना होगा।"[8]

जैसे जैसे सत्ता का हस्तांतरण वास्तविकता के नजदीक आ रहा था, गांधी जी के सामने एक नाजुक सी स्थिति पैदा हो रही थी। दशकों तक उन्होंने भविष्य के भारतीय राज्य के बारे में लिखा। लेकिन अब जब स्वतंत्रता निकट ही थी, तो ऐसा प्रतीत नहीं हो रहा था कि उनके विचार फलित होंगे। यह गांधी जी के लिए एक दर्दनाक दुविधा की स्थिति थी क्योंकि यहाँ उनकी राजनीतिक दृष्टि और राज्य को संचालित करने की वास्तविकताओं के बीच एक बुनियादी अंतर परिलक्षित हो रहा था।[9]

गाँधी के आदर्श राज्य का सामाजिक और धार्मिक परिदृश्य

गांधी जी ने शारीरिक श्रम, आत्मनिर्भर गांवों और सांप्रदायिक सहयोग की वकालत करने के साथ साथ भारत के विकास के लिए सामाजिक और धार्मिक पद्धति के बारे में भी दृढ़ता से महसूस किया। उनके धार्मिक चिंतन में तीन मुख्य लक्ष्य शामिल थे। इनमें अस्पृश्यता का उन्मूलन, जाति व्यवस्था के वर्ण भेद को बनाए रखना और भारत को सहिष्णुता, शील और धार्मिकता में समाहित करना शामिल था। भविष्य के भारतीय राज्य की कल्पना इन आधारभूत सिद्धांतों द्वारा समर्थित होंगी। हालाँकि गांधी जी ने दबे-कुचले वर्गों के उत्थान और उन्हें संबल प्रदान करने के लिए प्रयास किया, लेकिन उन्होंने समग्र रूप से जाति व्यवस्था के उन्मूलन का पक्ष नहीं लिया। गांधी जी ने परंपरा के कुछ पहलुओं का बचाव किया, विशेष रूप से वर्ण भेद व्यवस्था का। गांधी जी के भविष्य के भारत में प्रत्येक गांव को इन चार वर्णों के विभाजन में

व्यवस्थित किया जाएगा। समाज का प्रत्येक सदस्य इस सहकारी तंत्र में ईमानदारी से अपना कर्तव्य निभाएगा।[10] गांधीजी का मानना था कि कोई भी कार्य ऊँचा या नीचा नहीं होता है। गांधी जी जाति की संकीर्ण परिभाषा के स्थान पर प्राचीन वर्ण व्यवस्था का समर्थन करते थे जहाँ व्यक्ति को उसके कार्य विभाजन से उच्च या निम्न जाति का नहीं माना जाता था। भविष्य के भारतीय राज्य में गांधी जी ने धर्म के पालना की कल्पना की। उन्होंने लिखा कि मेरी पहली शिकायत यह है कि भारत अधार्मिक हो रहा है।ष हमें "परमात्मा से दूर होने" पर विराम लगाना होगा।[11]

निष्कर्ष

गांधी जी अतीत की ओर तेजी से वापसी करते हुए भविष्य की ओर अग्रसर हुए। हालाँकि मानक साहित्य कभी-कभी गांधी जी की अधिक अपरंपरागत धारणाओं की अनदेखी करता रहा है। लेकिन इस तर्क को पुष्ट करने के लिए साक्ष्य मौजूद है कि उनके मातृभूमि के भविष्य के बारे में दृढ़ विचार थे। इस विचारधारा के निचोड़ के रूप में उनके द्वारा पूंजीवाद, समाजवाद, लोकतंत्र और साम्यवाद सहित आधुनिक सभ्यता की निंदा को समझा जा सकता है। महात्मा गांधी बीसवीं सदी में एकमात्र शख्सियत थे, जिन्होंने भारतीय शिल्प को ग्रामीण अर्थव्यवस्था और राजनीतिक स्वतंत्रता की अवधारणा से सफलतापूर्वक जोड़कर इस पर लग रहे सम्पूर्ण ग्रहण से बचाया। गांधी जी का सुझाव था कि भारत को शुद्धता, नैतिकता और आत्म-अनुशासन के रास्ते पर लौटने की जरूरत है। आज, उनकी मृत्यु के लगभग सात दशक बाद, भारत एक शक्तिशाली वैश्विक अर्थव्यवस्था के साथ दुनिया के सबसे बड़े लोकतंत्र के रूप में गर्व से खड़ा है। ऐसा प्रतीत होता है, कि भारत ने स्वतंत्रता प्राप्ति के बाद गांधी जी के विचारों के विपरीत एक 'पश्चिमी' मॉडल का अनुसरण किया है, जिसका गांधी ने पूरे जीवन विरोध किया।इस प्रकार गांधी जी द्वारा परिभाषित सच्चा 'स्व-शासन' आज केवल 'हिंद स्वराज' और उनके एकत्रित ग्रंथों के पन्नों तक ही सीमित है।

संदर्भ

1. Gandhi, "*Hind Swaraj*" in Parel, ed., *Hind Swaraj: And Other Writings*, 39.
2. "Interview to Francis Hickman", *Collected Works,* 17 Sep. 1940. See Chatterjee, *Nationalist Thought and the Colonial World,* 88.
3. "Is *Khadi*Economically Sound?",*Collected Works*, Vol. 63, 77. See: Partha Chatterjee,"Gandhi and theCritique of Civil Society" in RanajitGuha, ed., *Subaltern Studies III:Writings on South Asian History and Society*, (Oxford: Oxford University Press, 1989)
4. ChistopheJaffrelot, *India's Silent Revolution: The Rise of the Lower Castes in NorthIndia*, (London: Hurst & Company, 2003), 27.
5. Gandhi, "*Hind Swaraj*", 33.
6. Rudrangshu Mukherjee, ed., *The Penguin Gandhi Reader*, (London: Penguin BooksLtd., 1993), Speech delivered 11 Dec. 1924, 237.

7. "Enlightened Anarchy: A Political Ideal", *Collected Works*, Vol. 59, 45. See: Chaterjee,*Nationalist Thought and the Colonial World*, 92.
8. Gandhi, "Independence", *Collected Works*, Vol. 85, 460. See: Chatterjee, "Gandhi andthe Critique of Civil Society" in Guha, ed., *Subaltern Studies III*, 161.
9. Chatterjee, "Gandhi and the Critique of Civil Society" in Guha, ed., *Subaltern StudiesIII*, 189.
10. Rudrangshu Mukherjee, ed., *The Penguin Gandhi Reader*, (London: Penguin BooksLtd., 1993), xv.
11. Gandhi, "*Hind Swaraj*" in Parel, ed., *Hind Swaraj: And Other Writings*, 42.

19

गाँधीः विश्वशांति और अहिंसक क्रांति के अग्रदूत

पूजा

महात्मा गाँधी संपूर्ण विश्व पटल पर सिर्फ एक नाम ही नहीं, अपितु शांति और अहिंसा का एक प्रमुख प्रतीक भी है। महात्मा गाँधी के पूर्व भी विश्व में शांति और अहिंसा की अवधारणा फलित थी, परन्तु उन्होंने जिस प्रकार सत्याग्रह, शान्ति व अहिंसा के रास्तों पर चलते हुए अंग्रेजों को भारत छोड़ने पर मजबूर कर दिया, उसका कोई दूसरा उदाहरण विश्व-इतिहास में देखने को नहीं मिलता। आज आधुनिक युग की सबसे बड़ी समस्या शांति की समस्या है। अब यह विश्वास दिन-प्रतिदिन बल-पकड़ता जा रहा है कि यदि मनुष्य ने अंतर्राष्ट्रीय झगड़ों को युद्ध के द्वारा सुलझाना नहीं त्यागा, तो संपूर्ण मानव-संस्कृति और मानव-जाति का विनाश हो जाएगा। विश्व शांति के संबंध में गाँधी जी का यह विचार था कि अब तक मनुष्य ने अपनी सामूहिक समस्याओं को गलत आधार पर, हिंसा, घृणा, द्वेष, और विग्रह आदि के द्वारा सुलझाने का प्रयास किया है। जीवन के प्रत्येक क्षेत्र में गाँधी जी का कार्यक्रम चाहे वह व्यक्तिगत हो, सामाजिक, राजनीतिक या आर्थिक हो, विश्व शांति का साधक रहा है। आर्थिक क्षेत्र में गाँधी जी विकेन्द्रित उद्योगों के पक्षपाती हैं। यदि उद्योगों का पूँजीवादी आधार पर केन्द्रीयकरण होता है, तो इससे शोषण और साम्राज्यवाद बढ़ता है। यदि उद्योगों का साम्यवादी आधार पर केन्द्रीयकरण किया जाता है, तो इससे नौकरशाही बढती है। ऐसी स्थिति में गाँधी जी का विकेंद्रीकरण सिद्धांत शांति की दृष्टि से सर्वथा युक्तिकर है। सामाजिक क्षेत्र में गाँधी जी ने उँच और नीच के समस्त भेदभाव हटाकर शांति की सराहनीय साधना की है। राजनीतिक क्षेत्र में गाँधी जी लोकतंत्र के समर्थक थे। लेकिन उनके लोकतंत्र में स्थानीय स्वायत्तता का बड़ा महत्व है। गाँधी जी ने कहा भी था कि विश्व की अव्यवस्था का मूल कारण मनुष्य के व्यक्तिगत और सामूहिक जीवन में सामंजस्य का न होना है। उनके अनुसार विश्व -शांति की समस्या का स्थायी हल तभी निकल सकता है जबकि मनुष्य के व्यक्तिगत और सामूहिक जीवन में संतुलन स्थापित

हो जाए। वे नैतिक मापदंड जो मनुष्य के व्यक्तिगत जीवन का नियमन करते है; अंतर्राष्ट्रीय क्षेत्र में भी प्रयुक्त किये जाने चाहिए।[1]

विश्व शांति के संबंध में गाँधी जी के विचार इसलिए भी प्रासंगिक है, क्योंकि उन विचारों को उन्होंने स्वयं अपने आचरण में ढालकर सिद्ध किया। उन विचारों को सत्य और अहिंसा की कसौटी पर जाँचा-परखा। वे हिंसा को एक क्षण के लिए भी बर्दाश्त करने को तैयार नहीं थे। आज भी हिंसा भरे वैश्विक माहौल में गाँधी जी के विचारों की महत्ता बढती जा रही है। हम हिंसा की नींव पर शांति का शहर खड़ा नहीं कर सकते है। यदि मानव जाति शांतिपूर्ण जीवन निर्वाह करना चाहती है, तो सभी क्षेत्रों में हिंसा को हराना होगा। साथ ही हिंसा के स्थान पर प्रेम और सहयोग के दर्शन को जीवन का अंग बनाना होगा। हमे त्याग का जीवन अपनाना होगा। हमे अपने दैनिक जीवन में गांधीवादी मूल्यों को अपनाना होगा। वास्तव में आज गांधीवादी मूल्यों को दोहराने की जरूरत है; न कि उनके चित्रों व मूर्तियों पर माला पहनाने की। अत: हम यह कह सकते है कि गाँधी का पूरा जीवन एक संदेश था।[2] आज हमें भी गाँधी विचारधारा की राह पकड़कर ही विश्व में शांति की स्थापना का मार्ग प्रशस्त करना होगा।[3]

शांति के मसीहा व सहस्त्राब्दि के नायक के रूप में भी अनेक देशों ने, गाँधी जी के चित्रों को आधार बनाकर डाक टिकट व अन्य डाक सामग्रियाँ जारी की हैं। दुनिया के अधिकांश देशों ने भी बापू की टिकट जारी कर उन्हें सम्मान दिया, लेकिन पाकिस्तान ने शांति के इस दूत की उपेक्षा की; क्योंकि पाकिस्तान में कभी भी शांति बहाल नहीं हुई।[4]

विश्व शांति आज समस्त जगत के लिए सबसे बड़ी चुनौती बनकर उभरी है। हमें इस बात की खुशी है कि हमारा देश भारत इससे दूर शांतिप्रिय है। उसने कभी भी कोई भी कार्य दूसरों को पीड़ित करने के लिए नहीं किया। वह हमेशा से ही स्वयं की शांति के साथ-साथ समस्त राष्ट्रों की शांति चाहता है। विश्व शांति का अर्थ है-चुपचाप अन्याय-अत्याचार सहन न करना और जानबूझकर ऐसे कार्यों को न करना जिनसे शांति भंग करने या होने का अंदेशा हो, जिससे कोई भी व्यक्ति, समाज, राष्ट्र या समस्त विश्व दुखी व परेशान न हो। अत: विश्व शांति अंतर-आत्मा से उपजने वाली भावना है, जो अहिंसा से संभव है क्योंकि विश्व शांति और अहिंसा में घनिष्ठ संबंध है। इतिहास साक्षी है कि किसी भी युग में किसी समस्या का समाधान युद्ध

1. विश्वप्रकाश गुप्त और मोहिनी गुप्त, 'महात्मा गाँधी: व्यक्ति और विचार', राधा पब्लिकेशन्स, नई दिल्ली, 1996, पृष्ठ. स. 164-165.
2. अनिल दत्त मिश्र, 'गाँधी: सिद्धांत और व्यवहार', पियर्सन पब्लिकेशन, पेपरबैक, 2012, Available at] http%@@www-uprtou-ac-in@other_pdf@PGFGS-pdf
3. अरविंद जयतिलक, 'विश्व शांति के लिए आवश्यक है गाँधी के विचार', देशबंधु, Influencing Public Opinion since, 1959] Available at, http%@@www-deshbandhu-co-in@vichar/विश्व-शांति-के-लिए-आवश्यक-है-गांधी-के-विचार--30262-2
4. डाक टिकटों में महात्मा गाँधी, Available at, 2019 https%@@bharatdiscovery-org@india@डाक टिकटों में महात्मा गाँधी

से नहीं होता क्योंकि युद्ध हिंसा है और हिंसा से शांति संभव नहीं। अगर यह सच होता तो आज पूरा विश्व शांतिमय होकर सुख की नींद सोता। विश्व शांति के लिए अहिंसा का मार्ग ही अपनाना एक सुखद कल्पना ही नहीं अपितु सत्य भी है। विश्व शांति और अहिंसा में गहरा संबंध ही नहीं अपितु ये एक दूसरे के पूरक भी है। अतः विश्व बंधुत्व और अंतर्राष्ट्रीयता की भावना ही इसको कायम रख सकती है और विश्व शांति के लिए यह परमावश्यक भी है, तभी यह शांति हमेशा के लिए कायम रह सकती है।

गाँधी अहिंसा को सबसे बड़ा कर्तव्य बताते है। मन, कर्म, वचन की स्वीकारिता ही अहिंसा का सिद्धांत है। यदि हम इसका पूरा पालन नहीं करते है तो हमें इसकी भावना को अवश्य समझना चाहिए और जहाँ तक संभव हो हिंसा से दूर रहकर मानवता का पालन करना चाहिए।[1] अहिंसा विश्व शांति का स्थायी उपाय है। अहिंसा में विश्वास रखने वाला व्यक्ति संसार के सभी धर्मों के प्रति समान श्रध्दा रखता है। अहिंसा का पुजारी शांति का दूत कहलाता है।[2] गाँधी अपने अहिंसक मार्ग के शांति सन्देश के साथ विश्व में प्रासंगिक है। आज सम्पूर्ण विश्व को गाँधी के सिद्धांतों पर चलने की आवश्यकता है। गाँधीजी की मान्यता थी कि हमें मानव को चिर–शांति प्रदान करने के लिए तानाशाही और शोषण तथा भय से मुक्त करने के लिए अहिंसा का अजेय अस्त्र अपनाना चाहिए।[3] गाँधीजी स्थायी शांति चाहते थे, उनकी नींद, सुख सब स्थायी शांति की खोज में बलिदान हो चुका था। शांति को शांतिपूर्वक कायम करना ही गाँधी का अहिंसात्मक मार्ग है। गाँधीजी पूर्ण रूप से आस्तिक थे। विश्व शांति के विरोधियों के लिए उनका यह विचार बन चुका था कि वे ईश्वर में विश्वास ही नहीं रखते। उनकी पावन दृष्टि में ईश्वर उपासक शांति का विरोधी हो ही नहीं सकता। ईसामसीह को सब ईसाई ईश्वर का पुत्र तथा शांति का अग्रदूत मानते है।[4]

वर्तमान में भी सत्य, अहिंसा व सत्याग्रह ही विश्व शांति स्थापित करने का एकमात्र रास्ता नजर आ रहा है।[5] गाँधी इस नई सदी में एक परंपरा का नाम है। गाँधी अब भारत के लिए एक संस्कृति है और उनका अहिंसा का मन्त्र अब पूरे विश्व में शांति का प्रतीक बन गया है। इस ग्लोबल होते विश्व में भले मूल्य और मानवीय परम्पराएं बदल रही है। विभिन्न देशों के भूगोल और सीमाएं बदल रही है परंतु गाँधीजी का दर्शन आज हर लब पर परिविर्तित हो रहा है। गाँधी आज हमारी आस्था का प्रतीक है। गाँधी दर्शन की इस रोशनी में एक नई दुनिया की तलाश की जा सकती है। गाँधी दर्शन इस नई सदी में भी उतना ही महत्वपूर्ण है, जितना पिछली शताब्दी

---

1. महात्मा गाँधी–शांति के दूत, भारत का राष्ट्रीय पोर्टल, 2014, www-india-gov-in
2. जय प्रकाश नाटानी, 'गाँधी, नेहरू और टैगोर', जयपुर, पॉइंटर पब्लिशर्स, 2002, पृ. 83–85.
   Ibid, पृ. 85.
3. मनोज कुमार सिंह और आशुतोष कुमार, 'महात्मा गाँधी: एक अवलोकन', नई दिल्ली, के. के. पब्लिकेशन्स, 2007, पृ. 158.
4. आराधना, 'महात्मा गाँधी के विचार और वर्तमान विश्व', दिल्ली, राहुल पब्लिशिंग हाउस, 2015, पृ. 44.

में था। आज इस तकनीक और विज्ञान की तेज गति के विश्व में गाँधी दर्शन उस पेड़ की भाँति है, जो अपने आस-पास अपनी छाँव में हरियाली और शांति का अनुपम परिदृश्य दिखाता है। गाँधी दर्शन आज विश्व दर्शन में शांति की एक धरोहर है जो शताब्दियों तक मानव समाज को एक नया रास्ता और दृष्टिकोण दिखाती रहेगी। गाँधी दर्शन प्रगति, विकास और शांति का एक मंथन है, अहिंसा का एक रोशन चिराग है और इस दर्शन में आज भी वो तेज है जो एक नई दुनिया को दिखता है, जिसमें आपसी भाईचारा और सौहार्द शामिल है।[1]

गाँधी दर्शन आज समय की आवश्यकता है। गाँधी दर्शन आज समूचे विश्व को एक नया रास्ता दिखा रहा है। अहिंसा का रास्ता ही आज इस आतंकवाद और परमाणु विनाश के कगार पर खड़े विश्व को बचा सकता है। गाँधी दर्शन आज शांति के मार्ग की अंतिम कड़ी है। अभी भी हम चुक गये तो शायद विनाश के अलावा बाकी कुछ नहीं रहेगा।

---

1. कृष्ण कुमार रत्तू, 'गाँधी दर्शन: नयी सदी के बदलते संदर्भ, जयपुर, बुक एन्क्लेव, 2002, पृ. 1

संदर्भ सूची

1. विश्वप्रकाश गुप्त और मोहिनी गुप्त, 'महात्मा गाँधी: व्यक्ति और विचार', राधा पब्लिकेशन्स, नई दिल्ली, 1996, पृ. 164-165.
2. अनिल दत्त मिश्र, 'गाँधी: सिद्धांत और व्यवहार', पियर्सन पब्लिकेशन, पेपरबैक, 2012, Available at] http%@@www-uprtou-ac-in@other_pdf@PGFGS-pdf
3. अरविंद जयतिलक, 'विश्व शांति के लिए आवश्यक है गाँधी के विचार', देशबंधु, Influencing Public Opinion since, 1959, Available at, http%@@www-deshbandhu-co-in@vichar@विश्व- शांति-के-लिए-आवश्यक-है-गांधी-के-विचार--30262-2
4. डाक टिकटों में महात्मा गाँधी, Available at, 2019 https%@@bharatdiscovery-org@india@डाक टिकटों में महात्मा गाँधी
5. महात्मा गाँधी-शांति के दूत, भारत का राष्ट्रीय पोर्टल, 2014, www-india-gov-in
6. जय प्रकाश नाटानी, 'गाँधी, नेहरू और टैगोर', जयपुर, पॉइंटर पब्लिशर्स, 2002, पृ. 83-85.
7. वही, पृ. 85.
8. मनोज कुमार सिंह और आशुतोष कुमार, 'महात्मा गाँधी: एक अवलोकन', नई दिल्ली, के. के. पब्लिकेशन्स, 2007, पृ. 158
9. आराधना, 'महात्मा गाँधी के विचार और वर्तमान विश्व', दिल्ली, राहुल पब्लिशिंग हाउस, 2015, पृ. 44.
10. कृष्ण कुमार रत्तू, 'गाँधी दर्शन: नयी सदी के बदलते संदर्भ, जयपुर, बुक एन्क्लेव, 2002
11. महात्मा गाँधी और विश्व, भारतकोश, 2019,
Available at] https%@@bharatdiscovery-org@india@महात्मा गाँधी और विश्व

20

मानवता के सच्चे साधक : गांधीजी

सुभाष चन्द्र डबास 'चौधरी'

गांधी सत्य-अहिंसा के सच्चे उपासक थे। उनकी अहिंसा और सत्य ईश्वर के पर्याय थे। गांधीजी पूरी तरह से आशावादी और कर्म में आस्था रखने वाले महापुरूष थे। उनके जीवन के समस्त कार्य मानव कल्याण के लिए समर्पित थे। उनका स्वराज, रामराज्य, सत्य, अहिंसा, असहयोग, सविनय अवज्ञा आंदोलन, छुआछूत एवं शोषण रहित समाज की कल्पना, सर्वधर्म समभाव की धारणा, स्वैच्छिक श्रम, अपरिग्रह और त्याग भावना, प्रार्थना, उपवास, समाज सेवा, स्वच्छता, आर्थिक-सामाजिक-राजनीतिक समानता, गोरक्षा, शाकाहार, बुनियादी शिक्षा, वकालत के द्वारा मानव सेवा, रंगभेद के खिलाफ लड़ाई, गिरमिटिया की खिलाफत, धर्म एवं राजनीति और लोकतंत्र को जोड़ कर देखना गांधीजी के मौलिक और मानवीय विचार थे। गांधीजी एक सत्यशोधक के रूप में एक साथ ही आध्यात्मिक और सामाजिक-राजनीतिक आयामों में संतुलन बनाकर चलने वाले अद्‌वितीय महापुरूष थे। ईश्वर में अटूट विश्वास रखने वाले गांधीजी का मानना था कि भगवान की मर्जी के बिना पत्ता भी हिलता।[1] भारत देश की आजादी की लड़ाई लड़ते हुए गांधीजी पूरी दुनिया में मानवता, शांति और समानता की स्थापना के लिए निरंतर प्रयास करते रहे; चाहे दक्षिणी अफ्रीका में गोरे काले रंगभेद की समस्या हो या नेटाल में गिरमिटिया की।

आचरण की शुद्धता और मन की पवित्रता गांधीजी के धर्म दर्शन का अहम् हिस्सा थे। उनका मानना था कि प्रार्थना और उपवास हमारे शरीर, मन और आत्मा को क्रमशः शुद्ध करते हैं। ऐसी आत्मिक और शारीरिक शुद्धता के बलबूते पर मनुष्य अनेक प्रकार के शारीरिक, मानसिक और आत्मिक विकारों से मुक्ति प्राप्त करता है। इन विकारों से मुक्त होना सच्चे इंसान बनने की ओर बढ़ना है; जहाँ हमारा विवेक अच्छे बुरे की पहचान करने लगता है और हम सच्चे मनुष्यता के मार्ग पर बढ़ने के योग्य बनते चले जाते हैं। गांधीजी का विश्वास था कि धर्म बुराई

से बचाने का काम करता है।[2] कवि इकबाल ने भी कहा है 'मजहब नहीं सिखाता आपस में बैर करना'। गांधीजी धर्म के इस महत्व को भलीभाँति समझते थे। उसके नैतिक बल को जानते थे। इसीलिए उन्होंने प्रार्थना, उपासना, मौन, उपवास आदि को अत्यधिक महत्व दिया और धर्म एवं राजनीति को जीवन में परस्पर जोड़कर देखा; बल्कि यहाँ तक कहा कि धर्म के बिना राजनीति का कोई अर्थ नहीं है। गांधीजी के लिए धर्म का वृहत्तर अर्थ कर्तव्यनिष्ठा है अर्थात लोक सेवा। इसीलिए धर्म, अर्थ, समाज एवं राजनीति से जुड़े किसी भी कार्य में इन सभी पक्षों का ध्यान रखकर नैतिकता के मार्ग पर आगे बढ़ना चाहिए।[3] राजनीति के बिना लोक कल्याण संभव नहीं है; किंतु नैतिकता पर आधारित राजनीति ही देश एवं दुनिया के लिए कल्याणकारी सिद्ध हो सकती है। लोकतंत्र में धर्म का नैतिक बल उसे और अधिक मानवीय और कल्याणकारी बनाने का काम करता है। भारत जैसे लोकतंत्र में राजनीतिक शक्ति जनता की दशा सुधारने का काम करती है। अहिंसा गांधी जी का भगवान है; मानवता की रक्षा का एक अचूक अस्त्र है। इसके द्वारा विश्व शांति संभव हो सकती है। विश्व में वर्ग संघर्ष को अहिंसा के द्वारा ही कम किया जा सकता है। गांधीजी का दृढ़ विश्वास था कि हमारी सभ्यता, संस्कृति, स्वराज और राम राज्य की अवधारणा आत्म त्याग पर बल देती है।[4]

अपरिग्रह का सिद्धांत आवश्यकतानुसार भंडारण और त्याग पर जोर देता है। गांधीजी चाहते थे कि अमीर लोगों को गरीबों के लिए त्याग करने की जरूरत है। इससे कोई अभावग्रस्त और भूखा नहीं सोएगा। गांधीजी ने श्रम के महत्व को समझा और रोटी के लिए किए गए श्रम को उत्तम समाज सेवा के रूप में देखा।

मनुष्य का हृदय परिवर्तन भी मानवता के उच्चतम मूल्यों को रेखांकित करता है और विश्वव्यापी संघर्ष को भी न्यूनतम करने के मार्ग को प्रशस्त करता है। गांधीजी रस्किन की पुस्तक 'अनटू दिस लास्ट' के संदेश को अत्यधिक महत्व देते थे। उनका मानना था "इस पुस्तक ने मेरे जीवन की दिशा बदल दी। हमें दुनिया से जो कुछ चाहिए वह पहले हम खुद दुनिया के दीनतम व्यक्ति को उपलब्ध कराएँ। सभी व्यक्तियों को समान अवसर मिलने चाहिए; अवसर मिले तो प्रत्येक व्यक्ति के आध्यात्मिक विकास की एक जैसी संभावना हैं। चरखा इसी भावना का प्रतीक है"।[5] गांधीजी का चरखा लघु कुटीर उद्योग, ग्रामोद्योग व ग्रामोत्थान, खादी, स्वदेशी एवं स्वावलंबन का पर्याय है। मजदूर किसान की श्रम शक्ति की पहचान है। मानव प्रेम एवं भाईचारे की भावना से ओतप्रोत है। जीवन की सहजता एवं स्वरोजगार का प्रतीक है। सही मायने में व्यापार, वाणिज्य के शांति–सौहार्द्र, अंत्योदय की क्रांति और आर्थिक विकास का सोपान है। जीवन की सरलता, भारत जैसे लोकतंत्र की कृषि प्रधान अर्थव्यवस्था, पर्यावरण एवं प्रकृति–प्रेम के मनोभाव भी इसी में निहित हैं। कुल मिलाकर शांति, संतोष, अहिंसा एवं सुख–समृद्धि के भावों का विस्तार दुनिया भर में इसी चरखे के द्वारा किया जा सकता है।

धार्मिक, सामाजिक, राजनैतिक और आर्थिक सभी प्रकार के शोषण से मुक्ति गांधीजी के समाजवाद और मानववाद की कल्पना थी। इसीलिए वे आर्थिक समानता को ही सच्ची

स्वाधीनता के रूप में देखते थे और पूंजीपतियों तथा जमींदारों को संपत्ति का ट्रस्टी बनने की बात पर जोर देते थे। सेवा और समानता का भाव यहाँ महत्वपूर्ण था। सच्ची अर्थव्यवस्था अहिंसा, मानवीयता और नैतिक मूल्यों पर आधारित होती है; उसी तरह जैसे परमात्मा के द्वारा प्रदत वायु, जल आदि जीवन की मूलभूत आवश्यकताएँ। गांधीजी भी जीवन की मूलभूत आवश्यकताओं के उत्पादन और साधनों पर जनसाधारण का नियंत्रण चाहते थे। ''सारी दुनिया का आर्थिक गठन ऐसा होना चाहिए कि उसमें किसी को रोटी-कपड़े की तंगी ना रहे। दूसरे शब्दों में, प्रत्येक व्यक्ति को अपने जीवन निर्वाह के लिए पर्याप्त काम उपलब्ध होना चाहिए। यह आदर्श सर्वत्र तभी प्राप्त किया जा सकता है, जब जीवन की बुनियादी आवश्यकताओं के उत्पादन के साधन v le t urk d sfu; ak k easgks*A[6]

गांधीजी का दृढ़ विश्वास था कि विश्व-शांति का आधार अहिंसा ही हो सकती है। जीवन का पहला और अंतिम नियम अहिंसा ही है। समुद्र जैसे विशाल, गंभीर और धैर्यवान मनुष्य में ही ऐसे गुण संभव है। अहिंसा, सत्य, त्याग एवं क्षमा जैसे कोमल मनोभाव आत्मा के गुण हैं। सच्ची शांति और 'वसुधैव कुटुंबकम' इसी से संभव है। गांधीजी का राष्ट्रप्रेम और सेवा भाव विश्व प्रेम और मानव कल्याण का पर्याय है; क्योंकि गांधीजी किसी अन्य देश-जाति का अहित करके अपने देश और जाति के हित की कामना नहीं करते। इसी में सच्ची शांति, रामराज्य, समानता और विश्व कल्याण की भावना व्याप्त है। गांधीजी का विश्वास था कि ''मेरा संदेश और मेरे तरीके सचमुच मूलत: सारी दुनिया के लिए हैं और मुझे यह देख कर बड़ा संतोष होता है कि बहुत बड़ी संख्या में पश्चिम के स्त्री-पुरुषों के हृदय में इसकी अद्‌भुत अनुक्रिया हुई है और ऐसे लोगों की संख्या दिनोंदिन बढ़ रही है''।[7]

गांधीजी किसी भी कार्य के संपादन अर्थात लक्ष्य-प्राप्ति हेतु इस्तेमाल किए गए साधन की शुद्धता पर बहुत जोर देते थे। उनका मानना था 'जैसा साधन, वैसा साध्य'। इसी सत्प्रेरणा के वशीभूत गांधीजी ने वकालत जैसे पेशे में सच्चाई और ईमानदारी को महत्व दिया। एक वकील के रूप में गांधी जी ने अपनी आत्मा को कभी नहीं बेचा; सदा अपने ईमान को बचाए रखा। गांधीजी वकीलों, दलालों और अदालत के मायाजाल, झूठे गवाह, भारी भरकम फीस, इंग्लैंड हो या अफ्रीका अपने मुवक्किल के लिए झूठ के निकृष्टतम हथकंडो से भलीभाँति परिचित थे और यह सब देख कर बहुत दुखी थे। उनका मानना था कि वकील की योग्यता लोक सेवा और राष्ट्र सेवा के काम आनी चाहिए न कि अपनी जेब भरने के लिए। गांधीजी ने आत्म त्याग और सेवा भाव के लिए वकीलों का आहवान किया और बताया कि दुनियाभर के 'मूर्धन्य वकीलों ने आत्म त्याग का जीवन जिया और अपनी प्रखर कानूनी प्रतिभा का उपयोग पूरी तरह देश की सेवा के लिए किया''।[8] न्याय-प्रक्रिया में वकील के कर्तव्य को स्पष्ट करते हुए गांधीजी ने बताया कि ''वह न्यायाधीशों के समक्ष मामला पेश कर दे और उन्हें सच्चाई तक पहुँचने दे। वकील का काम दोषी को निर्दोष सिद्ध करना कदापि नहीं हैं''।[9] दक्षिण अफ्रीका में गांधी जी द्वारा लड़े गए मुकदमे सेवा भाव के उत्कृष्ट उदाहरण हैं। जोहांसबर्ग की कुली

लोकेशन अर्थात भंगी बस्ती के मुकदमे में मकान मालिकों ने गांधी जी को अपना वकील बनाया। गांधीजी ने स्पष्ट किया कि "इस कार्य में धन कमाना मेरा उद्देश्य नहीं है। म्युनिसिपालिटी की तरफ से जो भी मिलेगा, उसी में संतोष होगा। आप हारे या जीते, यदि हर पट्टे के पीछे 10 पाउंड आप मुझे देंगे तो काफी होगा"।[10] गांधीजी ने स्पष्ट किया कि इसमें भी आधा धन किसी अस्पताल या सार्वजनिक कार्य में खर्च करने का उद्देश्य है। नेटाल के गिरमिटिया (वे मजदूर जो 5 साल या इससे कम की मजदूरी की शर्तों पर भारत से बाहर मजदूरी के लिए गए हो) पर लगे 3 पौंड के कर एवं प्रथा की समाप्ति के लिए गांधीजी ने संघर्ष किया और गोरे काले की रंगभेद नीति का विरोध किया। चंपारण में नील की खेती अर्थात् 'तीन कठिया' (जिसमें 3/20 अर्थात 20 कट्ठे अर्थात 1 एकड़ में से 3 कट्ठा जमीन में नील बोने) की प्रथा के खिलाफ संघर्ष गांधी जी के सेवा भाव का नमूना है। गांधी जी ने बृज किशोर बाबू और अन्य वकीलों को न्यूनतम फीस लेकर किसानों की सेवा के लिए प्रेरित किया। गांधीजी का यह प्रयास आज के भौतिकवादी और अवसरवादी युग में वकीलों के भीतर आत्म त्याग और सेवा भाव पैदा करने और न्याय प्रणाली की विश्वनीयता के मार्ग को प्रशस्त करता है। "हम इतने लोग, आप जो काम हमें सौंपेंगे वह कर देने के लिए तैयार रहेंगे"।[11]

जोहांसबर्ग की भंगी बस्ती की घनी आबादी, गंदे पाखाने, स्वच्छता की कमी, आसपास की सोने की खानों से उत्पन्न प्रदूषण ने गांधी जी को स्वच्छता के प्रति अधिक सचेत किया। भारत की धार्मिक नगरी काशी और हरिद्वार में गंदगी और रेल गाड़ी के पाखाने की संड़ाध ने गांधी जी को खिन्न कर दिया। "तीसरे दर्जे के डिब्बे में गंदगी और पाखानों की बुरी हालत तो जैसी आज है, वैसी ही उस समय भी थी। गांधीजी को ऋषिकेश और लक्ष्मण झूले के प्राकृतिक दृश्यों ने आकृष्ट किया और अपने पूर्वजों की कला पारखी धार्मिक दृष्टि को नमन किया; किंतु ऐसे रमणीय स्थान को लोगों द्वारा गंदा करना गांधीजी को असह्य था। "हरिद्वार की तरह ऋषिकेश में भी लोग रास्तों को और गंगा के सुंदर किनारों को गंदा कर देते थे। गंगा के पवित्र जल को दूषित करने में भी उन्हें किसी प्रकार का संकोच न होता था। पाखाना जाने वाले दूर जाने के बदले जहाँ लोगों की आमद रफ्त होती, वही हाजत रफा करने बैठ जाते थे। यह देख कर हृदय को बहुत आघात पहुँचा।[13] गांधीजी जानते थे कि सफाई का काम बहुत कठिन है और जीवन में जरूरी है। चंपारण के गाँवों में पाठशाला, सफाई एवं औषध-उपचार का कार्य स्वयंसेवकों की सहायता से आगे बढ़ाया और लोक सेवा के मार्ग को प्रशस्त किया। ग्रामोदय के क्षेत्र में गांधीजी ने ग्राम पाठशाला, ग्राम सुधार और गो रक्षा का कार्य स्वयं अपनी देखरेख में किया और गोरक्षा एवं हिंदी भाषा का प्रचार अन्य सहयोगियों को दिया। भारत जैसे कृषि प्रधान देश में गोवंश की वृद्धि, गो जाति का सुधार और दुग्धालय गांधीजी का उद्देश्य था। दक्षिण अफ्रीका में महामारी के समय डॉ गॉडफ्रे की देखरेख में प्लेग के बीमारों की सेवा शुश्रुषा गांधीजी ने जान जोखिम में डालकर की। 'मरीजों को दवा देना, ढाँढस बँधाना, पानी पिलाना और उनका मल मूत्र आदि साफ करना' गांधीजी का सेवा कार्य था।[14] डॉ बूथ की देखरेख में खुले एक छोटे

अस्पताल में गाँधीजी ने नर्स का कार्य एक स्वयंसेवक के रूप में किया और एक कोढ़ी व्यक्ति के घावों को खुद अपने हाथों साफ किया। गांधी जी की सेवा वृति की पूरी परीक्षा उनके अंतिम शिशु के जन्म के समय हुई, जब गांधी जी को "प्रसव के समय का सारा काम मुझे अपने हाथों ही करना पड़ा। सौभाग्य से मैंने इस विषय को 'माने शिखामण' पुस्तक में ध्यान पूर्वक पढ़ लिया था। इसलिए मुझे कोई घबराहट नहीं हुई"।[15]

मैक्स मूलर की पुस्तक 'हिंदुस्तान क्या सिखाता है?' और थियोसॉफिकल सोसायटी द्वारा प्रकाशित उपनिषदों के भाषांतर का अध्ययन करने पर गांधीजी के हृदय में हिंदू धर्म के प्रति आदर बढ़ गया। टालस्टाय और रस्किन की पुस्तकों ने गांधीजी पर गहरा प्रभाव छोड़ा। स्वयं गांधीजी ने महसूस किया– "विश्व प्रेम मनुष्य को कहां तक ले जा सकता है, इसे मैं अधिकाधिक समझने लगा"।[16] गांधीजी को महात्मा बुद्ध की करूणा, दया अनुकरणीय जान पड़ी जो "मनुष्य जाति को लाँघ कर दूसरे प्राणियों तक पहुँच गई"।[17] गांधीजी ने 'सत्याग्रह आश्रम' की स्थापना की, जिसके उपादान उन्होंने निश्चित किए–सत्य, अहिंसा, प्रेम, ब्रह्मचर्य, अपरिग्रह, श्रम की महत्ता, स्वदेशी, निर्भयता, अस्पृश्यता एवं सहनशीलता। इन उद्देश्यों की प्राप्ति के लिए गांधी जी ने पूजा, स्वच्छता सेवाएँ, समर्पित कताईबुनाई, कृषि, दुग्धालय–गो रक्षा, चर्म उद्योग, राष्ट्रीय बुनियादी शिक्षा आदि कार्य–सोपानों को निर्धारित किया। इस महत कार्य के द्वारा गांधीजी एक आदर्श लोकतंत्र, समाजवाद, रामराज्य और विश्व शांति की स्थापना करना चाहते थे। गांधी जी भारत देश की आजादी प्राप्त करने के बहाने संपूर्ण मानवता के बीच भाईचारे के लक्ष्य को पाना चाहते थे। वे दृढ़ता के साथ विश्वास करते थे कि 'देश सेवा और विश्व सेवा के बीच कोई विरोध नहीं है'।[18] गांधीजी की राष्ट्रभक्ति न तो एकांतिक थी और ना ही दूसरे किसी भी राष्ट्र के शोषण पर टिकी थी; बल्कि उनकी राष्ट्रभक्ति मानववाद और विश्व बंधुत्व की भावना से ओतप्रोत थी। भारतेंदु हरिशचंद्र ने अखबार और पत्रकारिता की शक्ति को पहचान कर नारा दिया था 'जहां तोप मुकाबिल हो, अखबार निकालो'। वहीं गांधीजी अहिंसा को सबसे शक्तिशाली मानते हैं– "अब मैदान में सिर्फ अहिंसा ही खड़ी रह गई है। यही एक चीज है जिसे अणु बम नष्ट नहीं कर सकता।...अब अगर दुनिया अहिंसा को नहीं अपनाती तो मानव जाति को आत्महत्या करनी पड़ेगी"।[19] विश्व शांति की बुनियाद अहिंसा पर ही संभव है। दुनिया के भविष्य का संदेश देते हुए गांधी जी ने कहा कि "विश्व परिसंघ का ढांचा केवल अहिंसा की नींव पर ही खड़ा किया जा सकता है; अंतरराष्ट्रीय मामलों में हिंसा को पूरी तरह त्याग देना होगा"।[20] मनुष्य केवल अहिंसा द्वारा ही हिंसात्मक, पाशविक एवं आतंकवादी गतिविधियों पर विजय प्राप्त कर सकता है; क्योंकि "घृणा को प्रेम से ही जीता जा सकता है। जवाबी घृणा केवल घृणा का विस्तार करती है और उसे गहराती है"।[21] वर्तमान समय में पश्चिमी जगत सच्चे ज्ञान एवं शुद्ध; सात्विक शांति के मार्ग के लिए बेचैन है। गांधीजी ने पश्चिमी भौतिकवाद के समक्ष भारतीय संस्कृति एवं पौर्वात्य आदर्शों को अनुकरणीय माना। जरदुस्त, बुद्ध, महावीर जैन, ईसा, राम, कृष्ण आदि एशिया के इन महापुरूषों के समान दुनिया में अन्य कोई

बराबरी में नहीं है। "मैं चाहता हूं कि आप एशिया के संदेश को समझें। आप इसे पश्चिम के चश्मे या अणु बम की नकल करके नहीं समझ सकते। खैर मुझे आशा है यदि आप बुद्धि ही नहीं बल्कि अपने हृदय को भी एकजुट करके पूर्व के इन मनीषियों द्वारा हमारे लिए छोड़े गए संदेश के रहस्य को समझेंगे और स्वयं को उस महान संदेश के सही उत्तराधिकारी सिद्ध करेंगे तो पश्चिम की हमारी विजय पूर्णता को प्राप्त हो सकेगी। इस विजय पर पश्चिम को भी प्रसन्नता होगी"।[22]

अब तक के विवेचन के पश्चात प्रश्न उठता है कि गांधीजी के मानवीय मूल्य आज कितने प्रासंगिक हैं? इसका एक ही जवाब हो सकता है कि गांधीजी के मूल्य शाश्वत हैं। गांधीजी का जीवन ही एक संदेश है। सत्य एवं अहिंसा में ऐसी शक्ति है; जो शक्तिशाली आसुरी ताकतों को चिर शांति की नींद सुला देने में समर्थ है। आज विश्व में कोरिया, सीरिया, इजरायल, पाकिस्तान, लेबनान कितने ही देश युद्ध एवं आतंकवाद के कारण बने हुए हैं और पूरी दुनिया इस विभीषिका को झेल रही है। अहिंसा, शांति, मानववाद और नैतिकता की शक्ति ही इनका हृदय परिवर्तन करा सकती है। भारत जैसे लोकतंत्र में अधिकारों के लिए निरंतर संघर्ष गांधीजी की कर्तव्यनिष्ठा के समक्ष शांत होने लगता है। तुम अपना कर्तव्य करो, अधिकार तुम्हारे पीछे दौड़े आएंगे'। दिल्ली में जेएनयू के छात्रों का संघर्ष, हड़ताल, आगजनी हमें गांधीजी की छात्रों संबंधी नीति पर सोचने को विवश करता है। छात्रों के लिए राष्ट्रधर्म, नैतिकता और शिक्षार्जन परम कर्तव्य है। आर्थिक स्तर पर विभिन्न घोटाले, स्वार्थ लिप्सा, अवसर वाद हमें गांधी जी के त्याग भाव और सेवा भाव को बार-बार याद दिलाता है। आज स्वच्छता और पर्यावरण की शुद्धता और सुरक्षा की माँग सर्वोपरि हो गई है। भारत देश में आज 'नमामि गंगे' और प्रधानमंत्री मोदी जी के स्वच्छता अभियान में गांधीजी के सपने साकार हो रहे है। देश और दुनिया में लगातार बढ़ती हुई प्रदूषण समस्या का हल भी गांधीजी के विचारों में खोजा जा सकता है। श्रमदान, शाकाहार, उपवास, प्रार्थना, आस्तिकता, आशावादिता, राष्ट्रप्रेम, सर्वधर्म समभाव के विचारों की आज के समय में सख्त जरूरत है।

अंत में हम कह सकते हैं कि गांधीजी मानवता के सच्चे साधक थे। उनके नैतिक और मानवीय मूल्य आज भी प्रासंगिक हैं। बल्कि कहे कि मानव जीवन को स्वस्थ एवं सुखद बनाने के लिए गांधी जी के विचारों एवं आदर्शों का अनुपालन आज अनिवार्य हो गया है। गांधी जी की सेवा वृति, स्वच्छता, सत्य-अहिंसा और नैतिकता क्रमशः राष्ट्र प्रेम, विश्व शांति, मानव प्रेम, प्रकृति प्रेम और मानववाद को शाश्वत बनाते हैं। 'वसुधैव कुटुंबकम' और विश्व शांति का संदेश भारत देश की पहचान है। गांधीजी इसी महान परंपरा को वर्तमान और भविष्य से जोड़ते देखना चाहते हैं। यही गांधीजी के राम राज्य की अवधारणा है और मानवता की प्रतीक है।

संदर्भ सूची

1. महात्मा गाँधी के विचार, पृ. 13
2. टू द स्टूडेंट्स, पृ. 62
3. हरि; 24-12-1938, पृ. 393
4. यंग, 23-12-1921, पृ. 59
5. हरि; 17-11-1946, पृ. 404
6. महात्मा गाँधी के विचार, पृ. 253
7. यंग, 17-9-1925, पृ. 320
8. महात्मा गाँधी के विचार, पृ. 474-75
9. यंग, 22-12-1927, पृ. 427-28
10. आत्मकथा, पृ. 261
11. वही, पृ. 373
12. वही, पृ. 217
13. वही, पृ. 359-60
14. वही, पृ. 264
15. वही, पृ. 183
16. वही, पृ. 144
17. वही, पृ. 145
18. हरि; 17-11-1933, पृ. 5-6
19. महात्मा गाँधी के विचार, पृ. 435
20. वही, पृ. 445
21. हरि; 7-7-1946, पृ. 212
22. महात्मा गाँधी के विचार, पृ. 435-36

21

भारतीय राष्ट्रवाद में गांधीवादी मूल्यों की भूमिका

संजय कुमार एवं रीटा जैन

गांधी जी के राष्ट्रवाद से सम्बंधित जो भी विचार मिलते हैं वो उनके सामाजिक,आर्थिक और राजनीतिक चिंतन में ही परिलक्षित होते हैं।महात्मा गांधी के राष्ट्रवाद संबंधी विचारों में व्यक्ति और मानवतावाद को ज्यादा महत्ता दी गई है। उनके अनुसार राष्ट्रीयता और मानवता एक–दूसरे के पर्याय हैं।उनका राज़्ट्रवाद "वसुधैव कुटुम्बकम" के दर्शन पर आधारित होने के कारण अंतर्राष्ट्रीयवाद के साथ भी घनिष्टता से जुड़ा हुआ है। उन्होंने साधन और साध्य की पवित्रता, अहिंसा और अपरिग्रह को अपनाते हुए विश्व बंधुता एवं शांति के लिए सकारात्मक तथा व्यावहारिक पक्ष को सबके सामने रखा। गांधीजी का राष्ट्रवाद पश्चिम की संकीर्ण राष्ट्रवाद की अवधारणा से सर्वथा भिन्न था। उनका राष्ट्रवाद समावेशी था न कि अनन्य। उनके राष्ट्रवादी विचारों में अहिंसा, सत्याग्रह, स्वराज और स्वदेशी के साथ–साथ स्वावलंबन और स्वानुशासन पर अधिक बल था। गांधीजी के राष्ट्रवाद में "सर्व जन हिताय सर्व जन सुखाय" का भाव निहित था। गांधी जी के राष्ट्रवाद को उनके सम्पूर्ण दर्शन को समझे बिना समझना कठिन हैं। गांधी जी ने राष्ट्र को प्रजा के साथ जोड़कर देखा एवं इन्हें एक–दूसरे का पर्याय माना। यह कहा जा सकता है कि उन्होंने राज़्ट्रवाद की व्याख्या भारतीय संस्कृति एवं सभ्यता के व्यापक संदर्भों में की थी।

गांधी जी उस प्रचलित धारणा को अस्वीकार करते हैं, जिसमें भारत को अंग्रेजी शासन के अधीन रहते हुए एक राष्ट्र के रूप में आकार लेते हुए बताया गया है। गांधी जी इस धारणा को भारतीय इतिहास की अंग्रेजी व्याख्या बताते हुए अस्वीकार कर देते हैं और हिंद स्वराज (1909) में वे इस संदर्भ में कहते हैं कि "मैं इसे गलत मानता हूँ। अंग्रेजों ने हमें सिखाया है कि हम पहले एक राष्ट्र नहीं थे और हमें एक राष्ट्र बनने में कई सदियाँ लगेंगी। यह आधारहीन है। हम उनके भारत आने से पहले एक राष्ट्र थे। हमें प्रेरित करने वाला विचार एक था। हमारे जीवन

जीने का तरीका एक जैसा था। हम एक राज़्ट्र थे यह इसलिए भी सत्य है; क्योंकि हम एक साम्राज्य की स्थापना करने में सक्षम थे। इसके बाद उन्होंने हमें विभाजित किया है।" महात्मा गांधी भारत को एक राष्ट्र के रूप में देखते हैं, और उनका यह दावा दो मान्यताओं पर आधारित है: पहली यह है कि प्राचीन भारतीय सभ्यता में विविधता और बहुलता को समायोजित करने की क्षमता है और दूसरी यह है कि प्राचीन भारत में संतों द्वारा तीर्थ के लिए कुछ निश्चित स्थानों की स्थापना ने अखिल भारतीय चेतना के विकास का आधार रखा था। गांधी जी कहते हैं कि उत्तर में हरिद्वार और दक्षिण में रामेश्वरम और पूर्व में जगन्नाथ जैसे तीर्थस्थल केवल धार्मिक लाभ के लिए ही नहीं, बल्कि 'एक विशाल क्षेत्र में बिखरे भारतीयों के बीच आम पहचान की भावना पैदा करने और बनाए रखने के लिए भी स्थापित किए गए थे। उन्होंने (संतों ने) देखा कि भारत प्राकृतिक रूप से एक अविभाजित भूमि है। इसलिए उनका यह तर्क था कि यह एक राष्ट्र होना चाहिए। उन्होंने इसी तरह का तर्क प्रस्तुत करते हुए भारत के विभिन्न हिस्सों में पवित्र स्थानों की स्थापना की और लोगों में राष्ट्रीयता के इस तरह के विशेष भाव को प्रस्फुटित किया; जिससे दुनिया अभी तक अनभिज्ञ थी।' गांधीजी का मानना था कि भारत की ताकत इसकी विविधता में एकता की संस्कृति में ही बसती है।

महात्मा गांधी जी का भारत के राष्ट्रवादी आन्दोलनों में योगदान

दक्षिणी अफ्रीका से भारत आने के बाद गांधी जी ने अपने राज़्ट्रवादी आन्दोलनों में सत्याग्रह, अहिंसा और अनुनय-विनय को साधन बनाया। अपने राजनीतिक गुरु गोपाल कृज़्ण गोखले के निर्देशन में उन्होंने भारत की मौजूदा राजनीतिक और सामाजिक स्थिति को समझा। गांधी जी ने भारत में राष्ट्रवादी अभियान का शंखनादचम्पारण के आन्दोलन से किया और "भारत छोड़ो" आन्दोलन का नेतृत्त्व करते हुए अंततः अंग्रेजों को भारत छोड़ने पर बाध्य करने में अहम भूमिका निभायी। महात्मा गांधी द्वारा 1917 का चंपारण सत्याग्रह भारत में उनका पहला सत्याग्रह आंदोलन था। इस सत्याग्रह ने अंग्रेजी शासन के सामने उनके आगमन को चिह्नित किया। इसके बाद खेड़ा जिले के किसानों के समर्थन में1918 में खेड़ा सत्याग्रह की शुरुआत की। इस सत्याग्रह में महात्मा गांधी गुजरात के खेड़ा नामक जिले में फसल खराब होने और प्लेग की महामारी फैलने के बावजूद अंग्रेजों द्वारा लगाए गए उच्च करों का विरोध कर रहे थे। गांधीजी द्वारा जलियांवाला बाग नरसंहार के बाद1920 से फरवरी 1922 तक अहिंसक साधनों से भारत में ब्रिटिश शासन का विरोध करने के उद्देश्य से असहयोग आन्दोलन चलाया। गाँधीजी के नेतृत्व में 1930 में सविनय अवज्ञा आन्दोलन की शुरुआत और अंग्रेजों के जन विरोधी नमक कानून के विरोध में प्रसिद्ध दांडी यात्रा की भी देश के राज़्ट्रीय आन्दोलन में उल्लेखनीय भूमिका रही है। महात्मा गाँधी ने क्रिप्स मिशन की विफलता के बाद अंग्रेजी सत्ता के खिलाफ अपना तीसरा बड़ा आंदोलन शुरू करने का निर्णय लिया। 8 अगस्त 1942 को कांग्रेस की अखिल भारतीय समिति के बम्बई अधिवेशन में "अंग्रेजों भारत छोड़ो" नाम से आन्दोलन का सूत्रपात हुआ; जिसका मुख्य लक्ष्य

भारत से अंग्रेजी सत्ता को समाप्त करना था। इसी आंदोलन के दौरान गांधीजी ने प्रसिद्ध ''करो या मरो'' का नारा दिया था।

गांधी जी के "राम-राज्य" की संकल्पना

गांधी जी के आदर्श राज्य की संकल्पना उनके "राम-राज्य" में ही विद्यमान थी। गाँधी जी का लक्ष्य राम के समान नैतिक जीवन जीने का था, क्योंकि राम उनके लिए नैतिक मर्यादा का स्रोत भी थे। राम राज्य को स्पष्ट करते हुए वे कहते हैं कि–'कुछ मित्र राम-राज्य का अक्षरार्थ करते हुए पूछते हैं कि जब तक राम और दशरथ फिर से जन्म नहीं लेते तब तक क्या रामराज्य मिल सकता है? हम तो राम-राज्य का अर्थ स्वराज्य, धर्मराज्य, लोकराज्य से करते हैं। वैसा राज्य तो तभी संभव है जब जनता धर्मनिष्ठ और वीर्यवान बने।" गांधी जी का स्वराज राम-राज्य ही था। गांधीजी के राम-राज्य में आर्थिक असमानता का कोई स्थान नहीं है। वे पूंजीवादी व्यवस्था में निहित आर्थिक विषमता को राम-राज्य के लिए चुनौती मानते थे। उनका मानना था कि शासक वर्ग के लोग, जमींदार वर्ग और पूंजीपति वर्ग मात्र न्यासी (ट्रस्टी) के रूप में कार्य करें। और यदि वे ऐसा नहीं करेंगे तो समय के साथ उनका अंत निश्चित है। महात्मा गांधी का मत था कि जब ग्राम-स्वराज (पंचायती राज) की स्थापना होगी तो लोकमत के सामने सबको झुकना पड़ेगा और सच्चे अर्थों में स्वराज की स्थापना होगी। गांधी जी समाजवाद के उसके जबरदस्ती थोपने और ईश्वर में विश्वास नहीं करने के लक्षण को अस्वीकार करते हैं। इस प्रकार गांधी जी का राम-राज्य मानवतावाद और नैतिकता पर आधारित है।

स्वानुशासन पर गांधी जी की संकल्पना

महात्मा गांधी की सोच थी कि एक अनुशासित राष्ट्र ही अपने लक्ष्यों की प्राप्ति कर सकता है। अनुशासित राज्ट्र के लिए यह जरूरी है कि वहाँ के नागरिक आत्मानुशासित हों। यह सार्वभौमिक रूप से माना जाता है कि दूसरों को संदेश देने से पहले स्वयं को सख्त आत्म अनुशासन का पालन करते हुए पूर्ण आत्म शुद्धि और आत्म परिवर्तन की प्रक्रिया से गुजरना चाहिए। आत्मप्रेरित अनुशासन ही मानवीय मूल्यों के लिए जगह बना पाता है। अनुशासन पर गांधी जी की अवधारणा आत्म-नियंत्रण पर आधारित है। आत्म-अनुशासन में आत्म-नियंत्रण से संबंधित तीन पहलू शामिल हैं-प्रलोभन का प्रतिरोध करने की क्षमता, संतुष्टि के विलंब को सहन करने का सामर्थ्य और स्वयं पर सिद्धि के सख्त मानकों को लागू करना। इस तरह का आत्म-अनुशासन गांधी जी के चरित्र परिवर्तन की शिक्षा की पहचान बन गया। उन्होंने आत्म-अनुशासन को विभिन्न अभ्यासों जैसे कि प्रार्थना, प्रतिज्ञा, उपवास और स्वीकारोक्ति के माध्यम से हासिल किया। उन्हीं के शब्दों में ''भारत का नेतृत्व करने का आह्वान मुझे अचानक महसूस नहीं हुआ। इसके लिए मैं उपवास और आत्म-अनुशासन के द्वारा तैयार हुआ हूँ।" गांधी जी ने अपने जीवन में तमाम गुणों में सबसे ज्यादा जोर अनुशासन पर दिया है। गांधी जी का

कहना था कि हर तरह के अनुशासनों का बराबर महत्व है। अगर इनमें से एक भी टूटा, तो सभी टूट जायेंगे। इसलिए यह आवश्यक है कि सभी अनुशासनों को एक समान माना जाए। यही ब्रह्मचर्य के पूर्ण अर्थ और महत्व को समझने में सक्षम बनाता है। ब्रह्मचर्य का मतलब है–हर तरह की इंद्रियों पर काबू पाना। अगर कोई मनुष्य सिर्फ एक इंद्री को काबू करने का प्रयास करता है, और अन्य सभी को स्वतंत्र छोड़ देता है, तो उसके सभी प्रयास व्यर्थ हो जाते हैं। इस संदर्भ में गांधी जी का कहना था कि "कानों से विचारोत्तेजक कहानियां सुनते समय, आंखों से उत्तेजक जगह देखते समय, जीभ से स्वादिष्ट भोजन का स्वाद लेते समय और हाथों से रोमांचक चीजों को छूते समय शेष इन्द्रियों को काबू करने की अपेक्षा करना, ठीक वैसा ही है जैसा आग में हाथ डालना और नहीं जलने की उम्मीद करना।" इस प्रकार गांधी जी कहते हैं कि हर प्रकार का अनुशासन आपस में एक-दूसरे से जुड़ा हुआ है। उनका मानना था कि किसी भी काम को अनुशासित रूप से पूरा किया जाए, तो उसमें कम समय में बेहतर नतीजे निकाले जा सकते हैं। सत्य, अहिंसा और आत्म अनुशासन संबंधी विचारों से गांधी जी पर आदर्शवाद की स्पष्ट छाप दिखाई देती है।

निष्कर्ष

गांधी जी के राष्ट्रवाद को उनके अहिंसा, स्वराज, सत्याग्रह, स्वदेशी और सर्वोदय के दर्शन में देखा जा सकता है। गांधी जी भी विवेकानंद और अरबिंदो की तरह इस बात को स्वीकार करते हैं कि आत्मानुभूति या आध्यात्मिक मोक्ष हेतु प्रयत्न करना मनुष्य के स्वभाव में है। महात्मा गांधी का यह भी मत था कि जब तक समाज में व्यक्ति का आध्यात्मिक या नैतिक बदलाव नहीं होगा; उस समय तक राजनीतिक स्वाधीनता अपने आप में अधूरी है। इस प्रकार वे न केवल नैतिक प्रगति पर जोर देते हैं, बल्कि गुलाम मानसिकता के निर्मूलन की भी वकालत करते हैं। गांधी जी का राष्ट्र स्वावलंबी और स्वानुशासित होगा। अर्थात गांधीजी का राष्ट्र राम-राज्य पर आधारित होगा।

संदर्भ सूची

1. मोहनदास कर्मचन्द गांधी, हिन्द स्वराज, 1909
2. एस.एल. नागोरी, कान्ता नागोरी, भारत का राष्ट्रीय आन्दोलन तथा संवैधानिक विकास : 1935 से 1950 तक
3. सम्पूर्ण गांधी वांग्मय (1958), प्रकाशन विभाग, सूचना एवं प्रसारण मंत्रालय, भारत सरकार
4. एम. के. गांधी, महात्मा गांधी के संगृहित ग्रन्थ, नई दिल्ली, प्रकाशन विभाग, सूचना और प्रसारण मंत्रालय, भारत सरकार वॉल्यूम 48
5. मीरा को बापू के पत्र

22
स्वाध्याय : युवा संस्कृति

अर्चना गौड़

गाँधी एक शख्सियत नहीं अपितु पूरा युग है। इस युग को हिंदी साहित्य के भक्तिकाल से तुलना करते हुए गाँधी का स्वर्णयुग कहने में कोई अतिशयोक्ति नहीं होगी। आज जब देश और लोकतंत्र जाति, वर्ण, धर्म में तेजी से बँटे जा रहे हैं; वहाँ गाँधी का एक विचार वाक्य विचारणीय है, "अपने मन का राज्य स्वराज्य है।"[1] इस विचार-वाक्य की आज के समय में प्रसंगगत अनिवार्यता है। सही मायनों में इस विचार-वाक्य में आये तीन शब्द अत्यंत महत्वपूर्ण हैं जिसे समझना जरूरी जान पड़ता है। पहला-मन, दूसरा-राज्य या राज, तीसरा-स्वराज्य। यदि पुराणों और गीता पर एक दृष्टि डाली जाय तो वहाँ मन को चंचल बताया गया है। मन को शरीर रूपी रथ में सारथी का स्थान दिया गया है, जो जब जैसे चाहे घोड़े की लगाम को खींच कर अपने अनुरूप यात्रा कर सकता है। लेकिन मन को निर्देशित करने वाला है कौन? मन को निर्देशित कौन करेगा? मन के अनुसार चलना ही क्या मन का राज्य है? क्या मन पर राज्य करने का अर्थ मनमानी है? जैसा चाहेंगे वैसा कार्य किया जाना ही मन पर राज्य किये जाने का अर्थ है। या फिर कर्तव्य बोध को जान कर, समझ कर विचार करके पूर्ण दृढ़ता के साथ कर्तव्य निर्वाह हेतु कर्तव्य पालन करना ही; जीवन यापन करना ही सही अर्थों में मन का राज्य है। गीता के अध्याय दो के 32 श्लोक में कहा गया है:-

सुखदु:खे समे कष्ट्त्वा लाभालाभौ जयाजयौ।
ततो युद्धाय युज्यस्व नैवं पापमवाप्स्यसि ॥38॥

अर्थात् :- सुख और दुख से छूटने के लिए भाव और बुद्धि दो मुख्य आधार स्तम्भ हैं। कर्तव्य बोध को सही दृष्टि से आँकने और उसका पालन करने वाला महत्वपूर्ण विचार है। यदि जीव फल की चिंता में पड़ जाता है; तो कर्म में निकृष्टता का प्रभाव जुड़ जाता है।[2]

यदि व्यक्ति मन से स्वकर्म में लग जाता है; तो सम्पूर्ण ब्रहमाण्ड उसे पूरा करने के लिए उसके अनुकूल हो जाता है। जिस प्रकार राम से मिलने की इच्छा शक्ति से भरत द्वारा नंगे पाँव पड़ना और उनकी व्याकुलता के भाव को समझ कर प्रकृति द्वारा हवा का मन्द गति शीतल प्रवाह से बहना, पेड़ों द्वारा छाया प्रदान करना, सरिता का मंथर गति से प्रवाहित होना ऐसा जान पड़ता है; मानो भरत की सुख-दुख की तीव्रता की अनुभूति कर सम्पूर्ण सृष्टि भरत को मंतव्य तक पहुँचने में सहायक सिद्ध हो रही हो:-

किए जाहि छाया जलद सुखद बहद बर बात
तस मगु भयउ न राम कह जस जा भरतहि जात[3]

रामचरितमानस और गीता में स्वधर्म के आचरण पर बल दिया गया। स्वधर्म पालन के लिये जिस देह-धर्म, निष्ठा एवम पवित्रता की आवश्यकता है; वह सुख और दुख को समान समझने से आती हैं। ये सम भाव ही है जो पूर्ण इच्छाशक्ति के साथ कर्तव्य निष्ठा का पालन करते हैं। वही मन का राज्य है। गाँधी के नजरिये से देखें तो ऐसा राज ही स्वराज्य है। स्व-स्वयं पर राज कर सके।

पर प्रश्न यह है कि क्या मन पर राज्य करना सरल है? इस प्रश्न को गाँधीजी ने निरूतर नहीं छोड़ा है। "धर्म की समस्या" में वे कहते हैं कि कर्तव्य का बोध सदा दीपक की भाँति स्पष्ट नहीं होता।"[4] बोअर युद्ध में हिस्सा लेने पर पोलक जैसे कई मित्रों ने प्रश्न ही नहीं उठाये बल्कि तार भेज कर आपत्ति जताई। पर गाँधी ने माना "युद्ध में शामिल होना मैंने धर्म माना। और आज भी उसका विचार करता हूँ तो मुझे अपनी विचार धारा में कोई दोष दिखाई नहीं देता। ब्रिटिश साम्राज्य के बारे में जो विचार थे उसका अनुसरण करते हुये मैने युद्ध कार्य में योग दिया, उसका मुझे पछतावा भी नहीं।"[5]

इस प्रकार जहाँ दृष्टि स्पष्ट हो, जहाँ करनी के पीछे पछतावा न हो, विचारधारा दोष मुक्त हो, कर्तव्य बोध की स्पष्टता हो, तीव्र इच्छाशक्ति हो, सुख दुख के प्रति सम् भाव हो, कर्म के प्रतिफल की कामना न हो, विशुद्ध कर्म हो; तो सम्पूर्ण ब्रहमाण्ड उसे पूरा करने में आपके समक्ष सहायक बन कर खड़ा होता है।

गाँधीजी के इस विचार-वाक्य की प्रासंगिकता स्पष्ट है। आज की युवा संस्कृति के परिवर्तित स्वरूप को गाँधी जी यदि देखते और जान पाते कि राम, अर्जुन, एकलव्य की धरती पर आज का युवा वर्ग भ्रमित, निस्तेजता, हतोत्साहित, कुपोषित, नशे का सेवक, धुँए में गारत करता जीवन यापन, मार्गदर्शक अपेक्षित जान पड़ता है। इस कारण ही मन के वशीभूत होकर मदिरापान का सेवन, चाऊमीन और पिज़्ज़ा की होड़, नॉर्थ ईस्ट के दूरदराज इलाकों के पहाड़ी गांव में भी मैगी और कोल्ड ड्रिंक के दीवाने एक सा खाना के व्यापार और उसके बाजार के आधीन होते जा रहे हैं। रातों को जागना, सुबह जल्दी न उठ पाना, मोबाइल, स्मार्टफोन, फेसबुक, इंस्टाग्राम, व्हाट्सएप ये सभी मन के वशीभूत होने का जीता जागता उदाहरण है। आज के युवा

वर्ग ने निर्णय की जिम्मेदारी स्वयं ना लेकर मार्गदर्शक पर छोड़ दी है। उन्हें आज काउंसलर की जरूरत है। निरंतर राह दिखाने वाले माता-पिता की आवश्यकता है। वह अपने रास्ते की जिम्मेदारी भी स्वयं नहीं लेना चाहता; जिसके वशीभूत स्ट्रेस, डिप्रेशन, एंजाइटी उसके जीवन में अपना महत्वपूर्ण स्थान बना चुके हैं। कर्म से पहले फल के विषय में सोच कर हतोत्साहित होना निराशा को जन्म देती हैं; जिसके कारण आत्महत्या का निर्णय ले लिया जाता है। ''हिंदुस्तान टाइम्स की 8 मई 2017 की एक रिपोर्ट के अनुसार प्रति घंटे में एक युवा आत्महत्या कर रहा है। 2010 से लेकर 2015 तक 39000 775 युवाओं ने आत्महत्या कर ली थी। भारत युवाओं का देश है। 2012 में अंतर्राष्ट्रीय विज्ञान पत्रिका लांसेट के अनुसार 15 से 29 वर्ष के आयु वर्ग में आत्महत्या करने वालों में भारत सबसे आगे है।[6]

आखिरकार ऐसा क्या है, जो हमारे युवा संस्कृति में नकारात्मक ऊर्जा प्रवाहित हो रही है जोकि निरंतर युवाओं में नकारात्मक सोच पैदा कर रही है प्रत्येक युवा किसी न किसी मानसिक दबाव का शिकार हैं। प्रेम की असफलता–ब्रेकअप उसे इतना मजबूर कर देता है कि वह आत्महत्या करने को उतारू हो जाता है। प्रतिदिन समाचार पत्रों में युवाओं के आत्महत्या करने की बढ़ती खबरें मन में आशंका पैदा करती है कि भारत का भावी भविष्य और संस्कृति किस ओर जाएंगे? आज इंटरनेट जाल ने युवा हृदय में आशा-अशांत भ्रम फैला दिया है। इस भ्रम जाल में स्मार्टफोन पर अपडेट बने रहने की अजीब प्रवृत्ति है। विशाल जाल, पब्जी और ब्लू व्हेल जैसे अजीब से खेलों ने युवा वर्ग की एक अलग ही काल्पनिक दुनिया खड़ी कर दी है। इस मीडिया इंटरनेट का विशाल जाल हमारे युवाओं को अंधे कुएं में धकेल रहा है। टेलीविजन को यूंही स्टुपिड बॉक्स नहीं कह दिया गया है। उसके काल्पनिक धारावाहिक भ्रम पैदा करने वाली खबरें नाहक ही युवाओं में नकारात्मक ऊर्जा का संचार कर रही हैं।''

Why would you expose yourself to so much nagative? Don't expose yourself to much of the garbage that is our there on t.v substitude your habit of watching T.V for a healthier habit like taking a walk, speeding more time with your family or readign a good book xxxx Don't watch the news for a week and see how you feel[7]

आज के समय में कठिनाई यह है कि हमारे युवा उपवास की संस्कृति के महत्व को सही रूप में जानने की इच्छा ही नहीं रखते। वे उपवास से अर्थ मात्र भोजन का उपवास मानते हैं; मन के उपवास की महत्ता को भूलते जा रहे हैं। यदि आज का युवा उपवास के महत्व को जान ले और यह उपवास भोजन का ना होकर मन का हो; तो बहुत बड़े पैमाने पर सकारात्मक ऊर्जा का संचरण होने की संभावना दिखाई देती है। यदि एक दिन स्मार्टफोन का उपवास ले, टीवी का उपवास ले, काम क्रोध का उपवास लें, निराशा और अवसाद का उपवास ले, एंजाइटी का उपवास ले, उसके स्थान पर प्रकृति से जुडे योग के महत्व को जानते हुए योग, प्राणायाम और साधना से जुड़े, स्वाध्याय और इच्छाशक्ति से जुड़े कर्म के फल से न जोड़कर कर्तव्यनिष्ठा से जुड़े–तो मन का राज्य संभव है। स्वयं गांधी जी ने कहा है ''अगर शरीर उपवास के साथ मन

का उपवास ना हो तो दंभ में परिवर्तित हो जाता है और हानिकारक सिद्ध होता है।[8]"

इसके साथ ही अगर युवा मनमानी की जगह मन का राज करे तो निसंदेह अपने कर्म के प्रति सावधान होकर यदि सच्चे मन से एक बार स्वयं से यह पूछ ले कि जो अपनी मनमानी से मैं कर रहा हूं। उसकी मुझे क्या कीमत चुकानी होगी? क्या मेरे परिवार, समाज और राष्ट्र के हित में यह है, तो उसे स्वयं उत्तर मिल जाएगा। उसकी नकारात्मक शक्ति सकारात्मक ऊर्जा में परिवर्तित हो जाएगी। आज का युवा यदि गांधी के विचार-वाक्य "अपने राज्य का, अपने मन का राज्य स्वराज्य है" को अपना ले; तो संपूर्ण ऊर्जा सकारात्मक होगी।

संदर्भ

1. गीताज्ञान : दीनानाथ दिनेश
2. रामचरितमानस : गीता प्रेस बुक
3. सत्य के प्रयोग : आत्मकथा गाँधी
4. हिन्द स्वराज : नवजीवन प्रकाशन मन्दिर, अहमदाबाद
5. 30 days change your habits, change your life

23

स्वराज पर गांधी के विचार : वर्तमान प्रासंगिकता

लाजपत राय

स्वराज पर चर्चा भारत के स्वतंत्रता संग्राम के समय से लेकर आज तक जारी है। उस दौरान बाल गंगाधर तिलक के शब्द 'स्वराज मेरा जन्मसिद्ध अधिकार है और मैं इसे लेकर रहूंगा।' इस नारे ने तब के स्वतंत्रता संग्राम के सेनानियों को जोश से भर दिया था। लेकिन जहाँ तिलक को उग्र दल के मुख्य नेताओं में एक क्रांतिकारी माना जाता था और उनके विचार कहीं-न-कहीं उग्रता के प्रतीक थे तथा राजनीतिक स्वतंत्रता के अर्थ में स्वराज की बात नहीं करते थे; बल्कि उनका स्वराज्य अध्यात्म तथा बहुआयामी स्वरूप वाला था।

गांधी यह सोचते थे कि अगर राष्ट्रीय संघर्ष कामयाब हो जाता है और स्वराज हासिल हो जाता है, तब भारत कैसा होगा? अगर हिंसक समूह अपने तरीकों से विजय हासिल कर लेते हैं, तो सत्ता प्राप्ति के बाद वे अपने लोगों के खिलाफ भी बल प्रयोग के समान तरीके अपनाएगें। दूसरी ओर मध्यमार्गियों की 'याचक' प्रवृत्तियाँ कोई नतीजा देने नहीं जा रही थी क्योंकि उनसे ब्रिटिश शासकों पर कोई असर नहीं पड़ने वाला था। इसका मतलब यह था कि कुल मिलाकर संघर्ष का इकलौता संभव तरीका था–कानूनों की शांतिपूर्ण ढंग से अवमानना, या सविनय अवज्ञा, जिसे गांधी जी ने हाल ही में 'सत्याग्रह' का नाम दिया था। नैतिक शुचिता का अनुपालन करने वाले नेताओं के आह्वान से एक बार जनता जुड़ जाए, तो इसका मतलब कामयाब होना तय था। इससे आश्वस्त होने के बाद गांधी जी ने खुलकर यह सवाल उठाया कि ऐसे साधनों से सफलता मिलने के बाद क्या होना चाहिए।''[1]

गांधी इस बात को जानते थे कि अंग्रेजी राज के साम्राज्यवादी और विनाशकारी नीतियों के कारण भारतीयों में घोर निराशा थी। गांधी इस बात से भी अवगत थे कि अंग्रेजी साम्राज्य को रातों-रात हिंसा के रास्ते से समाप्त नहीं किया जा सकता। गांधी का यह भी मानना था कि स्वतंत्रता तो अवश्य मिलेगी, लेकिन उस स्वतंत्रता के बाद कैसा स्वराज्य होगा? यहीं पर गांधी

के स्वराज्य से जुड़े विचारों से यह स्पष्ट हो जायेगा कि केवल राजनीतिक स्वराज्य नहीं बल्कि स्वतंत्रता के बाद सभी भारतवासियों के लिए कैसा स्वराज्य होगा, यह स्पष्ट कर देना चाहते थे।

स्वराज्य पर गांधी विचारों से सहज ही यह समझ आ जाता है कि गांधी हिन्दुस्तानियों को अपनी सभ्यता पर गर्व करना, उसमें जो समायोजन की भावना है उसे आत्मसात करना, आपसी प्रेम, भाईचारे और अहिंसा आदि की ओर वे तत्कालीन भारतीयों को प्रेरित करना चाहते थे।

आइये, स्वराज पर गांधी के विचारों को क्रमवार समझने का प्रयास करें:

स्वराज्य और सभ्यता

गांधी के अनुसार, "अगर स्वराज्य का अर्थ हमें सभ्य बनाना और हमारी सभ्यता को अधिक शुद्ध तथा मजबूत बनाना न हो, तो वह किसी कीमत का नहीं होगा। हमारी सभ्यता का मूल तत्व ही यह है कि हम अपने सब कामों में, फिर वे निजी हों या सार्वजनिक, नीति के पालन को सर्वोच्च स्थान देते हैं।"[2]

आत्म संयम पर आधारित स्वराज्य

गांधी अपने जीवन में नैतिक मूल्यों को बहुत ऊँचा स्थान देते थे। स्वराज्य का अर्थ स्पष्ट करते हुए गांधी लिखते हैं, "स्वराज्य एक पवित्र शब्द है। वह एक वैदिक शब्द है, जिसका अर्थ आत्मशासन और आत्म-संयम है। अंग्रेजी शब्द 'इंडिपेंडेन्स' अक्सर सब प्रकार की मर्यादाओं से मुक्त निरंकुश आजादी का या स्वच्छंदता का अर्थ देता है। वह अर्थ स्वराज्य शब्द में नहीं है।"[3]

राष्ट्र की भलाई पर आधारित स्वराज्य

गांधी के स्वराज्य में राष्ट्र की भलाई का ध्यान रखना परम आवश्यक था। गांधी लिखते हैं, "स्वराज्य की रक्षा केवल वहीं हो सकती है, जहाँ देशवासियों की ज्यादा बड़ी संख्या ऐसे देशभक्तों की हो, जिनके लिए दूसरी सब चीजों से अपने निजी लाभ से भी देश की भलाई का ज्यादा महत्व हो। स्वराज्य का अर्थ है देश की बहुसंख्यक जनता का शासन। जाहिर है कि जहाँ बहुसंख्यक जनता नीति भ्रष्ट हो या स्वार्थी हो, वहाँ उसकी सरकार अराजकता की ही स्थिति पैदा कर सकती है, दूसरा कुछ नहीं।"[4]

गरीबों का स्वराज्य

गांधी के स्वराज्य में अंतिम पंक्ति में खड़े गरीब व्यक्ति का भी महत्वपूर्ण स्थान था तथा वह कैसे प्रगति कर सकता है; इसका ध्यान रखने पर गांधी का बहुत जोर था। गांधी के ही शब्दों में, "मैं तुम्हें एक मंत्र दूँगा जब भी शंका हो अथवा अहं बहुत बढ़ जाये तब निम्नलिखित कसौटी अपनायें। किसी अत्यन्त गरीब और कमजोर आदमी का चेहरा याद करो, और अपने आप

से प्रश्न करो कि जो कदम उठाने का विचार कर रहे हो, वह उस व्यक्ति के लिए उपयोगी होगा अथवा नहीं? क्या उससे उसे कोई लाभ होगा? क्या उससे वह पुनः उस स्थिति में आ सकेगा कि अपने जीवन और अपने भाग्य को नियंत्रित कर पाये? दूसरे शब्दों में, क्या तुम्हारे कार्य से कोटि-कोटि भूखे और आध्यात्मिक रूप से वंचित लोगों को स्वराज्य मिल सकेगा? तब तुम देखोगे कि तुम्हारी सारी शंकाएँ और तुम्हारा अहं दूर हो जायेगा।[5]

स्वराज्य में गरीबों की स्थिति को और स्पष्ट करते हुए गांधी लिखते है, ''मेरे सपने का स्वराज्य तो गरीबों का स्वराज्य होगा। जीवन की जिन आवश्यकताओं का उपयोग राजा और अमीर लोग करते हैं, वही तुम्हें भी सुलभ होनी चाहिए। इसमें फर्क के लिए कोई स्थान नहीं हो सकता। लेकिन इसका यह अर्थ नहीं कि हमारे पास उनके जैसे महल होने चाहिए। सुखी जीवन के लिए महलों की कोई आवश्यकता नहीं। हमें महलों में रख दिया जाए तो हम घबरा जाएँ। लेकिन तुम्हें जीवन की वे सामान्य सुविधाएँ अवश्य मिलनी चाहिए, जिसका उपभोग अमीर आदमी करता है। मुझे इस बात में बिल्कुल भी सन्देह नहीं है कि हमारा स्वराज्य तब तक पूर्ण स्वराज्य नहीं होगा, जब तक वह तुम्हें ये सारी सुविधाएँ देने की पूरी व्यवस्था नहीं कर देता।''[6]

गांधी की कथनी और करनी में कोई अन्तर नहीं होता था। जब वे गरीब की बात करते थे तो वह केवल एक उपदेश नहीं होता था। वह स्वयं अपने जीवन के उदाहरणों द्वारा संदेश देते रहते थे। उदाहरण के लिए हम देख सकते हैं कि दक्षिण अफ्रीका से भारत वापस आने के बाद भारत को समझने के लिए जब उन्होंने भारत भ्रमण किया और यह पाया कि भारत में अत्यन्त गरीबी है; तब गांधी ने स्वयं को गरीबी और कम से कम जरूरतों का अभ्यास करना शुरू कर दिया। उनके चित्रों में उनके द्वारा पहने गये कपड़ों तथा निजी उदाहरणों से यह आसानी से समझा जा सकता है।

विविधता पर आधारित स्वराज्य

गांधी यह जानते थे कि भारत विविधता में एकता वाला राष्ट्र है और हजारों वर्षों से अलग-अलग लोग मिल-जुलकर रहते आये हैं। गांधी लिखते हैं, ''स्वराज्य में जाति आदि भेदों का कोई स्थान नहीं हो सकता। उस पर शिक्षितों या धनवानों का एकाधिपत्य नहीं होगा। वह स्वराज सबके लिए-सबके कल्याण के लिए होगा। सबकी गिनती में किसान तो आते ही हैं; शरीर से लाचार और भूख से मरने वाले लाखों-करोड़ों मेहनतकश मजदूर भी अवश्य आते हैं''[7] अर्थात् गांधी की नजर में नागरिकों की गरिमा अत्यन्त महत्वपूर्ण स्थान रखती है। चाहे वह व्यक्ति छोटे से छोटे पद या स्तर का हो।

सत्य पर आधारित स्वराज्य

गांधी अपने जीवन में सत्य को सर्वोपरि स्थान देते थे। उन्हीं के शब्दों में, ''मेरी कल्पना का स्वराज्य तभी आएगा; जब हमारे मन में यह बात अच्छी तरह जम जाए कि हमें अपना

स्वराज्य सत्य अहिंसा के शुद्ध साधनों द्वारा ही हासिल करना है, उन्हीं के द्वारा हमें उनका संचालन करना है और उन्हीं के द्वारा हमें उसे कायम रखना है। सच्ची लोकसत्ता या जनता का स्वराज्य कभी भी असत्यमय और हिंसक साधनों से नहीं आ सकता। कारण स्पष्ट और सीध ा है : यदि असत्यमय और हिंसक उपायों का प्रयोग किया गया, तो उसका स्वाभाविक परिणाम यह होगा कि सारा विरोध या तो विरोधियों को दबाकर या उनका नाश करके खत्म कर दिया जाएगा। ऐसी स्थिति में वैयक्तिक स्वतंत्रता की रक्षा नहीं हो सकती। वैयक्तिक स्वतंत्रता को प्रगट होने का पूरा अवकाश केवल विशुद्ध अहिंसा पर आधारित शासन में ही मिल सकता है।''[8]

धर्मनिरपेक्षता पर आधारित स्वराज्य

एक अत्यन्त धार्मिक व्यक्ति होने के बावजूद गांधी सभी धर्मों का सम्मान करते थे तथा स्वतंत्रता आन्दोलन के दौरान वो यह जान चुके थे कि अंग्रेजों की 'फूट डालो और राज करो' की विभाजनकारी नीतियों के कारण भारत में साम्प्रदायिकता धीरे-धीरे अपनी पकड़ मजबूत बनाती जा रही है। इसलिए गांधी अपने विचार और आचरण द्वारा साम्प्रदायिक एकता के लिए अन्त तक कार्य करते रहे। उन्हीं के शब्दों में, ''कुछ लोग ऐसा कहते हैं कि भारतीय स्वराज्य तो ज्यादा संख्या वाले समाज का यानी हिन्दुओं का ही राज्य होगा। इस मान्यता से ज्यादा बड़ी कोई दूसरी गलती नहीं हो सकती। अगर यह सही सिद्ध हो तो अपने लिए मैं ऐसा कह सकता हूँ कि मैं उसे स्वराज्य मानने से इन्कार कर दूँगा और अपनी सारी शक्ति लगाकर उसका विरोध करूँगा। मेरे लिए हिन्द स्वराज्य का अर्थ सब लोगों का राज्य, न्याय का राज्य है।''[9]

अहिंसा पर आधारित स्वराज्य

गांधी को भारत ही नहीं पूरे विश्व में अहिंसा का दूत माना गया है। उनका स्वराज्य भी निस्सन्देह अहिंसा पर आधारित स्वराज्य है। गांधी लिखते हैं, ''अहिंसा पर आधारित स्वराज्य में कोई किसी का शत्रु नहीं होता, सारी जनता की भलाई का सामान्य उद्देश्य सिद्ध करने में हर एक अपना अभीष्ट योग देता है, सब पढ़-लिख सकते हैं। बीमारी और रोग कम से कम हो जाएँ, ऐसी व्यवस्था की जाती है। कोई कंगाल नहीं होता और मजदूरी करना चाहने वाले को काम अवश्य मिल जाता है। ऐसी शासन-व्यवस्था में जुआ, शराबखोरी और दुराचार को या वर्ग-विद्वेष को कोई स्थान नहीं होता। अमीर लोग अपने धन का उपयोग बुद्धिपूर्वक उपयोगी कार्यों में करेंगे। अपनी शान शौकत बढ़ाने में या शारीरिक सुखों की वृद्धि में उसका अपव्यय नहीं करेंगे। उसमें ऐसा नहीं हो सकता, होना नहीं चाहिए, कि चंद अमीर रत्न-जड़ित महलों में रहें और लाखों-करोड़ों ऐसी मनहूस झोपड़ियों में, जिनमें हवा और प्रकाश का प्रवेश न हो। अहिंसक स्वराज्य में न्यायपूर्ण अधिकारों का किसी के भी द्वारा कोई अतिक्रमण नहीं हो सकता और इसी तरह किसी को कोई अन्यायपूर्ण अधिकार नहीं हो सकते। सुसंघटित राज्य में किसी के न्याय, अधिकार का किसी दूसरे के द्वारा अन्यायपूर्वक छीना जाना असंभव होना चाहिए और

कभी ऐसा हो जाएँ तो अपहर्ता को अपदस्थ करने के लिए हिंसा का आश्रय लेने की जरूरत नहीं होनी चाहिये।''[10]

कर्तव्यों पर आधारित स्वराज्य

गांधी का मानना था कि अधिकार के साथ कर्तव्य भी अत्यन्त महत्वपूर्ण हैं। प्रत्येक नागरिक को अपने कर्तव्यों का अवश्य पालन करना चाहिए। गांधी लिखते हैं, ''अहिंसा पर आधारित स्वराज्य में लोगों को अपने अधिकारों का ज्ञान न हो तो कोई बात नहीं, लेकिन उन्हें अपने कर्तव्यों का ज्ञान अवश्य होना चाहिए। हर एक कर्तव्य के साथ उसकी तौल का अधिकार जुड़ा हुआ होता है, और सच्चे अधिकार तो वे ही हैं जो अपने कर्तव्यों का योग्य पालन करके प्राप्त किये गये हो। इसलिए नागरिकता के अधिकार सिर्फ उन्हीं को मिल सकते हैं, जो जिस राज्य में वे रहते हों, उसकी सेवा करते हों। सिर्फ वे ही इन अधिकारों के साथ पूरा न्याय कर सकते हैं। जिन लोगों को अधिकार अपने कर्तव्यों के पालने के फलस्वरूप मिलते हैं, वे उनका उपयोग समाज की सेवा के लिए करते हैं, अपने लिए कभी नहीं। किसी राष्ट्रीय समाज के स्वराज्य का अर्थ उस समाज के विभिन्न व्यक्तियों के स्वराज्य (अर्थात् आत्म शासन) का योग ही है। और ऐसा स्वराज्य व्यक्तियों के द्वारा नागरिकों के रूप में अपने कर्तव्य के पालन से ही आता है। उसमें कोई अपने अधिकारों की बात नहीं सोचता। जब उनकी आवश्यकता होती है; तब वे उन्हें अपने आप मिल जाते हैं और इसलिए मिलते हैं कि वे अपने कर्तव्य का सम्पादन ज्यादा अच्छी तरह कर सकें।''[11]

सहनशील अन्तर्राष्ट्रीयवाद पर आधारित स्वराज्य

केवल वर्तमान समय में ही नहीं अपने समय में ही गांधी वैश्विक बन चुके थे। कारण स्पष्ट है–उनके लिए विश्व के सभी राष्ट्रों का महत्व भारत की तरह का ही था तथा वे राष्ट्रों के बीच आपसी संबंधों को महत्वपूर्ण मानते थे। उन्हीं के शब्दों में, ''पूर्ण स्वराज्य की मेरी कल्पना दूसरे देशों से कोई नाता न रखने वाली स्वतंत्रता की नहीं, बल्कि स्वस्थ और गम्भीर किस्म की स्वतन्त्रता की है...उसमें दूसरे किसी राष्ट्र या व्यक्ति को नुकसान पहुँचाने की सम्भावना नहीं है। कानूनी सिद्धान्त असल में नैतिक सिद्धान्त ही हैं। अपनी सम्पत्ति का उपयोग इस तरह करो कि पड़ोसी की सम्पत्ति को कोई हानि न पहुँचे। यह कानूनी सिद्धान्त एक सनातन सत्य को प्रकट करता है और उसमें मेरा पूरा विश्वास है।''[12]

स्वराज्य पर गांधी के उपरोक्त विचारों के अवलोकन से यह स्पष्ट हो जाता है कि अगर राजनेता उनके महान विचारों को वास्तविकता में अपने विचार और कर्म में सम्मिलित कर लें तो निस्संदेह गांधी के स्वराज्य पर विचार वर्तमान समय में भी प्रासंगिक हैं।

जब यह स्पष्ट हो जाता है कि भारत स्वराज्य प्राप्त कर लेगा। अर्थात् जब भारतीय स्वयं इस महान् राष्ट्र के कर्ता–धर्ता होंगे तब क्या होगा? आज स्वतंत्रता प्राप्ति के इतने वर्षों के बाद

हम यह कह सकते हैं कि हां हमने वो स्वराज्य प्राप्त कर लिया है; जिसकी ओर गांधी लगातार हमारा ध्यान आकर्षित कर रहे थे। अगर प्रभाष जोशी के विचारों को जानें तो इसका उत्तर ज्यादा आशाजनक नहीं है। उनके अनुसार, ''पहले अंग्रेज हम पर राज कर रहे थे। हमारे देश में एक प्रकार का साम्राज्यवाद और गुलामी उसी तरह है, जैसे अंग्रेजों के समय में थी। इसलिए गांधी ने स्वराज्य की बात, सिर्फ देश की आजादी के लिए नहीं कही, आजादी तो एक राजनीतिक बात है। वे स्वराज्य की बात करते थे। स्वराज्य का मतलब यह है कि इस देश का हर एक आदमी अपने जीवन के लिए किसी और पर निर्भर न रहे, उसका अपने ऊपर राज हो–ऐसा गांधी ने कहा। जो आदमी बाहरी चीजों पर जितना कम आश्रित होगा, उतना ही ज्यादा वो स्वतन्त्र और स्वराज्य वाला होगा।''[13]

आज किसान आत्महत्या कर रहे हैं। साम्प्रदायिक ताकतें सिर उठा रही हैं। अमीर और अमीर होता जा रहा है, गरीबों की संख्या बढ़ती जा रही है आदि। काश गांधी के विचारों को ईमानदारी से व्यवहार में लागू किया जाता तो पंक्ति के अंतिम छोर पर खड़ा व्यक्ति भी सही मायने में उस स्वराज्य का सम्मानित भाग होता।

शशि शेखर लिखते हैं, ''गोरखपुर में अकाल के गाल में समा जाने वाले नैनिहालों के रोते–चीखते परिजन, नोएडा में जे.पी. आम्रपाली सहित तमाम बिल्डर्स के शिकार मध्यवर्गीय लोग, कर्ज–माफी की घोषणा के बावजूद अपनी जान देने पर मजबूर किसान, केरल में साम्प्रदायिक हिंसा के शिकार लोगों के परिजन...। क्या गुजरे 70 सालों में हमने यही कमाया है?'' वे आगे लिखते हैं, ''आज जरूरत तो इस बात की है कि किसान अपनी फसल उगाए, तो उसे उचित मूल्य देने वाली मंडी हासिल हो। बच्चा जब इस देश की धरती पर जन्म ले, तो उसकी परवरिश के माकूल इंतजाम और पढ़ाई के लिए स्कूल हो। साथ ही अध्ययन के बाद जीवनयापन के समुचित साधनों के लिए उसे भटकना ना पड़े। इन व्यवस्थाओं के लिए शासकों–प्रशासकों को समय और स्कूल की जरूरत है। हमें सोचना होगा कि हर वक्त की हाय–तौबा कहीं हमारा ही मार्ग तो अवरूद्ध नहीं कर रही? हमारा लोकतन्त्र तो बहुत पहले ही भीड़तंत्र में तब्दील हो गया था। अब हम उसे शोरतंत्र बनाने पर क्यों आमादा हैं?''[14]

एक और उदाहरण रविन्द्र कोल्हे–जिन्होंने डाक्टरी की पढ़ाई के बाद शहर में पैसा कमाने की बजाय गांव में लोगों की सेवा का निर्णय लिया; अपने अनुभवों को साझा करते वक्त वे बताते हैं, ''हमने बीमारियों की असल वजह तक पहुँचने की कोशिश से पता चला, बिमारी की असली वजह गरीबी है। लोगों को भरपेट खाना नहीं मिल पाता, इसलिए उनकी प्रतिरोध की क्षमता बहुत कम थी। सर्दी में ठंड से मौतें होती थीं, क्योंकि गाँव वालों के पास शरीर ढकने के लिए पर्याप्त कपड़े नहीं होते थे।''

उपरोक्त पंक्तियाँ हमें यह सोचने के लिए बाध्य करती हैं कि यह वो स्वराज्य नहीं है, जिसका निर्माण गांधी करना चाहते थे।

संदर्भ सूची

1. इरफान हबीब, कहां खो गए वे आदर्श, आउटलुक, 28 अगस्त, 2018 पृ. 26-27
2. यंग इंडिया, 23-1-1930
3. यंग इंडिया, 19-3-1931
4. यंग इंडिया, 28-7-1921
5. मो.क. गांधी, सम्पूर्ण गांधी वाग्मय, खण्ड 89
6. यंग इंडिया, 26-3-1931
7. वही
8. हरिजन 27-5-1931
9. यंग इंडिया 16-4-1931
10. हरिजन 25-3-1939
11. वही
12. यंग इंडिया 26-2-1931
13. प्रभाष जोशी, हिन्द स्वराज्य और आधुनिक सभ्यता का संकट, आलोचना त्रैमासिक, अक्टूबर-दिसम्बर 2010, दिल्ली, राजकमल प्रकाशन पृ. 13
14. शशि शेखर, भीड़तंत्र से शोरतंत्र तक हिन्दुस्तान, 20.8.2017, पृ. 10

24

वैश्विक सिनेमा और गांधी

राजेश कुमार

महात्मा गांधी के जीवन दर्शन और चिन्तन ने समस्त विश्व को प्रभावित किया है। यही कारण है कि गांधी जी आज भी हमारे विमर्श का विषय बने हुए हैं। आज के समय वैश्विक मूल्यों का जिस तरह से ह्रास हुआ है, ऐसे में गांधी जी और प्रासंगिक हो गये हैं। दुनिया के लगभग सभी बुद्धिजीवियों ने गांधी जी के जीवन का अध्ययन और विश्लेषण किया और उन सभी का निष्कर्ष एक ही था कि गांधी जी के जीवन सिद्धान्तों को आत्मसात करना। गांधी जी के व्यावहारिक रूप से समाज, साहित्य, सिनेमा और सारी कला विधाओं को प्रभावित किया। सिनेमा एक ऐसा क्षेत्र है जिसे गांधी दर्शन ने न केवल प्रभावित किया बल्कि उसे और जिज्ञासा और सम्भावनाओं से भर दिया। सिनेमा ही एक ऐसा माध्यम है, जिसकी पहुँच उस आम जनसमुदाय तक है, जिसके अवचेतन में गांधी जी 150 साल बाद भी जमे हुए सौहार्द भाव को राजनैतिक स्वतन्त्रता से अधिक महत्व देता है।

गांधी जी का मानना था कि भारत में मानव-श्रम से विकसित किए जाने वाले लघु कुटीर उद्योग के बल पर ही स्वराज की परिकल्पना साकार हो सकती है। आधुनिक मशीनीकरण देश की जनता के लिए किसी भी प्रकार से हितकारी नहीं है। 1931 में गोलमेज वार्ता के समय चार्ली चैपलिन ने गांधी जी से मुलाकात के दौरान जानना चाहा कि वे मशीन का विरोध क्यों करते हैं? मशीन तो मनुष्य के श्रम को कम करती है, जिससे मनुष्य खाली समय में अपने व्यक्तित्व का विकास कर सकता है। इस पर गांधी जी का जवाब था कि मशीनों पर पूंजीपतियों का अधिकार है और पूंजीपति आम जनता का शोषण करते हैं। आज यही प्रमाणित हो रहा है कि मशीन अपना काम कर रही है, परन्तु व्यक्तित्व का विकास नहीं हो रहा है। गांधी जी से प्रभावित होकर चार्ली चैपलिन ने 'मॉर्डन टाइम्स' नाम की फिल्म बनाई; जिसमें उन्होंने दिखाया कि अति आधुनिकता के दौर में आदमी केवल मशीनी पुर्जा बन कर रह गया है और उसके

अन्दर संवेदनशून्यता का विकार पैदा हो गया है।

जीवन में सत्य का आचरण और अंहिसा का धारण महात्मा गांधी के जीवन प्रेरक संदेश रहे हैं। इनकी महत्ता का अनुमान इसी से लगाया जा सकता है कि सेंसरशिप होने के बावजूद धार्मिक आख्यानों के माध्यम से इन्हें प्रचारित किया गया। 1920 में द्वारका प्रसाद संपत ने 'महात्मा विदुर' नामक फिल्म में नायक गांधी जी के चश्में, धोती और लाठी को धारण करके धर्म के माध्यम से गांधी जी के चिन्हों की लोकप्रियता की प्रस्तुति करता है। आज के समय में गांधी जी के विचारों का ही नहीं उनके चिन्हों का अध्ययन भी आवश्यक है। थाई फिल्म 'Ong Bak' में नायक गाँव से चोरी की गई प्राचीन बुद्ध की प्रतिमा के सिर और उससे जुड़ी सामग्री को बचाने का इसलिए प्रयास करता है कि बुद्ध के सन्देश कालान्तर में तभी प्रभाव पैदा कर पायेंगे, जब उनके प्रतीकों को सहेजा जायेगा। यही गांधी जी के परिप्रेक्ष्य में कहा जा सकता है। उपरोक्त फिल्म में सत्य, अंहिसा, प्रेम और अन्याय का विरोध आदि का प्रचार धर्म की आड़ में करना उस समय की जरूरत थी और भारतीय ज्ञान-परम्परा में तो कई सारे शास्त्रों की शिक्षा धर्म के माध्यम से देने का प्रचलन रहा है।

व्यवस्था यदि जनता के पक्ष में न हो तो इसका विरोध करने का नया प्रयोग गांधी जी ने असहयोग आन्दोलन के रूप में दुनिया को दिया; जिसका प्रभाव आज के समय में वैश्विक स्तर पर देखा जा सकता है। यह हिंसात्मक नहीं है, बल्कि परिवर्तन करने वाला है। गांधी जी के असहयोग आन्दोलन का असर अवाम पर इतना था कि देवकी बोस ने आन्दोलन में शामिल होने के लिए एम.ए. की परीक्षा का बहिष्कार तक कर दिया और कालान्तर में गांधी जी के आदर्शों से प्रेरित होकर उन्होंने 'चण्डीदास' नाम की फिल्म में गांधी जी के 'अस्पृश्यता का विरोध' सिद्धान्त को प्रस्तुत किया। इसके एक दृश्य में दिखाया गया कि एक ब्राह्मण और एक धोबिन एक घाट पर खड़े हैं और शान्त और स्थिर जल उनकी छवियों को अलग-अलग बयान कर रहा है। इतने में एक लहर आती है और दोनों छवियों को गढ़-मढ़ कर देती है। ऐसी कालजयी प्रस्तुतियाँ किसी भी कालखण्ड में वर्ग-भेद और अस्पृश्यता को खत्म करने में सफल सिद्ध हो सकती हैं। 1959 में बनी 'सुजाता' फिल्म में बिमल रॉय ने छुआछूत जैसी कुप्रथा को उजागर किया है और यह बताने का साहस जुटाया है कि भारत जैसे आदर्श समाज में यह कुप्रथा स्वीकार नहीं की जा सकती, जिसकी संस्कृति ही 'वसुधैव कुटुम्बकम' की रही है।

अनुपम खेर की 'मैंने गांधी को नहीं मारा' में डार्ट (Toy Gun) के खेल के दौरान गांधी जी का अनुयायी गांधी जी के पोस्टर पर डार्ट लगते ही चिल्ला उठता है कि उसने गांधी को नहीं मारा, संयोगवश उसी समय समाचार आता है कि गांधी जी की हत्या कर दी गई। प्रस्तुत कथा में अनुपम खेर अभिनीत प्रोफेसर डिमेंसिया का शिकार होता है और वह अपने आप को इस अपराधबोध से निकल नहीं पाता है। वह इस बात से भी भड़क जाता है, जब वह देखता है कि एक आदमी ने किस तरह से अखबार में छपे महात्मा गांधी के पोस्टर पर किस निर्लज्जता से ऐस्ट्रे को रखा है। हम गांधी जी और उनके चिन्हों को संजोकर क्यों नहीं रख पाने में कामयाब

हो रहे हैं। यह सब बार बार क्यों बताया जाता है कि ये महज वस्तु नहीं हैं; बल्कि गांधी जी के विचार हैं और आज के समय में ही नहीं अपितु हर बार इनका पाठ जरूरी है।

भारत और दक्षिण अफ्रिका के सहयोग से बनी श्याम बेनेगल की 'द मेकिंग ऑफ महात्मा' गांधी जी के आरम्भिक जीवन को चरित्रार्थ करती है, जब वे अफ्रिका आये थे। यह फिल्म फातिमा मीर द्वारा लिखित 'The Apprenticeship of a Mahatma' पुस्तक पर आधारित है। यह गांधी जी के 'महात्मा' बनने का आख्यान है, जिसकी शुरूआत अफ्रिका में हो चुकी थी। जहाँ उन्होंने नस्लवाद और स्थानीय समुदाय और एशियाई लोगों के बीच पनपे वैमनस्य को समाप्त करने का काम किया। 'Gandhi to Hitler' नामक फिल्म सिनेमा के पर्दे पर आई जिसमें गांधी द्वारा हिटलर को लिखे गये पत्रों को रेखांकित किया गया है। इस फिल्म का व्यापक स्तर पर विरोध किया गया कि इसमें अधिकतर हिटलर के जीवन को दिखाया गया है। नाजीवाद का हौवा उस समय जनमानस पर इतना भयानक असर पैदा कर रहा था कि यह माना जाता था कि हिटलर का अन्त मुश्किल है। यही जानकर उनके मरने से दो दिन पहले ही उनकी प्रेमिका एवा ब्राउन ने एक बंकर में छिपे हिटलर से शादी की। यदि वह ऐसा नहीं करती तो शायद उन्हें भी आज कोई नहीं जानता। गांधी जी के ये पत्र हिटलर को अहिंसात्मक तो नही बना सके, परन्तु दुनिया से तानाशाही को खत्म करने में जरूर सहायक सिद्ध हुए।

'Coming of Age' नामक पुस्तक में सिमॉन द बोआ ने लिखा है कि गांधी जी 'काउंटर क्लोजर के शिकार हुए हैं। सिमॉन ने भविष्य में होने वाली गांधी संबंधी औपचारिकताओं को बहुत पहले जान लिया था कि आदमी द्वारा निर्मित व्यवस्था में मौजूद आदर्शों को अपनी सार्थकता सिद्ध करनी पड़ेगी। 'Gandhi's Truth' नामक किताब अहिंसात्मक आतंकवाद के अवयवों पर आधारित है, जिसे जर्मनी मूल के अमेरिकी मनोवैज्ञानिक एकिक एच. एरिक्सन ने लिखा। जिसे बाद में दर्शन और धर्म की श्रेणी में पुल्तिजर सम्मान मिला। इस किताब ने भारत में चले स्वतन्त्रता आन्दोलन के दौरान की गतिविधियों को मनोवैज्ञानिक माध्यम से व्याख्यायित किया, कि कैसे 1857 के संग्राम में देश का अवाम शामिल नहीं था और किसी भी समय तीस हजार से अधिक अंग्रेज भारत में नहीं रहे, परन्तु उन्होंने ऐसी व्यावस्था को रचा था कि भारतीयों की मदद से ही भारत पर राज कैसे किया जाता है। इसलिए हमारे कई सारे आन्दोलन सही उद्देश्य और बलिदान के होते हुए भी इस आधार पर असफल हुए कि उनमें जन भागीदारी नहीं थी। जब ऐसे आन्दोलनों को जनता का साथ मिला तो स्वयं अंग्रेज को लगने लगा कि अब भारत पर राज करना मुश्किल है, क्योंकि उनका सारा शासन तंत्र भारतीय मन की संस्कृति पर था। इसलिए भारतीय इतिहास का पाठ कराते हुए यह बताना जरूरी है कि भारत को आजादी देना अंग्रेजों की मजबूरी थी, क्योंकि अब भारत के लोगों को बाँटकर राज करना उनके लिए बेहद मुश्किल था।

वी. शान्ताराम द्वारा निर्मित 'दो आँखे बारह हाथ' फिल्म गांधी जी के 'क्षमा और शील' सिद्धान्त पर आधारित है। 1957 में बनी यह फिल्म क्लासिकल सिनेमा की सबसे चर्चित फिल्म

है, इसकी कथावस्तु का आधार ही यह है कि कठोर अपराधी के जीवन को कैसे बदला जा सकता है। दयाशील जेल वार्डन आदित्यनाथ गांधी जी का यह सन्देश देने में कामयाब होता है कि जीवन में सृजनशीलता के माध्यम से ही अपराधबोध को खत्म किया जा सकता है और समाज मानव श्रम को महत्व देने की ओर अग्रसर होता है।

1982 में ब्रिटिश और भारत के सहयोग से बनी 'गांधी' फिल्म आजाद भारत की सबसे चर्चित फिल्म रही। जॉन ब्रेली द्वारा लिखित इस फिल्म का निर्देशन सर रिचर्ड एटनबरो ने किया; जिसमें महात्मा गांधी के कालजयी पात्र को बेन किंगसले ने अभिनीत किया। यह अपने आप में असाधारण प्रस्तुति थी; जिसमें गांधी के हर एक पक्ष को बड़ी सिद्दत के साथ रेखांकित किया गया। इस फिल्म को बनने में लगभग पन्द्रह साल लगे; तब तक नायक बेन किंगसले अपनी युवा उम्र से अधेड़ में पहुँच चुका था और गांधी जी के सभी आदर्शों को आत्मसात कर चुका था। इंग्लैण्ड में जब इसे अकादमी अवार्ड के लिए चुना गया तो वहाँ की सरकार ने निर्माता को 'सर' की उपाधि से नवाजा गया। लेकिन नियति का खेल अजीब होता है कि निर्माता को अपने जीवन का अन्तिम समय वृद्धाश्रम में गुजारना पड़ा। आज पूरे वैश्विक परिदष्टश्य में देखा जाये तो गांधी जी के मूल्यों पर जीने वाला वृद्धाश्रम का ही जीवन जीता है। यह अपने आप में बौद्धिक समाज के लिए चुनौती है।

2007 में आई 'गांधी, माई फादर' फिल्म के माध्यम से गांधी जी को पारिवारिक रूप से जानने में मदद मिलती है। इसमें गांधी जी के पुत्र हरिलाल की असमर्थता और जीवन के प्रति व्याकुलता को दिखाया गया है। गांधी जी को सार्वजनिक जीवन में ही नहीं व्यक्तिगत जीवन में भी संघर्ष करना पड़ा था। अक्षय खन्ना द्वारा अभिनीत पात्र हरिलाल की इच्छा है कि वह विदेश में जाकर अपने पिता की तरह बैरिस्टर की शिक्षा हासिल करे, परन्तु गांधी जी चाहते हैं कि हरिलाल मेरे आदर्श और जीवन मूल्यों का प्रचार भारत में करे। यहीं पर पिता और पुत्र के बीच दूरियाँ बढ़ जाती हैं और हरिलाल न केवल अपने आप को जीवन के प्रति हारा हुआ युवक समझता है बल्कि अनेक व्यसनों का शिकार हो जाता है। उसमें आज के भारतीय युवक का बिम्ब दिखाई देता है। हरिलाल अपना धर्म बदलकर मुसलमान बन जाता है, इससे आहत होकर उसे पत्नी छोड़कर अपने पिता के घर चली जाती है। यह फिल्म महज हरिलाल की जीवन कथा को नहीं प्रस्तुत करती है, बल्कि उन आदर्शों की प्रासंगिकता को जनता के सामने प्रस्तुत करने में सफल होती है जिन पर मानव जीवन की सार्थकता और उसकी तात्कालिक जरूरतों को दर्शाया गया है। गांधी जी को जानने के कई आयाम हैं। 'हे राम' में गांधी जी को आलोचनात्मक दृष्टि से चरित्रार्थ किया गया है, जिसमें नायक को यह समझाने का प्रयास किया गया है कि उनकी पत्नी का शोषण और हत्या के लिए गांधी जी उत्तरदायी हैं; जिनकी सोच ने देश में साम्प्रदायिक परेशानी पैदा की। '' एक अमेरिकन थ्रिलर है जो नाथूराम गोडसे के जीवन के अन्तिम नौ घण्टों का चित्रांकन है, इस फिल्म की काफी आलोचना की गई, परन्तु निर्माता जिस तरह से गांधी जी के जीवन को बताना चाहता है, आम जन उस तरीके से हर

बार नहीं समझ पाता है। 2009 में तेलुगू फिल्म 'महात्मा' आई जिसमें एक उपद्रवी गांधी जी से प्रभावित होकर हिंसा के पथ का त्याग करता है।

गांधी जी के चरित को भारतीय जनसमुदाय ने ही नहीं महत्व दिया, बल्कि उस समय स्वयं अग्रेंज भी इसके प्रति गंभीर थे। उनकी फिल्म डिवीजन में गांधी जी द्वारा संचालित 1914 से 1946 तक के आन्दोलनों पर वृतचित्र आज भी महत्व रखता है। यह विधा दृश्य के माध्यम से इतिहास को कैसे समझा जा सकता है, बताने में सक्षम है। गांधी जी को अलग-अलग रूपों में सहेजने का काम जारी है। मुम्बई के जे.जे. स्कूल ने उनके चित्रों की प्रदर्शनी लगा कर उनके प्रति आदरांजली व्यक्त की है। महज किताबों के अध्ययन और उनके विमर्श एवं समालोचनात्मक दृष्टिकोण से आज भी भागदौड़ भरी जिन्दगी में लोगों को गांधी जी के बारे में बताना पर्याप्त नहीं होगा। हमें उन सभी माध्यमों का प्रयोग करना होगा, जो जनता की पहुँच में हैं और इनमें एक सिनेमा व्यापक, विस्तृत और प्रभावकारी माध्यम है। यह गांधी जी के आदर्शों को रटाता नहीं है, बल्कि जनता को उस गूंगी-बहरी व्यवस्था के खिलाफ खड़ा करने का साहस पैदा करता है, जो सदियों से जनता का न्याय के नाम पर शोषण करती आई है।

जैसा कि उन्होंने कहा था कि मेरा जीवन ही मेरा आदर्श है। यही विश्वभर का सिनेमा दिखाने में प्रयासरत है। गांधी जी का अभी तक पूरा चित्रांकन नहीं किया गया है। उनके द्वारा लिखे गये पत्र अभी सिनेमा की पहुँच से बाहर हैं, बायोपिक सिनेमा थ्रिलर और जीवन के रहस्य पर काम करता है, जो दर्शकों में कौतुहल पैदा करने में सक्षम है। परन्तु, आज दर्शक की रूचियाँ बदली हुई हैं, इसलिए वह तमाम पक्षों को जानना चाहता है, जो सर्वांगीण जीवन को कड़ियों में बयान करते हों।

25

खेती-किसानी में गांधीजी की प्रासंगिकता

अटल तिवारी

महात्मा गांधी ने गाँव और खेती-किसानी के विकास का एक खाका बुना था। देश के विकास का मॉडल क्या होना चाहिए? उसकी शुरुआत कहाँ से होनी चाहिए? उसके केन्द्र में किसे रखा जाना चाहिए? गाँव और खेती-किसानी से जुड़े ऐसे अनेक बिन्दुओं पर गांधीजी ने विचार रखे थे। उन्हीं में से तीन बिन्दु थे-सहकारिता, देशी बीज और मशीनों का इस्तेमाल। इन बिन्दुओं पर रखे गए गांधीजी के विचार 21वीं सदी की खेती-किसानी में कितने प्रासंगिक हैं, यह देखने की आवश्यकता है।

गांधीजी मानते थे कि देश के लोगों के लिए खेती ही एकमात्र अटूट और अचल सहारा है। उस समय परिवारों में लगातार हो रहे विभाजन का असर खेती पर पड़ रहा था। परिवारों के साथ खेती वाली जमीन का भी विभाजन हो रहा था। जोत छोटी होती जा रही थी। गांधीजी छोटी जोत में आने वाली समस्याओं को समझ रहे थे। इसीलिए वह सामुदायिक खेती पर जोर दे रहे थे। उनका कहना था कि जब हम अपनी जमीन को सामुदायिक पद्धति से जोतेंगे, तभी उससे फायदा उठा सकेंगे। गाँव की खेती अलग-अलग सौ टुकड़ों में बँट जाय, इसके बनिस्बत क्या यह बेहतर नहीं होगा कि सौ कुटुम्ब सारे गाँव की खेती सहयोग से करें और उसकी आमदनी आपस में बाँट लिया करें? गांधीजी जिस तरह की सामुदायिक खेती की बात करते थे, उसे एक उदाहरण से समझा जा सकता है।

एक गाँव में दो-तीन एकड़ जमीन वाले छोटे दस परिवार सामुदायिक खेती के लिए तैयार हो जाएँ तो वे मशीनरी आदि का मालिक की तरह इस्तेमाल कर सकेंगे। सुचारु रूप से संचालन के लिए उन्हीं परिवारों के सदस्यों को लेकर एक छोटी कमेटी बना ली जाए। कमेटी में शामिल परिवारों की लेनदारी-देनदारी जमीन की जोत के हिसाब से तय हो। गाँव से लेकर राज्य स्तर तक उनकी यूनियन हो। सामुदायिक खेती करने वालों के लिए सरकारी नीति बने। सब्सिडी की

सुविधा मिले। मण्डी की शत-प्रतिशत व्यवस्था हो। फसल के सालाना भाव, उतार-चढ़ाव तय किए जाएँ। बेचने वाले को घाटा हो, तो उसकी भरपाई मण्डी परिषद करे। ग्रामवासी इस तरह की पहल दिखाएँ तो हर घर मशीनरी खरीदने से मुक्त हो जाएगा। उसकी मरम्मत और देखरेख पर आने वाले खर्चे से भी बच जाएगा। यह सारा काम समूह में होगा तो जाहिर है कि उस पर खर्च कम आएगा। वैसे गांधीजी की सहकार की कल्पना इससे भी आगे की थी।

गांधीजी का मानना था कि सब मालिक मिल-जुलकर जमीन पर अधिकार रखें और जोतने, बोने, फसल काटने वगैरा का काम भी मिल-जुलकर ही करें। इससे मेहनत, पूँजी, औजार वगैरा की बचत होगी। मालिक मिल-जुलकर खेतों में काम करेंगे और पूँजी, औजार, जानवर और बीज वगैरा पर भी उनका मिला-जुला अधिकार होगा। 'मेरी कल्पना की सहकारी खेती जमीन की शकल ही बदल देगी और लोगों की गरीबी और आलस को भगा देगी। यह सब तभी सम्भव होगा जब लोग एक-दूसरे के मित्र बन जायेंगे और एक परिवार के सदस्य बनकर रहने लगेंगे।' गांधीजी के इस वाक्य की अंतिम पंक्ति ही भारतीय समाज के लिए चुनौती है। अगर सब एक-दूसरे के मित्र हो जाएँ तो बहुत सारी समस्याओं का समाधान अपने आप हो जाएगा। उसके लिए किसी का मुँह नहीं ताकना पड़ेगा। जब छोटे-छोटे स्वार्थों के लिए लोगों में वैमनस्यता चरम पर पहुंच चुकी हो। एक-दूसरे को गिराने-उठाने-फँसाने की कुचक्र चालें चली जा रही हों। पंचायतों में बड़े पैमाने पर आ रहा धन मारपीट और हिंसा को बढ़ाने में योगदान दे रहा हो, तब इस सहकार की बात करना बेमानी हो जाता है। इसके लिए लक्ष्य तय करके पहले भारतीय समाज का मन मस्तिष्क बदलने के लिए काम करना होगा तभी गांधीजी वाले सहकार के बारे में सोचा जा सकता है।

गांधीजी की सोच थी कि गाँव और किसान अपनी जरूरतों के लिए किसी पर आश्रित न रहे। वह कहते थे-ग्राम-स्वराज्य की मेरी कल्पना यह है कि वह एक ऐसा पूर्ण प्रजातंत्र होगा, जो अपनी अहम जरूरतों के लिए अपने पड़ोसी पर भी निर्भर नहीं करेगा; और फिर भी बहुतेरी दूसरी जरूरतों के लिए-जिनमें दूसरों का सहयोग अनिवार्य होगा-वह परस्पर सहयोग से काम लेगा। इस तरह हर एक गाँव का पहला काम यह होगा कि वह अपनी जरूरत का तमाम अनाज और कपड़े के लिए कपास खुद पैदा कर ले। गांधीजी, गाँव और किसानों के काम आने वाली हर चीज पैदा करने अथवा परस्पर सहयोग से हासिल करने की बात करते थे। किसान भी इसका ध्यान रखते थे। वे फसलों के लिए सभी बीज तैयार कर लेते थे। जिनके बीज खुद नहीं तैयार कर पाते थे, वह पड़ोसी से ले लेते थे अथवा उनसे बीजों की अदला-बदली कर लेते थे। मोटे तौर पर उन्हें बीजों के लिए पैसा नहीं खर्चना पड़ता था। लेकिन अनाज के मामले में समृद्ध होने के लिए हरित क्रान्ति के दौर में जेनेटिक बीजों को बढ़ावा दिया गया। निश्चित रूप से इससे फसलों के उत्पादन में बढ़ोतरी हुई, लेकिन बड़ा नुकसान यह हुआ कि धीरे-धीरे किसानों के देशी बीजों का लगभग खात्मा हो गया। वे बीजों के लिए बाजार के भरोसे हो गए। देशी-विदेशी कंपनियों ने बीजों पर कब्जा जमा लिया। सरकारों ने बीजों के मामले में अनेक कानून बनाकर

व समझौते कर मोनसेंटो और कारगिल जैसी बहुराष्ट्रीय कंपनियों को इजारेदाराना अधिकार दे दिए। कंपनियों ने चालाकी दिखाकर पहले सस्ती दर पर बीज दिए। तत्पश्चात जब वे निश्चिंत हो गईं कि किसानों के परंपरागत बीज खत्म हो चुके हैं तो वे जेनेटिक बीजों की मनमानी कीमत बढ़ाने लगीं।

आज हालात यह हैं कि किसान फसल बीजने के लिए कंपनियों की ओर टकटकी लगाए रहते हैं, जिन बीजों के लिए कभी उन्हें धेला भी नहीं खर्चना पड़ता था; आज उनकी मुँहमाँगी कीमत देने को मजबूर हैं। इन बीजों की गाँवों तक दुकानें खुली हैं। हाट-बाजार और पुरई-पुरवा तक में कंपनियों के प्रचार वाहन घूम रहे हैं। उनके कर्मचारी बीजों के फायदे गिना रहे हैं। वे बीज के साथ-साथ कीटनाशक, रासायनिक खाद आदि की पूरी किट उपलब्ध करा रहे हैं। इसी कारण बीजों का आयात बढ़ता चला गया। 2014-15 में जहाँ 22,292 टन बीजों का आयात था, वहीं 2015-16 में यह बढ़कर 23,477 टन हो गया।

सरकारों ने खेती-किसानी में आने वाली समस्याओं को नजरअंदाज कर इन बीजों को बढ़ावा दिया। बेहतर होता कि अधिक उत्पादन के लिए जेनेटिक बीजों की वकालत करने के बजाय सरकारें देशी बीजों को ज्यादा उत्पादन देने लायक विकसित करतीं तो वह गांधीजी की सोच के मुताबिक खेती-किसानी और गाँव के विकास में कहीं अधिक योगदान दे पातीं।

ऐसा भी नहीं है कि देशी बीजों को विकसित करने के प्रयास नहीं हुए। मध्य प्रदेश निवासी आकाश चौरसिया देशी अरहर की खास प्रजाति विकसित कर अच्छा उत्पादन ले रहे हैं। कृषि वैज्ञानिक डॉ. आर.एच. रिछारिया ने धान की करीब 17 हजार किस्में और उपकिस्मों को सूचीबद्ध किया था, जिसे छत्तीसगढ़ में संरक्षित रखा गया है। उत्तर प्रदेश के सीतापुर जिले के 176 किसानों ने अनेक बीजों का संरक्षण कर बढ़ावा देने का प्रयास किया है। इसी राज्य के निवासी करनजीत सिंह और सुधीर त्यागी गन्ने की खेती में रिकॉर्ड बना रहे हैं। ये कुछ उदाहरण भर हैं, लेकिन सरकारों ने इन्हें बढ़ावा नहीं दिया। इससे किसी को ऐतराज नहीं है कि देश की जरूरत के हिसाब से फसलों का अधिक से अधिक उत्पादन हो, लेकिन वह देशी बीजों के जरिए होता तो देश, गाँव और किसान के लिए कहीं अधिक सकारात्मक होता। किसान को दूसरों का मुँह नहीं जोहना पड़ता। उसकी जेब पर भार कम पड़ता और फसल की उत्पादन लागत भी कम आती।

गांधीजी खेती-किसानी में मशीनों के अंधाधुंध इस्तेमाल के विरोधी थे। वह लिखते हैं-'उनका (कुछ लोगों) स्वप्न है कि भाप और बिजली का बड़े पैमाने पर उपयोग करके मशीन की ताकत से खेती की जाय। जल्दी-जल्दी फसल लेने के लालच में जमीन के उपजाऊपन का व्यापार करना अन्त में बरबाद कर देने वाला सिद्ध होगा और वह सिर्फ संकुचित दृष्टि वाली नीति होगी। इसका नतीजा यह होगा कि जमीन का उपजाऊपन कम होता जायगा। अच्छी जमीन से खुराक पैदा करने के लिए पसीना बहाने की जरूरत होती है। लोग शायद इस दृष्टि की टीका करें और कहें कि यह दृष्टि प्रगति विरोधी है और इससे काम धीमा होगा। मैं भी इससे जल्दी

कोई नतीजा निकलने की आशा नहीं रखता। फिर भी जमीन और उस पर रहने वाले लोगों की समृद्धि की कुंजी इसी में है।'

मशीनों के परिप्रेक्ष्य में कही जाने वाली गांधीजी की इस बात को दूसरी तरह से देखना होगा। आज बड़ी जोत वाले किसान अगर ट्रैक्टर सहित आधुनिक यंत्रों का इस्तेमाल नहीं करेंगे तो वे खेती का काम समय से नहीं कर पाएंगे। खर्च भी अधिक आएगा। उत्पादन पर भी असर पड़ेगा। लेकिन इसका मतलब यह नहीं कि मध्यम और छोटी जोत के किसान भी मशीनों का शत-प्रतिशत इस्तेमाल किए बिना खेती नहीं कर सकते। छोटी जोत के लिए तो आज भी ट्रैक्टर की अपेक्षा बैल और भैंसा ही उपयोगी हैं। मध्यम जोत के लिए एक संतुलन बनाने की जरूरत है। इसमें शक नहीं कि ट्रैक्टर से खेती करना आसान हुआ है, लेकिन उससे कुछ समस्याएं भी पैदा हुई हैं। मसलन-जमीन में पानी ग्रहण करने की क्षमता कम हुई है। इसी कारण अब बाढ़ ज्यादा बढ़ी विभीषिका लेकर आती है। ज्यादा बरसाती पानी आपदा बन जाता है। फसलों की सिंचाई बार-बार करनी पड़ती है। असल में नवउदारवादी दौर में सरकारों ने सभी किसानों को मशीनीकरण की अंधी दौड़ में फँसा दिया। पहले बैंकों से बड़ी जोत वालों को ट्रैक्टर के लिए कर्ज मिलता था। बाद में एक एकड़ तक की जोत वालों को कर्ज दिया जाने लगा। परिणामतः जमीन के मालिकाने के आकार के हिसाब से ट्रैक्टरों की संख्या जरूरत से कहीं अधिक हो गई। लोग कर्ज के दलदल में समाते चले गए। ट्रैक्टरों को काम मिलना मुश्किल हो गया। कहने का मतलब यह कि जिन्हें मशीनीकरण के जाल में फँसने की जरूरत नहीं थी, देखादेखी में वे भी उसमें फँसते चले गए।

हालांकि जिस तरह से प्रचारित किया गया कि गांधीजी मशीनों के पूरी तरह खिलाफ थे, वह सच नहीं है। गांधीजी खुद एक सवाल, क्या आप तमाम यंत्रों के खिलाफ हैं, के जवाब में कहते हैं-वैसा मैं कैसे हो सकता हूँ, जब मैं जानता हूँ कि यह शरीर भी एक बहुत नाजुक यंत्र ही है? खुद चरखा भी एक यंत्र ही है। छोटी दांत कुरेदनी भी एक यंत्र है। मेरा विरोध यंत्रों के लिए नहीं है बल्कि यंत्रों के पीछे जो पागलपन चल रहा है, उसके लिए है।...आज तो करोड़ों की गरदन पर कुछ लोगों के सवार हो जाने में यंत्र मददगार हो रहे हैं। यंत्रों के उपयोग के पीछे जो प्रेरक कारण है, वह श्रम की बचत नहीं है बल्कि धन का लोभ है। दरअसल गांधीजी खेती-किसानी में मशीनों के अंधाधुंध इस्तेमाल के विरोधी थे, लेकिन मशीनों से पूरी तरह नफरत करते थे, ऐसा नहीं है। मशीनों का इस्तेमाल करने से गांधीजी जिस खतरे की बात कर रहे थे, 21सवीं सदी में वह खतरे नासूर बनकर सामने हैं। आज जिस तरह से हर काम में मशीनों का अधिकाधिक इस्तेमाल हो रहा है, उसने बड़े पैमाने पर हाथों से काम छीना है। भयानक बेरोजगारी वाले देश में क्या यह उचित है? इसलिए आज के समय में मशीनों का अंधाधुंध प्रयोग जहाँ लंबे समय की खेती के लिए नुकसानदायक साबित होगा, वहीं मशीनों से शत-प्रतिशत दूरी बनाना भी खतरनाक है। बेहतर होगा कि बीच का रास्ता अपनाते हुए संतुलन बनाकर काम किया जाए और खेती से लंबे समय तक लाभ उठाया जाए, यही गांधीजी के विचारों की प्रासंगिकता है।

सन्दर्भ स्रोत

1. महात्मा गांधी, *ग्राम स्वराज्य* (संग्राहक : हरिप्रसाद व्यास), नवजीवन प्रकाज़न मंदिर, अहमदाबाद, 2010, पृ. 105
2. वही
3. महात्मा गांधी, *मेरे सपनों का भारत* (संग्राहक : आर.के. प्रभु), नवजीवन प्रकाज़न मंदिर, अहमदाबाद, 2015, पृ. 101
4. अरविन्द कुमार सिंह, देशी बीज अपनाएंगे तभी मिटेगी हर पेट की भूख, बढ़ेगी किसानों की आमदनी, 7 मार्च 2018, देखें-https://www.gaonconnection.com/kheti-kisani/only-native-seeds-can-provide-food-security
5. अरविन्द कुमार सिंह, देशी बीज अपनाएंगे तभी मिटेगी हर पेट की भूख, बढ़ेगी किसानों की आमदनी, 7 मार्च 2018, देखें-https://www.gaonconnection.com/kheti-kisani/only-native-seeds-can-provide-food-security
6. महात्मा गांधी, *ग्राम स्वराज्य* (संग्राहक : हरिप्रसाद व्यास), नवजीवन प्रकाशन मंदिर, अहमदाबाद, 2010, पृ. 92

26

वैश्विक शांति और गांधी

पिंकी कुमारी

"मैं अपने हृदय की गहराई से यह महसूस करता हूँ...कि दुनिया रक्तपात से बिल्कुल उब गई है। दुनिया इस असहाय स्थिति से बाहर निकलने का रास्ता खोज रही है और मैं विश्वास करता हूँ तथा उस विश्वास में गर्व भी अनुभव करता हूँ कि शायद मुक्ति के प्यासे जगत को रास्ता दिखाने का श्रेय भारत की प्राचीन भूमि को ही मिलेगा।" इस वक्तव्य से गांधी जी कि दृष्टि स्पष्ट हो जाती है कि वह विश्व को एक नई रोशनी ही दुनिया को दे सकता है। गांधी जी ने इस वक्तव्य से यह भी स्पष्ट कर दिया है कि भले विश्व कितना भी उन्नत व प्रगतिशील क्यों न हो जायें फिर भी वह भारत की तरफ देखता है और यह आशा रखता है कि भारत ही विश्व को कुछ नया दे सकता है क्योंकि भारत के आदर्शों में विचारों में वह शक्ति है जिससे विश्व को प्रभावित किया जा सकता है। गांधी जी इसी सोच का परिणाम है, जिन्होंने पूरे विश्व को प्रभावित करने का काम किया है।

गांधी जी एक ऐसे व्यक्ति थे जिनको अपनी भारतीय संस्कृति व परम्परा पर गर्व था, इसीलिए समाज का ऐसा कोई भी विषय नहीं बचा, जिस पर गांधी जी अपने विचार व्यक्त न किये हो, राजनीति, धर्म सम्प्रदाय, सद्भावना, व्यक्ति, समाज, सत्ता, गरीबी, शिक्षा, नारी अनेक विषय है इसके अलावा छुआछुत, गरीबी शोषण, हिंसा, चोरी आदि। गांधी जी भारत को ही नहीं बल्कि विश्व को भी समझाना चाहते थे कि हिंसा पर आधारित राज्य कभी उन्नति नहीं कर सकता है। बल्कि जो राज्य स्वराज पर आधारित होगा वही फलीभूत भी होगा।

यदि राज्य के साधन पवित्र है तो वह साध्य तक आसानी से पहुँच सकता है। इसके लिए उन्होंने साधनों की पवित्रता पर जोर दिया।

मैं अपने लेख के माध्यम से गांधी जी के विचारों पर प्रकाश डालना चाहूँगी, जिनसे ये पता चलता है कि गांधी जी हमेशा चाहूँगी, जिनसे ये पता, चलता है कि गांधी जी हमेशा विश्व में

एक स्थायी शांति चाहते थे। मनुष्य के विकास के लिए, राष्ट्रों के लिए वैश्विक शांति क्यों आवश्यक है?

किसी भी लेख का एक उद्देश्य होता है कि वह कुछ नया लोगों तक समाज तक पहुँचाने का प्रयास करे अतः मैं अपने इस लेख के माध्यम से यह बताने की कोशिश कर रही हूँ कि समाज में राष्ट्र में या विश्व में गांधी जी का स्थान इतना उच्च क्यों है? क्योंकि गांधी जी एक बहुआयामी व्यक्तित्व है, वह यह बताने का प्रयास करते हैं कि व्यक्ति को व्यक्ति से प्रेम व सद्भावना से रहना चाहिए, व्यक्ति एक महत्त्वपूर्ण इकाई है, क्योंकि व्यक्ति ही समाज व राष्ट्र का निर्माण करता है। जैसा व्यक्ति ही समाज व राष्ट्र का निर्माण करता है। जैसा व्यक्ति वैसा समाज होगा तो यह आवश्यक है कि समाज ही राष्ट्रों का निर्माण भी करता है।

जब गांधी जी का जन्म हुआ था तब किसी को यह पता नहीं था कि यही छोटा सा बालक आगे चलकर जीवन में सत्य के मार्ग चलेगा और विश्व को अपना अनुकरणीय भी बना पायेगा। गांधी जी हमें जीवन के हर एक क्षेत्र में दिखाई देते है चाहे वह मानवीय पहलू हो या फिर व्यक्ति की दुःख तकलीफ। जब गांधी के जन्म दिन को 'अहिंसा' दिवस के रूप में संयुक्त राष्ट्रसंघ ने घोषित किया तब हर भारतीय के लिए यह गर्व का विषय था कि भारत ने विश्व पर अपनी साख बनाई है। तब पूरा विश्व ही गांधी जी के अहिंसा सिद्धांत से अवगत भी हुआ तथा स्थयी शांति और समस्याओं के विषय में भी सोचने लगा। गांधी जी के द्वारा दिये गए भाषाओं अंशों पर टिप्पणियों लिखी जाने लगी। गांधी जी ने किसी भी वाद के साथ अपना संबंध नहीं जोड़ा बल्कि व सत्य को कमजोर नहीं बल्कि शक्तिवादी का हथियार भी मानते है। सत्य में वही ताकत है जो उसे सदैव जीवित रखती है। गांधी जी अपने-आपको नये-नये प्रयोगों के साथ जोड़कर देखते है। जिस तरह बौद्ध धर्म में भी यह शिक्षा दी जाती है कि हिंसा न करना, चोरी न करना, और आवश्यकता से अधिाक संग्रहण न करना ही उत्तम जीवन का लक्ष्य है फिर भी मनुष्य हो या राष्ट्र लालच के वशीभूत होकर ही एक दूसरे पर अपना अधिापत्य जमाते हैं जो युद्धों को जन्म देती है। यदि विश्व से युद्ध, भय, डर हिंसा समाप्त करना है तो स्वयं हमें इन आदर्शों पर निर्भर होना पड़ेगा।

आज विश्व के प्रत्येक कोने में अनेक समस्याएं नजर आ रही है, गरीबी, भूखमरी, शोषण, पर्यावरण, लैंगिक भेदभाव या िर जल संरक्षण की समस्या, इन सबका एक ही कारण है कि हिंसा व्यक्ति में समा चुकी है। और यदि यह ऐसा ही रहा तो संघर्ष विश्व में बढ़ते जायेगें और समस्या बहुत ज्यादा विकराल रूप धारण कर लेगी। बुराई के साथ खड़ा होना न्याय नहीं है बल्कि डर के आगे खड़ा होना ही सत्य है। क्योंकि गांधी जी प्रतिहिंसा की बात नहीं करते है बल्कि वह अपने शत्रु के हृदय को परिवर्तित करने की बात करते है। इसीलिए उनका सत्य डरपोक का हथियार नहीं बल्कि शक्तिशाली का यंत्र है। उनका मानना है कि कभी किसी को लालच देकर हम अपना नहीं बना सकते हैं बल्कि स्वयं परिवर्तन की चाह होनी चाहिए।

कभी भी अन्यायी या आतंकी के समाने घुटने टेकना उचित नहीं है बल्कि अपने

स्वाभिमान के लिए डटकर खड़ा होना आवश्यक है।

गांधी जी का मानना था कि एक सच्चा सत्याग्राही ही पूरे साम्राज्य को चुनौती दे सकता है। हिंसा सदैव प्रतिहिंसा को बढ़ावा देती है और जो उचित नहीं है। स्थायी शांति के लिए अहिंसा आवश्यक है। गांधी जी के इसी अहिंसा के सिद्धांत को अपनाकर दलाई लामा ने तिब्बत की स्वतंत्रता के लिए प्रयास किये। अहिंसा की ताकत से नेल्सन मंडेला भी प्रभावित हुए तथा अफ्रिका के लोगों के लिए संघर्ष किया। इसका परिणाम यह निकला कि बराक ओबामा अश्वेत राष्ट्रपति बने। अहिंसा का परिणाम ही था भारत का स्वतंत्रता आंदोलन चला। जब राष्ट्र आपस में उलझते है तो यह कोशिश की जाती है कि समस्या का हल बातचीत या मधयस्थता से शांतिपूर्वक साधानों से निकले न कि हिंसात्मक कार्यवाहियों से।

जब हम विश्व में गरीबी, हिंसा, शोषण, प्रतिहिंसा आतंकवाद की अनसुलझी समस्याओं को देखते है तो यह अदांजा स्वंय लगता है कि अहिंसा एक महत्वपूर्ण साधन है। सभी समस्याओं का जन्म असंतोष और संग्रहण पद्धति से ही होता है, जब वस्तुओं पर भी किसी एक वर्चस्व होगा, तभी संघर्ष होते हैं, तभी युद्ध होते है, कितने निरपराधा व्यक्ति युद्ध में मारे जाते है कितने ही हिंसा के शिकार बनते हैं।

आज स्थिति यहां तक पहुँच गई है कि हमने पर्यावरण व खनिज पदार्थों का दोहन इस तरह से किया है कि पृथ्वी संकट के बादल मंडराने लगे हैं। ओजोन विच्छेद इसका एक कारण है। फैक्ट्रियों से निकलने वाले कूड़े के निस्तारण से नदी प्रदूषण व जल संबंधी समस्याएं उत्पन्न हो गई है। जिनका हमारे पास कोई हल नहीं है। वनों की अंधा-धुंध कटाई से संकट के बादल है। असमय वर्षा, बाढ़, ग्लेशियरों का पिघलना, जुताई की खेती का कम होना खाद्यान संकट की तरु इशारा कर रही है।

गांधी जी ने सत्य और अहिंसा को अपने जीवन में अहम स्थान दिया तभी तो 1920 में जब असहयोग आंदोलन चल रहा था तब हिंसक घटना से हुई मौतों का जिम्मेदार स्वयं को मानते हुए उन्होंने आंदोलन स्थगित कर दिया। इस घटना से यह प्रेरणा मिलती है कि वह हिंसा को अपने जीवन में किसी हद तक भी स्वीकार नहीं करते थे। जब भारतीय जनता पर नमक कर लगा, तब गांधी जी ने ही डांडी मार्च किया और गुजरात के तटों पर सर्वप्रथम नमक बनाया। ऐसा इसीलिए किया क्योंकि नमक एक साधारण व्यक्ति के जीवन से जुड़ा पहलू है। जब नटाल में शादियों की मान्यता के लेकर विवाद चला तब गांधी जी ने बा को शामिल किया आंदोलन चलाने में क्योंकि वो स्त्री अधिकारों की बात थी और बा ने उनके प्रयत्नों में उनका साथ दिया क्योंकि वह उनके स्वाभिमान का प्रश्न था। स्वदेशी को अपनाने की बात हो या अपरिग्रह यह सब हमें संयमित जीवन की शिक्षा देते है। आज विश्व में समस्याओं को देखते हुए और मानव जीवन को बचाने के लिए गांधी जीवन प्रेरणा का स्त्रोत है। सभी राष्ट्रों और युवाओं को हिंसा पथ से हटाने के लिए आवश्यक है कि अहिंसा को अपनाना चाहिए। उनके विचारकों, लेखकों ने उन्हें, अनेक नाम पदवी दी है। जब हम गांधी की बात करते है सिद्धांतों की बात करते हैं तो

वह संत दिखाई पड़ते है। जब सर्वोदय की बात करते है तो एक समाज सुधारक की तरह दिखते हैं, और जब विश्व में फैली समस्याओं को देखते है तो वह एक विद्वान नजर आते है। जब राजनीति में संयम की बात करें तो वह आध्यात्मिक गुरु की तरह दिखते हैं।

गांधी जी एक सामाजिक व्यक्ति ही नहीं बल्कि राजनीतिक, आर्थिक, आध्यात्मिक भी नजर आते है। ऐसे लगता है कि अनेक मानवों का समावेश एक व्यक्ति में है इसीलिए उन्हें बहुआयामी व्यक्ति भी कहा जाता है। गांधी जी ने लगभग 150 वर्षों पहले यह जान लिया था कि आने वाला समय, संघर्षों का होगा, समस्याएं होगी, विश्व में गरीबी, भूखमरी, व शोषण व हिसा होगी, विश्व में आतंकवाद जैसी पर्यावरण जैसी समस्या होगी तथा विश्व के कोने-कोने में अशांति होगी। एक दूसरे से आगे निकलने के लिए एक दौड़ होगी। यदि समय रहते समस्याओं को सुलझाया नहीं जायेगा तो विश्व में अशांति का बोलबाला होगा अत: आवश्यक है समस्याओं को पहचानकर उनका समाधान करना। यदि कोई बुराई है कि तो उसे स्वीकार करके समाधाान ढूढ़ना।

गांधी जी ने इसलिए सत्य व अहिंसा पर बल दिया ताकि व्यक्ति किसी का शोषण न करे। अत: यह स्पष्ट है कि उन्नति व विकास का मार्ग वैश्विक शांति से ही प्राप्त हो सकता है। उन्होंने राष्ट्र, व विश्व के विषय में अपने विचार व समाधाान भी प्रस्तुत कियें।

सन्दर्भ स्रोत

1. deshbandhu-co-in-Vichar
2. www-pib-nic-in-hindifeature
3. http://www-jagranjunction-com
4. http://www-mea-gov-in-speeches&statement
5. http://www-India-gov-in-spotlight
6. http://lokmathnews-in
7. http://www-jagran-com
8. http://www-hindi-news18-com
9. गांधी जी, मेरे सपनों का भारत, नवजीवन प्रकाशन, अहमदाबाद, 1960
10. विष्णु प्रभाकर, भाग-1, गांधी आख्यान माला, (अवधारणा और आयाम), अर्जुन पब्लिशिंग हाऊस, नई दिल्ली, 2011

List of Contributors

1. **Prof. Gianluigi Segalerba,** University of Vienna, Austria
   Email: gianluigisegalerba@gmail.com
2. **Prof. AnantaKumar Giri,** Madras Institute of Development Studies, Chennai, Email: aumkrishna@yahoo.com
3. **Prof. (Dr.) Harpreet Kaur,** Principal, Mata Sundri College of Women, University of Delhi, Email: harpreetjaswal5@gmail.com
4. **Prof. Rakesh Kumar Gupta,** Principal, Ram LalAnand College, University of Delhi, Email:rgupta1965@yahoo.com
5. **Dr. Prerna Diwan,** Associate professor, Ram LalAnand College, University of Delhi, Email: dr.pdiwan@gmail.com
6. **Rajdeep Pathak,** Programme Executive, Gandhi Samriti and DarshanSamiti, Rajghat, New Delhi,
   Email: rajdeep.pathak@gmail.com
7. **Dr. Suman Khanna Aggarwal,** Former Associate Professor, University of Delhi, Email: sumanka5@yahoo.co.in
8. **Dr. Rajni Mudgal,** Assistant Professor, Bansthali Vidyapith, Rajasthan, Email: rajnimudgal212@gmail.com
9. **Manisha Pal,** Research scholar, Centre for Historical studies, JNU, New Delhi, Email: manishapalinportuguese@live.com
10. **Rajeev Ranjan,** Science Teacher, RPVV, Sector-10, Dwarka, New Delhi, Email: rajivranjanpatna4@gmail.com
11. **Dr. Shakti P. Rout,** Assistant Professor, Ram LalAnand College, University of Delhi, Email: cherryphd@gmail.com
12. **Dr. Krishan Gopal Tyagi,** Assistant Professor, Ram Lal Anand College, University of Delhi, Email: krishanjnu@gmail.com

13. **Rajinder Singh,** Assistant Professor, Ram Lal Anand College, University of Delhi, Email: rschauhan096@gmail.com

14. **Dr. Swagata Karmakar,** Assistant Professor, Ram Lal Anand College, University of Delhi, Email: sway.swagata@gmail.com

15. **Prof. Radhey Shyam Sharma,** Department of Environmental Studies, University of Delhi, Email: radheyss26@gmail.com

16. **Dr. VandanaMishra,** Assistant Professor, Department of Environmental Studies, University of Delhi, Email: mistletoe_h@gmail.com

17. **Dr. Beena,** Assistant Professor, Satyawati College (Evening), University of Delhi, Email: beena1987@gmail.com

18. **Utsav Krishan Murari,** Research Scholar, Centre for Mass Communication Media, Central University of South Bihar
Email: utsavkarishan@cusb.ac.in

19. **Dr. Chandan Kumar,** Assistant Professor, Patliputra University
Email: chandankumar621988@gmail.com

20. **Dr. Hoimonti Barua,** Research Scholar from Bangladesh, Centre for South Asian Studies, JNU, New Delhi
Email: hoimonti.barua@gmail.com

21. **N. Shradha Varma,** Assistant Professor, Department of Economics, Maitreyi College, Delhi University.

22. **Dr. Subhash Chander Dabas' Choudhry',** Associate Professor, Ram LalAnand College, University of Delhi
Email: dr.subhash22@yahoo.com

23. **Dr. Sanjay Kumar,** Assistant Professor, Ram Lal Anand College, University of Delhi, Email: sanjayrladu73@gmail.com

24. **Dr. Rita Jain,** Assistant Professor, Ram LalAnand College, University of Delhi, Email: rita_jain7@yahoo.com

25. **Dr. Archna Gaur,** Assistant Professor, Ram LalAnand College, University of Delhi, Email: dr.archnagaur@gmail.com

26. **Dr. Lajpat Rai,** Assistant Professor, Satyawati College, university of Delhi, Email: lajpatrai.du@gmail.com

27. **Dr. Rajesh Kumar,** Assistant Professor, Ram Lal Anand College, University of Delhi, Email: rsgautam74@gmail.com

28. **Dr. Atal Tiwari,** Assistant Professor, Ram Lal Anand College, University of Delhi, Email: atal.tewari@gmail.com

29. **Dr. Pinki Kumari,** Research Scholar, Gandhi Bhawan, University of Delhi, Email: pinkikumari2108@gmail.com

30. **Pooja,** Research Scholar, Department of Political Science,University of Delhi, Email : Poojascholar26@gmail.com Phone: 9958714006

31. **Sudhir Kumar Garwal,** Assistant Professor, Department of Political Science, Dasbandhu College, University of Delhi, Delhi
Email: sudhirgarhwal@gmail.com